Talking with a Child

JAMES D. WHITE

ILLUSTRATIONS BY JOE ORLANDO

MACMILLAN PUBLISHING CO., INC.
New York
COLLIER MACMILLAN PUBLISHERS
London

Macmillan Publishing Co., Inc.
866 Third Avenue, New York, N.Y. 10022
Collier Macmillan Canada, Ltd.

Library of Congress Cataloging in Publication Data
White, James D
Talking with a child.
Includes index.
1. Children—Language—Handbooks, manuals, etc.
I. Title.
LB1139.L3W46   1976   372.6   76-19052
ISBN 0-02-626570-2

First Printing 1976

Printed in the United States of America

Contents

Foreword

I never intended to be a snoop and an eavesdropper. When I was a child in Knoxville, Iowa, and the conversation-makers asked me what I wanted to be when I grew up, I can't ever remember replying, "A snoop and an eavesdropper."

But here I am, and that's what I did.

I sat in parks, city squares, airport terminals, and similar public places in dozens of states and a dozen other nations. Around half of this world, I watched adults and children enjoy, ignore, tolerate, or antagonize each other. I heard the language exchanged between them. I noted their actions and their expressions.

Afterward, privately, I recreated those actions and repeated the language I'd heard to learn what I might feel or be likely to say during similar moments.

I snooped and I eavesdropped.

But I've been called other names, too, perhaps more suitable ones. When I was a *child,* I continuously imagined the day when I wouldn't be called a child any more. I remember specifically ordering coffee in restaurants, hoping that I wouldn't be mistaken for a child. It's the same dream shared by millions of children who want to be "on their own." It was your own dream as well, very likely.

One day, I became a college *student,* eager at times, less than serious when love and other follies competed for study and term-paper time. I earned my share of degrees from Drake

University, Des Moines, and Columbia University Teachers College, New York. A half-dozen gifted teachers in each affected my career. I thought then as I think now what brilliants we all could be if every teacher were both knowledgeable and energetic, as interested in basic skills as in coffee breaks.

I tried hard as a *teacher* for eleven years, and I hope I was a good one. I met with students in secondary school, elementary school, graduate college, and adult education. I earned my stripes, though, as a speech and hearing *therapist*. I learned more than I taught from handicapped children who needed to be convinced that the rewards of using language were worth the tremendous efforts. I tried not to lose hope in overly emotional, cruelly pushy, or indifferent parents. Mostly, I was grateful for perceptive parents who were willing to create a new language atmosphere for their child's benefit.

I was also called a *supervisor* during some of those school years. But supervisors may be neither fish nor fowl, as the saying goes, and I found myself too often at the whim of the administration, responsible for too many and too much and with authority for practically nothing. Those were difficult times, and my sympathies go to supervisors anywhere in similar circumstances.

For another eleven years I was a *consultant* in reading and the language arts for a major educational publisher. My travel log indicated 60,000 to 70,000 miles during a typical year. I visited students, teachers, parents, administrators (supervisors, you'll be pleased to know that I got in my zingers on your behalf!), and state education departments. I couldn't be doing what I do now, if I hadn't done what I did then. Approximately two million miles of travel to forty-five states and twelve other countries offered me perspective, a chance to "get it all together." During those years I was also called *lecturer, keynote speaker, convention-goer,* and *lover* of the good life. I also came to be called *friend* by some of the finest educators in the profession, people whom I continue to admire as vital and amiable.

The years change people. People change. I changed. I left that life to be called *writer* and *author.* A basic series in grammar and composition. Stories and guides for teaching reading. Materials to accompany a best-selling dictionary for children. A remedial reading program using some of the best-known superheroes in comic folklore—Superman, Wonder Woman, Batman, and their superfriends. I believe that if I died and were assigned to the Devil, he would put me to work writing teacher's guides forever. Very hard work for such an underrated and maligned classroom aid.

All in all, answering to one or another of these names, I studied the language exchanges between adults and children ever since I left that Iowa hometown more than thirty years ago.

Those years of education and experience have resulted in the above confession and the following book.

Through the months of work relating to this book, I was encouraged by several doctors and other adults to keep adults—parents, mainly, but not necessarily—and kids together, talking to each other, sharing things. They all knew the problem—something invariably seems to go wrong, parents and children stop talking to each other, adults and children develop an "us-against-them" attitude, and stony silences exist where warm language exchanges have long since perished.

Well, I can assure you that each line of these pages is dedicated to avoiding or, at least, postponing the day when adults and children discover that language between them doesn't work any more.

This book represents my perspectives, which have been distilled from experiences in working not only with children but also with adults who were interested in and concerned for children. The book is intended to help adults to have a pleasant, positive time sharing language. The goals of these suggestions are:

- to have FUN, a really good time with children;
- to make language experiences more pleasant than unpleasant;
- to give children a chance to talk rather than merely to listen; and
- to share rather than merely to confront.

Your immediate hope is for the child to feel satisfied after talking with you and to look forward to (or, at least, not to mind) talking with you again.

You are anointed if you really enjoy spending time with children, feel completely at ease in their company, and really want them to exchange language with you. May you enjoy a thousand different moments as you watch children who are learning to speak for themselves. After all, what is the name of the game, if not to promote in children confidence and independence?

Finally, I'm a total of the parts created by those of you who have touched and taught me, for you have all contributed to this book. I'm grateful for every touch. My thanks go specifically to Chris Athey, Froebel Institute, London, for her research and fresh attitude toward the development of humor in children; to Joanne Bernstein and Stephen Gullo, Brooklyn College, for their comments about helping children to cope with loss; to Kathleen Fischer for her assistance regarding sexism in choosing a vocation; to the late Haim G. Ginott; and to hundreds of adults and children who allowed me within earshot while I was gathering material.

I'm also grateful for the personal help and approval of Calvin W. Burt; Marion Collins Carson; Susan C. Jurgensen; Stanley S. Loeb; Mary G. Mallace; Dorothy Porter; Ray Roberts; James S. Russell; my dear friends in the English and reading associations, wherever you are. And a special thank you for Martha and Harold E. White, who got it all together for my benefit.

Talking with a Child

1

Out of My Mind

Ben Finchley purchased this book at one of those bazaars which line the passenger area of an airline terminal. He was somewhat early, and his flight was somewhat late. He settled into a plastic chair where he commanded a reasonably good view of the airport runways, as if his supervision would somehow hasten his plane's arrival. As he turned the first pages of the book, he also gave the main runway a sweeping look. But Ben's eye was caught by a strange child . . . looking rather intently at him. It was clearly Ben's move.

Obviously, Ben had indicated some interest in talking with children, since he was holding this book in his lap. So, here he went.

"Hello." Nice start, if spoken with a sincere smile.

"Umf—" After all, it was only a child.

"What's your name?" It didn't occur to Ben Finchley to introduce himself.

"Roobly Moo Va Doo Doo." Or something like that. Ben didn't ask the child for either a repeat or clarification.

"How old are you?" And how did it deeply matter?

"Six." Clearly understandable, but not much to make a conversation.

"Where do you go to school?" Somehow, he felt that the child expected this to be Ben's next question. Ben began to feel he was losing on points.

3

"Padocket Road School." As if the child had been through this scene before and often. Ben thought, As in puck-puck-puck-padocket? He didn't believe that, but he didn't believe the kid's name either. The conversation wasn't going at all well.

"When's your birthday?" Was this to be Ben's last try?

"The flimpth of March." So it sounded.

"Oh, that's nice." With a smile and a half-wave of the hand indicating dismissal, Ben retreated to the book in his lap.

Ben had concluded another odd and unsatisfying attempt at words with another Roobly Moo Va Doo Doo. Why, Ben wondered, don't children learn to converse intelligently? Whatever happened to dialogue? Why can't children even pronounce their names?

And yet, Ben didn't pronounce his name at all. Asking the child's often-heard questions, Ben struggled feebly to weave a conversation, using the ragged and bare threads of name, age, and school. And Ben managed no more than to terminate with an oh-that's-nice, a guaranteed conversation cooler.

Ben Finchley's next search of the runways revealed no arrival that, for him, meant departure. But there were at least three dozen other activities out there competing for conversation. So much there to share with a child, but Ben didn't really *see* what he saw.

I invented the story of Ben and Roobly Moo, of course. But I didn't invent the creeping discomfort which grows as language goes badly between an adult and a child who seem to want to talk with each other. That discomfort, I can assure you, is very real. I've seen it occur enough times and in enough places that I can share it when a tense adult and a child meet in a situation which invites or even requires dialogue.

As a result, talking with a child, anybody's child, is what this book's all about. (Not so incidentally, watch out for oh-that's-nice! It means you're sagging verbally on your side of the dialogue.)

When I was in the third grade, my teacher, Miss Kading—she never would have dreamed of being titled *Ms.*—became sick and tired of my excessive blather in her classroom. Using brown paper towels held together by paper clips, she fashioned an ingenious little gag which fit over the top of my head and

4

around my mouth, and she directed me to wear it for the rest of the afternoon. Not physically painful, it hurt my pride and reminded me to keep my trap shut while others in class had an opportunity to talk . . . when granted her permission.

The experience had two effects. First, I have been reminded ever since that if I can manage to keep that same now-grown trap shut, other adults and children have interesting things to say. Second, I think she paid me an extraordinary compliment by reminding me that I was sufficiently verbal—excessively so perhaps, but nevertheless facile.

But beyond that, Miss Kading, my dear, I'm here to tell you that the gag didn't work. I still talk too much, and I'm dedicated to helping children to become talkative as well, because you and I both know that gabby kids fare better than silent ones in the classroom.

Teachers of young children know that the talkers—as opposed to the quiet, mousy ones—are more likely to be known as the brighter pupils. A free and frequent exchange at home is likely to be solid insurance for a child's successful mastery of reading and writing in the classroom. Through anecdotes, explanations, examples, and suggestions, this book is intended for adults who want children to develop an ease in using and understanding the language.

Notice how many adults, teachers, and parents seem to ignore children. Notice how little the adults really talk together with children in public places. Hear how the adults' bossy commands outrageously outnumber all other kinds of language spewed at children. No wonder a child's dream is to grow up and not be a child any more!

It takes gumption to tell you how to have private language experiences with a child. As you read, please keep in mind these five gumptious assumptions:
- You are well-intentioned toward children;
- you want children to be open, comfortable, and communicative at home;
- you want children to be reasonably able in school;
- you want them to be successful and satisfied in their own adult lives;
- you want them to handle the language ably.

Several of the current child psychotherapists suggest negative avoidance techniques, such as how to keep a child from wetting on the dog or attacking a baby sister with a toy truck. This book, however, is intended to help you in exchanging language with the child who does not necessarily need a problem solved or a behavior corrected, but who either seeks or accepts your company for a while.

Some authors of books about children quite carefully divide their chapters and suggestions by the children's developmental ages. We'll be more informal here about delineating experiences by age, since children don't know how old they're supposed to be before they ask questions, revel in sensory experiences, and seek language exchanges with others.

Throughout this book, you means *you*, whoever you are—mother, father, grandparent, godparent, adult family member, adolescent, neighbor, teacher, babysitter, passenger sitting next to a youngster, or any adult who wants to make (or can't avoid making) conversation from time to time with a child. There's no rule that says you must be a parent in order to talk amiably with a child. Naturally, you'll find some of the situations in here a little too cozy if you are not a member of the child's family. Nevertheless, each experience and suggestion may give you some idea of how to enjoy a language exchange, no matter who you are or where you are.

The child may be your son, daughter, grandchild, other young relative, pupil, the kid you sit with, or any young friend. The English language does not make it easy for me to talk about a *child* without indicating whether it's a *him* or a *her*. Instead of saying *he or she* every time I mention one child, I'll trade off, using *he* one time and *she* another time. Either way, please remember that the child mentioned is the one you have in mind, too, even though the sex references don't always agree.

The stereotyped mommy-daddy-brother-sister-baby-dog-cat family unit is pretty hard to find. When we talk about a *family,* we mean the unit you know, which is composed of those adults and children—whether they're related or not—who share shelter, food, common needs, companionship, and love. On these pages a family means those people, young, old, and older, who "go home" to each other.

6

None of the language experiences I discuss are to be so finely structured and crankingly obvious to the child as to seem like some kind of private tutelage. They're intended to be more pleasant than unpleasant, more vocal than silent, more side-by-side than face-to-face.

Some adults and child experts recommend a given period of time—thirty minutes a day, say—for being "together" with children. Imagine! Only thirty minutes a day! How would you feel if the child you know received only thirty minutes of school a day? In thousands and thousands of homes the television sets get more attention than that! And how many adults are annoyed—and jealous—of the hypnotic hold of the TV? Sharing language doesn't take much effort, and it can happen almost anywhere and anytime that an adult and a child want to be together.

God gave us two ears and one mouth, as the saying goes, so that we can hear twice as much as we talk. Do as you see fit with your own two ears and your one mouth, but give the kids a chance, too. They have voices, and they have the greatest things to say.

Sure, there are times for relaxing alone and for doing things that only one can do. But getting your scenes together can be pretty easy, and the results—for both of you—can be worth much more than the effort.

I was invited to a teachers' workshop day in a school system on Long Island. I was going on about language experiences intended to turn on gifted children, and I was growing louder and more spirited as the workshoppers and I fed on each other's ideas. One lady, speaking for her friend as well as herself, said, "Of course, we take somewhat of a different viewpoint on these suggestions."

I effused, "Yes? What is your view?"

"Well," she mewed, "we're parents."

I was stopped. I couldn't make the connection. Several teachers, any of whom may also have been parents, seemed as stymied as I felt. I spoke an unworthy response: "We certainly wouldn't have known merely by looking at you."

"Humph!" the friend spatted. "How's a parent supposed to look?" Knowing that we were headed far off our course, I concluded, "Deciding how teachers and parents are supposed to look may be a topic for another day." And with a marked deflation in enthusiasm, we returned to gifted children.

But that exchange still echoes in my mind. I don't know how to spot a parent without a child or a teacher without a class. But I can tell you how hundreds of parents and teachers sound within range of their children. And my ongoing game consists of eyeing a child in a playground, beach, or shopping center and guessing, then waiting for proof on which adult is the child's parent or teacher.

It's a revealing game. Try it.

2

A Time for Togethering

You cannot develop the language of a child any more than you can digest the child's food. The child has to do it. You can provide attractive bites of lunch and interesting bits of conversation, hoping that the child will eat one and hear the other; but, once inside, the bites and the bits must become the child's own.

On the other hand, a child cannot develop his own abilities to understand and use the language by talking to himself. Language is a human game for two or more players. It implies that there is someone at "the other end." Of course, we often see children talking to dolls, dogs, toys, or even imaginary playmates; the play situation may seem satisfactory to the children for a while, but they are quite likely to welcome human company and prefer two-way language.

When the person at the other end of the language exchange does all of the talking, there's not much to do at the child's end except to listen. It's surprisingly easy to find a child who is annoyingly silent before a talkative adult, yet who may at another time talk endlessly to a toy or a pet.

A sadder situation is the one in which the adult seems "too busy" or too disinterested to share any language experiences with the child. In such a context, some children conclude that the development of language is unnecessary or even undesirable. A lack of development in language skills can be tragic. Both research and experience indicate that growing children who lack a command of the essential elements of verbal communication are likely to be loners, or worse yet, they may fall back on their abilities to deal with other people in assaultive, physical ways.

In these what-the-hell days, you'd think that talking to one's self may be more of a psychological aberration than playing sexually with one's self. Attitudes seem to grow more and more casual about what one does with "one's own" in private—and even in some public—places. But some children and certainly many adults who converse with themselves are still thought to harbor potentially serious social or mental disturbances. In either circumstance, it is not difficult to understand that a little physical or verbal something may be preferable to nothing.

Talking with a child will take your time. When you try to talk with somebody who can't seem to give you enough time to concentrate on what you are trying to say, do you find yourself getting angry? I do. So do children. People seem to have the time to do what they consider really necessary and important to do, in spite of how busy they often say they are. A satisfying talk with a child is time-engendering. A pleasant moment leads to the desire for another one, and another . . . and another. Having a little fun makes the time worth while, which makes you find the time for a little more fun. It's the right kind of a vicious circle. The rule of thumb is to talk with children oftener for shorter moments rather than fewer talks for longer spells.

Having words with a child can help to take your mind off yourself, provided that you pursue topics which interest the child rather than those which preoccupy you.

But you have to care enough.

Reading the Child's Scene

A dramatist once said that the trouble with real life is that there's not enough plot. Nevertheless, our lives seem to go by in acts and scenes. Children seem to measure the acts in their lives as the periods of time from hamburger to snack to hotdog. Our own scenes seem more difficult to measure, since

This morning my Dad and I had words . . .

. . . but I didn't get to use mine!

there are so many of them. You can rather easily determine the child's scene—the time of day; the child's place; any children, pets, dolls, or toys, or other "supporting cast" of players; the child's activities; and conflicts, if any. If you know the child's routine, you can quickly decide if he is following or departing from normal activities.

Many people go through their lives looking for *action*. You'll have a more interesting time, though, especially when you're observing a child, if you look for the child's *reactions*. How is the child replying to her scene? Is she satisfied by being alone doing something that only one can do well? Is she absorbed, busy, without stress, "away somewhere" in thought or actions? Does she seem to be lonely, withdrawn, and bored?

Try to place yourself mentally in the child's scene from the child's own point of view. Imagine yourself physically in the child's position. Try the child's expression on your own face. How do you think you'd feel, and what might you be thinking, if you looked the way the child looked?

You need only a moment from a short distance away to determine the child's scene and to decide whether you will enter it. Longfellow wrote in a poem, "A boy's will is the wind's will, and the thoughts of youth are long, long thoughts." Perhaps your child's thoughts are long and private, with a sign hung outside his mind that says *Do Not Disturb*.

Changing the Scene

Let's say you're at a party or some group meeting. You and a couple of friends are standing in a small circle in the middle of the room talking about something. Perhaps you're in the middle of one of your favorite stories. Have you ever noticed what happens to your story when another person, friend or acquaintance, steps up to the circle and enters the group? An awkward moment. Do you go back and start your story again? Do you review the story so far? Do you ignore the entrance of the person upon the scene until your story is finished? Do you try to retrieve the bits and pieces of the conversation after hellos and introductions?

Your own conversational scenes change as people enter and leave them. A thoughtful person, of course, would wait at a social distance until your story is ended and the scene is right for an entrance.

The scene surrounding the child is no different. Before you change it, you may decide why you want (or need) to enter the child's scene. Does the child seem to need your company, or do you feel the need for the child's company? If you're lonely and want to be with the child, by all means enter the child's scene and say, "I just wanted to be with you for a while," or "I felt lonely for a moment, and I wanted your company."

Do you have something to ask, tell, or command? If so, can it wait awhile? Patience is surely one characteristic of a mature person. If you insist that the child wait outside your scene until an appropriate time instead of bothering you, you must give the child the same consideration. If the child is absorbed in an activity, can't you write a note to yourself to speak to him later? Or you can write a brief note to the child and tack it on a bulletin board.

Note Boards Work Both Ways

You have your own busy scene at times, and the children can have theirs. They can be as annoyed at interruptions as you can. One important reason for reading a child's scene is to determine when not to interfere with what a child seems satisfied doing alone. An adult can interrupt the privacy and concentration of a child numerous times in a period of twenty minutes, yet snap a curt "Can't you see I'm busy?" when the child attempts to interrupt the adult's reading, rest, or recreation. Respect for the other's privacy and time works both ways.

A note board, complete with pencils and paper, can become the household message service. If you don't want sharp tacks and pushpins around, screw eight or ten cuphooks into a piece of plywood or scrap lumber, and attach it low enough to be handy for any child. Scribble a note reminding yourself to tell the child something later instead of disturbing him now. If the child is beginning to read, leave clearly printed, simply worded notes which may be directions, questions, or messages of love or appreciation. You'll be grateful for this note board when the child begins to draw and seeks your approval of each master-piece. Instead of having to brush him off with a "that's nice" every few minutes, the child can hang the pictures on the note board for an art show when you can take the time to admire and discuss them all. You can leave notes for the child in glyphs if he is too young to read—a quick sketch of a waste basket to be emptied, an apple in the fridge, a "smile" face to let the child know your cold is better. You'll be surprised at your growing reputation among the young for your ability as an artist!

Chew a Cert

Nobody's asking you to take a shower and change into your parlor clothes every time you expect to speak with a child. But if you expect to join a child for an activity that will bring the two of you close together for a while . . . check your breath. Especially if you wear dentures. If the child will be in your lap while you look at pictures in a magazine, play finger games, or learn how to make music with a comb and tissue paper, the most memorable part of the experience for the child may be the lingering smell of garlic, tuna fish, or liquor. This may sound like a tawdry commercial for mouthwash, until you re-member your own childhood days when you were overcome by the foul odor from the mouth of a well-meaning adult.

Sliding into the Child's Scene

Kevin, who works in a bakery, said to Debbie, "I saw your mother in the shop yesterday."

"What did she say to you?" Debbie asked.

"Oh, not much. Why?"

"Then she wasn't my mother."

It's not illegal or immoral to be known as a talkative person, depending, of course, on what you decide to be talkative about.

When you enter a child's scene, you can try to slip in unobtrusively to share the child's interest and activity, or you can stomp into it with great vocal accompaniment. Actually, you probably choose an entrance that lies somewhere between these two. This is the time when you use what you learned by observing the child's scene for a few moments to determine whether and how you might move into it. If the child must know something or do something that will stop her activities, you might spend a moment or two talking to her about them before you shift the topic. You have changed the scene anyway, merely by entering it, but you needn't destroy it abruptly. You may wish to give the child a message or direct her to do a task, or discuss misbehavior and punishment. But once you've done so, it would be most difficult to share any sincere interest in whatever she was doing before you interrupted. Instead, talk about her activity for a few moments, then simply say that you must now talk about something else.

Keep in mind that you do not need a strong voice to talk to a child by your side, especially if you have vocal chords that can be heard halfway up the next block. Intimacies are generally shared in quiet voices. Your own soft tones may influence the child to use the same tone in his voice, although that's not a promise. I sat near a mother and her young son on a bus and overheard the son ask, "But why do I have to stay with Margaret?"

"Because I have to go to the hospital to see Mrs. Kuns," the mother said.

"What happened to Mrs. Kuns?"

"She scrubbed her kitchen floor and fell on it before it was dry. She broke her hip."

"Why can't I go to the hospital to see her?"

"Because the hospital won't let boys your age in Mrs. Kuns' room. You have to stay with Margaret." At that moment the mother noticed that I was much too interested in the exchange between her and her son. She turned to the son. "You should talk more quietly, because you're bothering the other passengers."

The son, taking his cue magnificently, shouted very loudly, "But I want to go with you!" And the battle began. My fault, I

15

suppose. I wonder what might have happened if the mother had used example rather than admonishment to quiet the boy's voice.

When you simply want to join the child and share in his activity, how and where you sit will have an effect on the scene. One rule of thumb is to sit so that your faces are on about the same level. The child will have difficulty "togethering" with you if he can see and talk only to your knees. Second rule of thumb is to sit so that you and the child both face the activity—the book, the blocks, the modeling clay, the pennies, or whatever—from the same direction. When you are feeling sociable with the child, face what he faces; don't face him straight on, implying the possibility of a confrontation, unless you're planning to be opponents in a friendly game. Or, of course, unless you're planning a confrontation!

Listen!

At first, play a private game with yourself. When you decide to join the child, promise yourself that you *won't* say the first word after you sit down. If you're ignored for a few moments, fret not. That only gives you more time to observe the action and to enjoy the child's reaction. If you get a smile, smile back. But bite your tongue till you can't stand the pain; keeping quiet may help you to get into the child's interest instead of changing the scene with your own vocal entrance. If the child is molding something with modeling clay, you might start your own clay figure. Perhaps the child asks, "What do you want?" You can say, "I want to be with you awhile and to do what you do," or make some other cordial reply that indicates you're interested in the child's activity. But, whatever the opening, see if you can wait long enough for the child to speak first, giving you a cue on where to go from there.

Active listening means more than muttering a repertoire of senseless bromides during the pauses in another person's talk. You're losing quite steadily when you use almost exclusively a stream of conversation killers such as these with a child: "Huh-uh . . . That's nice . . . Too bad . . . Oh . . . Uh-huh . . .

Hm-m-m . . . Well . . . I see . . ." These are moments in a conversation when you're expected to nod your head, smile, frown slightly, or make some noise to indicate that you're awake and comprehending. But these words, and nothing more on your side of the talk, tend to place an increasingly heavy burden on the young child, who runs out of verbal gas for lack of substantial responses from you.

Active listening means that you steer the young speaker with comments and questions that encourage him to continue talking. His story may be guided by the interest you indicate in your responses. Mark was telling his Aunt Bella about his mishap with his bike. He was riding in another neighborhood and bent a wheel when it dropped into a slotted storm drain along the curb. "And I had to drag that darn bike all the way home." Bella avoided two pitfalls—one, to say "Too bad," which would have surely killed Mark's story; and the other, more tempting, "You shouldn't have been riding so far from home." Instead, Bella asked one of several acceptable encouraging questions which enabled Mark to elaborate his story: "How far did you have to go?"

You must hear the child's story and attempt to follow the sequence. If you can, comment or question in order to get the events straight in your own mind. Ask what happened then. You can, if you wish, shift the child's story from action to reaction and back again—"How did you feel about that? And then what did you do?" There's no need for you to milk a story (and the teller) to the point of exhaustion. You can, however, help a young talemaker to become aware of details and reactions by your own careful listening and responding. Your efforts will be rewarded in a satisfying way—with better and better stories.

For many children, talking with an adult who listens, really listens, is a rare and a very special form of attention. Senior adults in the family and neighborhood who show any affection seem to attract children. Parental authority doesn't complicate the relationship. And each seems to satisfy the need for companionship in the other. If eavesdropping is any basis for judgment, the do's and don'ts of behavior pass from parent to child, but the richness of a culture and its language skips to every other generation. The affinity of child for friendly senior citizens could be the main reason.

When Words Aren't Needed

Daryl was visiting his grandmother for a couple of weeks while his parents enjoyed a second honeymoon at home. Everything was fine at grandmother's house . . . that is, until the first pang of homesickness swept across him. The symptoms of the listless, moody kid were pretty obvious.

"Do you want to call your mother?" offered an understanding grandmother.

Daryl answered, "No, but I'd just like to see her face a minute."

Almost every one of us at some time and place has become suddenly aware of a strange child, standing a short distance away, gazing at us intently. Perhaps in some areas of the country where fear of strangers is not a major problem, the child has walked up to us, indicating a desire to enter our scene. The child may talk; on the other hand, the child may remain completely silent. Many of us are conditioned by the same fear of strangers, and we hesitate to talk to the child, thinking that a nearby adult will accuse us of accosting or molesting. But words aren't needed. We share a silent something with the child before winks or smiles are exchanged and the child steps out of our scene.

You know that you frequently satisfy a child merely by *being there*. I often think that a child desires to have an adult nearby in order to have somebody to ignore. But it isn't really an ignoring that you get. The child likes to observe your scene just as you like to observe the child's scene. You can, if you wish, sit still and let the child observe what he wants to see. You can, if you wish, throw a wink, a smile, some physical reassurance that everything is okay between the two of you. An arm around the child can show that you're sorry for a minor mishap. A pat can show that you understand when a spoonful of pudding drops in the child's lap. A small strut or other piece of foolishness can show that you like being observed. Remember that touching communicates as well as language, and even better in some situations. Physical communication that somehow says "We're buddies, aren't we?" is as strong as speaking or listening and generally less often employed.

Margot and her seven-year-old son David rode their bicycles together but silently to the school playground, a distance of about a mile. David found his private freedom by crawling up-downthrough the monkey bars. Margot surprised herself by pumping up high on one of the playground swings. Each of them seemed alone and free, yet each occasionally glanced to see if the other was having a good time. The reassurances were smiles and waves, not words. But for a half-hour, they were very much together.

3

Man So Loved the Shell...

. . . That he gave it a name.
It was his way of getting closer to it,
Paying homage to it,
Of summoning it up in his thoughts
Even when the creature itself was absent.
The act of naming is the act of loving—
Be it a decimal point, a part of speech,
Or a shell.
And the act of loving requires preparation—
Warmth, caring, ease,
Sensitivity, tenderness,
Skill.

—Haim G. Ginott
Teacher and Child

Perceiving—What Is It?

To perceive means to receive or to become aware of something through one's senses. When children perceive, they see, hear, taste, smell, or feel things, actions, and qualities. *To perceive* means primarily to become aware of things *now*, to have the ears, eyes, and the other perceivers going in a sort of continual, ever-sweeping scan of the surroundings. It doesn't really mean memory or mental pictures recorded from our scannings in the past. Even though we might say "I can hear it now" or "In my mind's eye I see," these phrases are generally used to introduce some tale from our memory rather than a description of a perception. We might say that a child is *perceptive;* that is, that the child might be more than usually aware of things, that the child's perceptions are extraordinarily keen. Something may be *perceptible* merely by being noticeable through one or more of a person's senses. *Perception,* then, is the act of the process of knowing about something through the senses.

The users of our language have confused the meanings of *touch* and *feel.* Although *feel* may imply more of an examination using the hands, the two words mean very much the same thing within the sense of perceiving. A child may touch something with his hand, his arm, or his knee; in like manner, he may feel something on his hand, his arm, or his knee. Both actions imply sensory awareness and may be called perceiving. However, the meaning of *feel* has been mishmashed by users to include the emotions, so that one may feel anger. The word is also used to mean *to believe* or *to hold an opinion.* In the sense of perception, though, we use *feel* to mean that which can be sensed by the hand, the skin, or some other tactile system, as the feel of ice on a sensitive tooth or the feel of hunger in an empty stomach.

Even though the child finds the smell of popping corn quite different from the smell of leftover fish in the garbage bucket, it's the same smell-perception system that works always. You employ the same eye-perception system when you see strange shapes in clouds and when you watch a person undress in the apartment across the court, although your responses may be quite different. I was told many years ago about little Callie who received her first wristwatch and a bottle of rosewater at the same time as birthday presents. After she put on her new watch and doused herself with the cologne, she announced to her party, "Now, when you hear something and when you smell something, it's me!"

The eyes and the ears seem to be the two "big ones" of the perception systems. A person can perceive visually quite apart from the other perception systems—a colorful picture on the

wall, a balloon floating higher and higher in the air, blood ooz-
ing from under an adhesive bandage. We find that some children are visually oriented because they wish to examine closely
every bit, corner, and angle of something. Visual perception
seems to be the most heavily employed system, yet a child can be
at quite a disadvantage relying so fully upon it. Another child
may be oriented heavily toward touching—feeling everything
possible with the hands, turning it over and over and over for
the feel, however, rather than the look.

The other perception systems may work in isolation, but we
tend to use them in combinations. When you hear a strange
noise outside your house, don't you generally walk to the window to see what it might be? Have you seen children who will
not eat strange foods until they've smelled them? One very
popular game with a young child involves putting a number of
commonly known objects in a paper bag; the child reaches for
one object at a time, feeling it without seeing it in order to
identify it, then pulling it out of the bag to see if his identification was correct.

In addition to the five senses already mentioned, there is a
perception of the body's place in space, the sense of balance or
equilibrium. It's the perception system that allows a person to
remain standing with eyes closed or to walk across a room in
the dark. As Ronnie and his dad were strolling along the sidewalk, Ronnie noticed that the man in front of him walked
slightly lopsided. Ronnie called his dad's attention to the man's
gait. At the corner, when the man went one direction and Ronnie and his dad went the other, Ronnie was shocked to see that
the man had lost one arm at the shoulder. When Dad suggested that Ronnie walk with one arm held very closely across
the front of his body, Ronnie learned the importance of both
arms in maintaining physical balance.

There is also a motion-perception system, the one which tells
us whether the vehicle is moving or standing still, even when
we don't seem to get any cues from the other senses. These
may be the two senses which delight children (and nauseate
adults) in rides on the merry-go-round, the flying parachute,
and the roller coaster during visits to amusement parks. Some

people will submit to being whirled but not up-ended; others will go upside down, but don't like swingy, circular rides. Perception systems determine what constitutes a good time at a carnival.

A person with a physical disability involving one of the perception systems can learn to compensate somewhat by raising the level of awareness in the other senses. Perhaps you've seen a book in the stores called *If You Could See What I Hear,* written by Tom Sullivan, who became blind shortly after birth and grew to become a champion wrestler, an honor student, a musical composer, and a happily married man. Great title, isn't it?

When you take a child for a physical examination, notice how the doctor checks carefully all of the child's perception systems. The doctor will probably examine the child's eyes, nose, mouth, and ears with a fancy flashlight. The child's ears may also be checked with a tuning fork or perhaps an audiometric test. The doctor moves a finger from side to side to see if the child's eyes follow it properly; other vision tests are sure to be included. The examination may also include checking the child's physical reflexes with a small rubber hammer, a sharp pin, or a feather.

After all this, please keep in mind that normal children are born with normal perception systems; however, the skills needed to use those systems competently are not innate, they are learned. You are needed, if the child is to become *perceptive.* Awareness of color differences, of varying sizes and shapes, of textures in natural and man-made materials, of scents and odors, of natural sounds and musical rhythms, of bland and spicy foods, and of hot and cold grows as the child develops the perception systems—with your help.

Perceiving Things

Ladybug, pocket, tire, cabbage, fossil, peanut, flashlight, pterodactyl, shortstop, volcano, cop, puck, caboose, popcorn, echo—each of these words names a thing. The name of a thing provides the gateway to language about that thing; children cannot talk about a thing they cannot name. At the beginning, the name must come from an adult who speaks the language that the child is learning to speak. Sometime much later, children may devise their own jargon—pig Latin, "op," code—or specialized slang, probably in an attempt to exclude outsiders from their language group. However, if the child's native tongue is to be useful in a family and the ethnic group, then the child must hear and imitate the agreed-upon names that things are called.

I was on my way to visit friends in New Jersey when the bus passed a water reservoir. Near the edge of the water was an aerator spouting a mushroom-shaped fountain of water. One of the two boys in the seat behind me said, "Look at the thing in the thing!"

His friend said, "What thing?"

"That thing in the water."

"Oh, yeah," said the friend. A few moments passed.

"What do you call that thing?" said the first boy.

"What thing?" said the friend. By the time they had another round or two about that thing, the bus was well beyond the reservoir.

Most things can be counted. The name for a thing generally has forms for naming one or more than one. The regular way to talk about more than one is formed by adding -s or -es to the name for one thing. Children who are learning to talk must hear both forms from adults if they are to use the names themselves. There is in the human mind some kind of system for making generalizations about words; after children have heard a sufficient number of regular forms, they can offer the names of more-than-ones without having to hear them previously.

All is fine in the naming until a child comes across an irregular form—names like *foot/feet, child/children,* and *woman/women.* The child isn't likely to offer an irregular form for a regular name—such as *hice* for *house*—because his generalizing scheme will probably work in favor of *houses.* On the other hand, the same scheme may lead him to offer *mouses* instead of *mice,* and *tooths* instead of *teeth,* if he has not heard you use the correct forms sufficiently. You may, if you wish, chortle to friends about the "cute" way the child said *foots, gooses,* and *mans;* but you won't be doing the child any favors if you leave the irregular forms uncorrected.

24

It's been said that every culture develops a large vocabulary for those things which are considered "close to its cultural core." If that's true, then Americans must be engrossed in the sexual organs and their functions. From tallywhacker, peetail, coozie, and twat right on through the more literary horn, instrument, engine, gates, vessel, and tender folds, the American names for the male and female genitals would probably not fit on this page. If you wish to include all of the randy names for the breasts and the anal area, you have the raw material for quite a dictionary. Who remembers when we used to "go to the basement" in grade school? Children in school still ask to go to the bathroom, even though there is no tub or shower.

You won't regret giving the child the straight, dictionary names for vagina, penis, testicles, and anus, since they name parts of the body as evident as a knee, a navel, or a chin. Body wastes are named urine, stool, bowel movement, or feces. Dodging around these names will only imply that they "aren't nice." And they're okay. Young children "sit on the pot," older children "go to the toilet." It seems unfair to confuse body functions with habits of cleanliness by talking about going to the bathroom, especially if you are in a department store or a restaurant. As soon as children are old enough to read, teach them the names they can expect to see on restroom doors. Worse yet, I am repulsed when a child has to go and "make a present"—an absolutely unexplainable confusion of generosity and normal body function; and I refuse to write a thank-you note.

Perceiving the qualities of a thing help the child to identify it. The child's perception systems zero in on an object, which, until this time, has been merely a thing. The see-system says it's red and round. The hear-system has nothing to report at this time. The feel-system says it's smooth, cool, and waxy. The smell-system says sweet. The taste-system says, You're right, smell, it is sweet, and it's fruity. The hear-system, when the taste-system bites it, says it's crisp, then pulpy. But it's still a thing until an adult supplies its name—*apple* (or *Apfel, pomme, poma,* depending on what language the adult expects the child to learn). The quality of the apple serves as some basis for determining the name for another thing perceived later having closely similar qualities. It's easy to understand why a child may call a tomato an apple until after she sees the inside of the tomato, compares the tomato with the apple, and tastes the tomato. Perception systems may report, This is not like the apple we perceived before; what is it? The child's generalizing scheme helps to classify perceptions so that objects perceived later may be tested by the perception systems to see if they fit any previously named group.

The perceived qualities themselves can be named. We're interested now in those qualities which can be perceived and measured or corroborated, particularly colors, shapes, and sizes. I have been asked by many parents and teachers, especially art teachers, about coloring books which label the colors that the child is expected to fill inside the lines. They ask if such coloring activities may inhibit the child's creative tendencies. Keep in mind that this type of coloring book helps the child to learn the names of colors. It doesn't matter much whether the child colors inside or outside the lines, if he cannot identify colors by their names. Provide color-identification books and large sheets of blank paper, since learning to perceive colors by name encourages creating colorful works of art.

You've probably noticed the large number of educationally oriented toys for younger children that involve the sorting of blocks or tiles by shape—triangles, squares, stars, circles, ovals. Children who play with these types of toys will undoubtedly be able to classify the shapes before they name them, but you will also help them to name the shapes and to find household objects of similar shapes. The length and the mass of a thing may, of course, be weighed or measured, but you must see these things from the child's size and point of view, rather than your own. Perhaps you used to play on an enormous front porch of somebody's house when you were a child, and then you discovered years later how small that porch really was. Do you remember that some tables were so big you could crawl under them to make a playhouse?

Perceiving qualities can also help a child to differentiate between two similar things. Patty saw Barb in the parking lot and said, "That's my mother's car."

Honey, I think the baby needs changing.

"Which one?" asked Barb.

Patty replied, "The little baby green one."

The names of the qualities became important after the things themselves have been identified.

A child cannot become skillful in perceiving and naming things by talking to herself; the input of the word must come from you. Generalizing and classifying follow sufficient perceiving and identifying. As more names become associated with the child's perceptions, the more verbally facile the child is likely to become.

Perceiving Things That Move

Nag, racehorse, steed, bronco, plug, and *charger* name six different horses. These names suggest some differences when the horses are standing still, although you and the child may have some difficulty in deciding which is the nag and which is the plug. When they move, however, a racehorse and a bronco move with quite different actions. Each of these names for the horses implies something about the actions they can do. You can help a child to develop a specific vocabulary when you use different names for things within a group that imply something special about the actions these things can do.

More specific names for things come directly from the names of the actions they perform. *Pacer, trotter,* and *jumper* name more horses, but these names are more closely associated with what the horses are trained to do. Point out, when the names offer an opportunity, how -*er* or -*or* on the end of many words may be used to name something according to the action it can do. An elevator and an escalator both raise people, but in different actions. A driver and a diver can both be people (check out that -*er!*), but they perform quite different actions. As a matter of fact, a driver can be a diver, but probably not at the same time. Note, too, that the thing doesn't have to be moving in order to earn its name, but this kind of name strongly implies the ability of the thing to do the action; the racer doesn't have to be whooshing around the Indy track, but it has to look like it could, or did, or will.

Words like *fast, zigzag,* or *lively* are used to name the qualities

28

of a moving thing. Some qualities can be associated to things from memory; but keep in mind that perceiving is current, and qualities which imply the action when perceived as moving don't necessarily apply to that thing when it's still. A child can say that turtles are small from her memory and past experiences in watching turtles, but she can't very accurately say that the "now" turtle is slow unless she perceives it moving. Developing a vocabulary involves identifying the names of things and qualities which imply both stillness and motion.

The actions of moving things may be named:

> The horse bit the rider's leg.
> The ladybug flew away home.
> The dog sniffed around the tree.
> The plane is landing (lands).
> The rabbits are eating (eat) the lettuce.
> Your cats are fighting (fight).

Knowing the names of actions is as important as knowing the names of things. Language would halt the world into the stillness of a globular mausoleum, if it could not provide words that name the hundreds of movements we go through each day. Try to remember your own helpless feelings when you struggle to talk about your perception of things and actions to someone who does not understand your language. Your arms begin to flail in order to provide the words which the tongue cannot name.

Actions do not perform themselves; things do actions. When a child talks about the actions he perceives, he must first name the thing that's acting. When he recalls an action, he must first bring to mind a doer. Both names have to "be there," the doer and the action—and the makings of a sentence are brought together.

The quality of an action can be named, but this quality must not be confused with the size, shape, color, or other qualities of the doer.

The gray horse limps slowly on the painful leg.

Slowly names the quality perceived in the limp, not the horse. (*Gray* names the color of the horse, and *painful* names a quality of the leg, if you care.) The names for an action's qualities usually answer the questions Where?, When?, and How?

> The skydiver landed there. (Where?)
> We heard the ambulance then. (When?)
> It sped away quickly. (Where? How?)

Personally, I'm not enthusiastic about stuffing a child full of qualities for actions. Answers to How?—words that generally end with -*ly*—can become so manufactured that a listener may begin to wince at a bombardment of them splattered through a narration. Answers to Where? and When? come more effectively in groups of words rather than in single words, and those word groups have a fine way of taking care of themselves. Simply ask children such questions as "Where did you see it? When did it happen? How did she do it?"

Later in the book we'll talk more about how a well-named action can make the use of its qualities redundant.

It doesn't seem to confuse children that the names of many actions have become the names of related things. When you go for a walk together, you *walk,* although you can walk without going for *a walk.* And you can't very well go for a walk in a car. When you go for a walk, you can look in store windows, sit on a bench and rest awhile, count robins, eat ice cream cones, turn an ankle, and buy a quart of milk on the way home. Of course, each action along the way can make a language experience for you and the child, if you'll simply keep your perceivers busy scanning the surroundings.

Look at the whole cluster that comes from the name of one action, *laugh: laughter, laughing, laughingstock, laughingly, laughable, laughably, laughableness* (it's a word, all right, but it sounds so manufactured coming from a child!). Some people call these clusters "word families" because they come from the same base word. If the child enjoys words as words, then naming word families can be good fun and a good reason for poking around in a dictionary.

Notice so far that we haven't once used the words *noun, adjective, verb,* or *adverb* when we were talking about names. These are grammatical terms that belong in the study of a textbook;

they are not words which need to enter the language experiences between you and the child. The terms may not be needed again in this book, unless we're absolutely cornered and without an alternative. You probably won't need them, either, in your conversations with children.

The Gift of Memory

Think of a child's mind as an intricate card-index system that files and records names, meanings, and sometimes associated experiences as well as mental sketches or images. The system, we hope, groups perceptions in such a way that the past may help to name the "now" perception. Perhaps the child has never seen a particular framework of Lucite, but the size, the shelves, the space between the shelves, plus whatever other things the child's perceptive scanners take in, go to the right corner of that magnificent retrieval system, which replies, "Uh-huh, from what we can make of it and what we know of other stuff like it, it's a bookcase."

The mind can work the other way, too. For example, when you or the child hears the word *birthday*, the data-retrieval system may go, "Ah-hah! Cake, hugs, hot dogs, presents, games, sick stomach." It may also run a short mental montage of bits and pieces about a memorable birthday. It may also report, "Yes, the day when you were nine, your father died."

Concepts are responses that may be triggered by words or associated experiences, a way of "getting the facts"—names, meanings, and memories—from the retrieval system. When somebody says "peppermint," what you get back may be called a concept. The word *lemon* may give you a slight pain behind the ears. The name *polka dot* may retrieve nothing from the child's mind, since although the child may be wearing a polka-dot shirt, nothing from the past connects the name with the thing. This is where the child suddenly becomes unique and individual. No two mental data-retrieval systems are exactly alike, and they are not preprogrammed. One word may easily get back a hundred different concepts from a hundred different children. A word can only be a word until it's used to name a thing, and the meaning of that word is decided by the thing it names. The catch is that the concept in the mind decides for each person the meaning of a name. It's that grouping and generalizing system that makes any language possible. Even though persons may have different meanings attached to things they name, they can agree on certain words of a language to name things which have fairly common meanings in each person's mind.

People may use and understand language because their memories provide a day-to-day consistency on which to base meaning. Young children cannot always understand language, because they do not have a sufficient number of words to name the things, actions, and qualities they perceive. Older people often have difficulty with the language because the "mind goes," and they cannot remember the names of things from day to day. The *mem* in *remember* is the same as the *mem* in *memory*. Our memories permit us to remember names from one person, time, and place to the next. The ability to remember and the agreed-upon consistency in naming things are two major factors which make a language possible.

Superthings

Close your eyes for a moment and think about a rodeo. What you get back from your mental retrieval system is a conglomerate of concepts associated with a rodeo based on your memories of pictures, TV programs, films, your past experiences at the real events, as well as your own expectations of what a rodeo might be. If you and a child tend toward creating fantasies, you might picture bits and pieces of something that happened at a fictional rodeo, or you might see yourself on a bucking horse, the strong and able ambulance driver, or perhaps the bronco itself (who knows what lurks in the mind!). Your concepts of a rodeo probably don't stand still, do they? You can think of a rodeo as an event—a collection of things to see and hear, plenty of actions and qualities to keep those perceptive scanners busy. A superthing.

Here are some other superthings:

party	parade	carnival	park
circus	chess	convention	pool
zoo	beach	jungle	airport

Here are some two-word superthings:

baseball game	amusement park
street fair	track meet
shopping center	construction site
swimming pool	fire station

These are the kinds of superthings you generally like to take children to for the experiences and, we hope, the language that goes with them.

But you don't always have to be on the run looking for events for children. You can turn ordinary, everyday things into superthings; children certainly can. Notice how they become intensely interested for long periods of time in staring into a brackish puddle, in dismantling an old appliance, in watching a fire. An anthill, a barn, a back yard, a garage, a vegetable garden, a set of trains may become superthings. As you and the child perceive almost anything more and more closely, you may discover that the whole thing is made of parts, and the parts themselves may be talked about as superthings which also contain smaller parts. Perhaps you and the child hear a folksong, and you listen very carefully for some repeated phrase that you wait to sing together. You may perceive more closely, learn that the tune is divided by melody and the accompaniment; the musical score includes notes for both voices and instruments; the instrumental portion may be divided by the parts played on the piano, the guitar, and the fiddle; the piano music is divided by notes and rests; and the notes are divided by . . . And so it goes, as far into detail as you and the child care to go, each part becoming a superthing composed of smaller parts. Think, then, as a scientist who becomes fascinated to learn that the atom, generally thought to be the smallest part of matter, is also a minute superthing which within itself contains parts. Are those parts superthings, too? How far can it all go?

The rule of thumb is to think of almost anything as a superthing composed of parts which may be perceived, named, and *talked about* with the child. On the other hand, naming the parts without identifying the superthing itself leaves you and the child to pleasant moments of making riddles. Try, for example, naming some things and actions that you may perceive at a filling station without identifying them by name. It doesn't take much experience at this little game before you and the child discover that you must name smaller and smaller parts of bigger and bigger superthings. Notice sometime, as you watch television quiz games, the enormous amounts of money that some contestants win at this very same game.

Acquiring Language

If there were nothing in this world to perceive, there would be no need for language. Language is a way of replying to things. One may look at a stone, say "stone," and almost expect it to move as if it knew its name. Some expert gardeners tell us that plants grow best when we talk to them. I'm not much of an apartment window gardener, but I'm absolutely hell with avocados, and I'm convinced that avocados are masochistic. I talk rough to them and I push them around, and they grow for me like crazy. Animals make satisfying company to many children and adults because they respond. You can look at a dog, say his name, and the dog picks up his ears, wags his tail, and comes to you for a pat on the head. More than that, a dog may know your directions and even respond to your conversation. But things, avocados, and animals generally do not completely satisfy a person's need for language.

Language development requires the input of words. Children talk best when they have people to talk with and when they continually receive new language resources in a verbal atmosphere. We said before that children cannot develop a language by talking to themselves. They need other people who will listen to them, encourage them to talk, and offer them quantities of language with which to work.

Each of us employs a combination of physical language and verbal language. We can tell a person in both physical and verbal ways that we love them (and the right combination is swell!). Unfortunately, we can also get pushed around physically and with words, and in many cases, the words can wound almost as much as a karate chop. We usually hope that conflicts between people and nations may be resolved verbally without having to resort to physical communication.

As children acquire language, they may express their needs and desires verbally, but they tend to resort to physical actions when their words don't seem to be successful or when they don't have adequate language to express what they want to say. Often, you can help a child by offering him a sentence which expresses what he may have tried to communicate in some behavior. Children learn from you how language may be used as a socially acceptable substitute for certain physical behaviors.

Not all of the words in our language are things, actions, and qualities. Hundreds of words—like *and, or, instead, although, meanwhile, through, into, around*—help to create a connection between words and the relationship of the ideas which they express. These connecting words help to glue ideas together into phrases and sentences. They help us to arrange one word after another into a relationship called syntax (if you care about the term). It's a great day when a child says her first word; it's perhaps an even greater day when she utters her first meaningful sentence.

Lucille Hilty is one of the best kindergarten teachers I ever knew. She keeps the developmental abilities of her pupils in mind when she divides her class between the "can-do's" and the "not-yet's." She keeps in mind, too, that a child can be a "can-do" in one ability and a "not-yet" in another. We'll take a lesson from Lucy throughout this book, and we won't limit or organize our language experience by developmental age groups. For example, even though a four-year-old may not fully understand our monetary system and probably won't select two nickels as proper change for a dime, it won't hurt a bit to talk about it now and then in order to give him a language background necessary for understanding. As he goes along with you to shop, he can understand eventually that things in stores have value and that money is the anticipated exchange for needed or fancied items. Questions and informative comments from you may never be wasted, even though the child's responses do not warrant pursuing this particular language experience. It's better for you to talk in a friendly, steady stream of language than to have the child follow you in silence. It's so easy to turn a "not-yet" into a "can-do."

A child's keen perception of things, actions, and qualities is a basic part of a child's life-long ability to use language. Perceptions lead eventually to preferences which affect a child's attitudes and behaviors. There's no such thing as acquiring too much language.

4

Sentences That Tell Stories

If you could be anything in the world other than yourself,
what would you be, and why?

A fly on the wall so I could watch people when they
think they're alone.

A merry-go-round so that I'd always be where people
are having a good time.

A cloud so that I could travel everywhere and never
have to stay home.

A drop of blood so that I could see what's inside a person's body.

A mean giant so that everybody would say "yes
ma'am" and be afraid of me.

A piece of seaweed at the bottom of the ocean so I
could have some peace and quiet.

Who hasn't played this game? After a few rounds, the players
often get really specific by limiting the "ifs" to living animals,
plants, other persons; sometimes, but not very frequently, a
round involves nonliving, "plain ol' *thing*" things.

Preferences by the players almost always are related to something that the choice can do . . . a matter of *power* in the action
of a thing.

The Power of Things

As we talk on these pages about *power,* we'll limit ourselves to perceivable things, and we'll deal later with the names of abstract things like grief, integrity, and friendship.

Remember that grouping and generalizing scheme in the mind that was so important to naming perceived things? Here it is again. Children learn to categorize things according to their powers to do actions.

Things that make noises.
Things that walk.
Things that swim.
Things that move on wheels.

These groupings don't hold things tightly. A bike and a car can move on wheels, a car and a jet use fuel, a jet and a bird can move through the air, a bird and a zebra can walk on the ground, a zebra and a giraffe walk on four legs, not two . . . New groupings may continue on and on as the perceived things hop in and out of categories by their similar powers to act. (To be fair about all of this, I suppose, only some things can "hop"!)

Grouping things in temporary categories provides a fine game of riddles as well as a basis for constructing sensible (or nonsensical) generalizations about what things can do. Your conversations about perceived things will help the child to build a more permanent, reliable framework of things' powers to act.

Perhaps the most obvious grouping comes from the child's realization that some things have life and other things don't. In order to identify the *thing* things, the lumpy stuff, we'll group them under "objects." As the child acquires more and more names for animate things, the need for breaking down that too-inclusive group becomes apparent.

Some of the animate things are human, and some are not. Perceptions and discussions will help the child to divide the mass of animate-but-not-human things into two more groups. One group includes plants, the other animals.

Four main categories of things emerge, then, as the child makes generalizations on a thing's power to act:

Objects—rocks, ice cubes, postage stamps

Plants—moss, trees, poison ivy (but not the product of plants, such as tomatoes, peanuts, pine cones, in case your conversations with the child get picky)

Animals—whales, eagles, woodchucks

Humans—of all races, creeds, colors

One class is not meant to imply strength or superiority over another class. Water moccasins and some mushrooms can kill humans. A barbed-wire fence can make a nasty cut on a cow's neck. Children play a finger game in which paper covers rock, scissors cut paper, and rock breaks scissors, yet all three may be grouped in the class of objects. No, comparing the powers of the classes is not the point of the grouping; instead, the categories help the child to assign actions to things and to test the reason of the sentences that tell what a thing can do or what it did.

Categorizing may continue to extremely intricate and minute detail, as the child gains more and more vocabulary, takes a growing interest in perceiving things, and makes generalizations. One child may develop an interest in grouping reptiles, mammals, and marsupials. Another may perceive the differences of arthropods (crustaceans, arachnids, and myriapods—how about *that!*). It seems that almost every subgroup in every class of things may become in itself a class to be divided even further. Like the atom, which may become a "superthing" to a scientist, these detailed classes within groups may become an enormous challenge to a curious and perceptive mind in a growing child.

The Doers and the Done-Untoers

My father, the country doctor and the rural philosopher, has said, "This world is divided into two kinds of people, the doers and the done-untoers." Each of us undoubtedly slips from one category to the other, depending upon the time and the circumstance. I doubt if there is any such thing as a one hundred percent doer, although it may be somewhat easier to find a one hundred percent done-untoer. The power of a thing lies in the quantity and the diversity of the action it can perform, its ability to be a doer.

Plants grow. That very act is the plant's power we can name as we perceive it to take root, sprout, bud, bloom, produce, and, of course, die.

Animals have an added advantage in their powers to move. Even though they move, feed, procreate, and fight in varied ways, the powers of animals increase in quantity and diversity. They are definitely doers.

We can name thousands of actions that humans can do, partly because we can speak from firsthand experience, partly because we can perceive human actions more closely, and partly because humans can *tell* about their actions to each other. Humans seem to be the doingest doers—not, mind you, because of the superiority, but because of the number and variety of their actions.

Objects, the lumpy stuff, take the short end of the stick when it comes to powers to act. Sure, the rock can lie there in the sun, but the power of objects is relatively limited, and they are mostly a large group of done-untoers.

Doers Make Story Sentences

When a child names a thing and then names an action that it did, she identifies the basic ingredients for telling a very short story—actually, a story so compact that it can fit into the confines of a unit called a sentence, a "story sentence."

Story sentences must contain at least a thing and an action which the thing did, does, or is doing. Even though it means a thing, *the dog in the road* is less than a sentence because the storyteller has not named the action. Another storyteller has offered less than a sentence with *rode on the Ferris wheel*, because no doer was named. As one child said, "Ya gotta have it both."

You can easily conclude, then, that things which can act in numerous and diverse ways are likely to be the most interesting doers in stories. If you had a choice, would you rather tell a child a story—a collection of story sentences—about a seashell or a dragon? A stalk of corn or a jet pilot? A broom or a wild dog? Your preference will probably go to the animals and the people rather than the plants or the objects. Your choice will undoubtedly be influenced by your consideration of what these things might *do* to make a more active, lively tale.

Borrowing Power from Another Class

Early childhood may be one of the very best times from the standpoint of language, because that remains a time in a child's mind when things have powers that might boggle an adult's reason. Flowers dance, cats wear hats, country mice hitch rides on trucks to visit their city cousins, a hippo makes a debut at Carnegie Hall, weeping willows cry, and a sheet of paper giggles every time it's tickled by a ball point pen.

Children correct the limitations of the powers of any class. For the purpose of a good story, a child can authorize almost anything to do what it needs or wants to do. That every animal in a story can talk is taken for granted. How else can it tell what happened or is happening? Henny Penny must run screaming through the barnyard to tell others that the sky is falling. The beautiful bird must cry happy tears as he lifts his slender neck and exclaims, "Well . . . I'm a *swan!*" It bothers children not a bit that the swan speaks English in a tale originally written in Danish. Never is there a time when more powers are borrowed back and forth from one category of things to another.

Children create metaphors (you may appreciate the term; children couldn't care less) as they ascribe an action of something in one class to something in a different group. Lisa, very tired, told her aunt, "My bed is crying because I'm not in it!" The borrowing of power enables the doer in a story to perform numerous and varied actions which, in real life, it could not do.

The language is soaked with thousands of metaphors which borrow meanings and apply them in imaginative ways to other things, actions, and qualities. The scarecrow wanted a brain, the tin man wanted a heart, and the lion wanted courage; Dorothy, the least imaginative character in this wildly metaphorical tale, only wanted to leave Oz and to go home to Kansas.

When you are about to tell a story to a child, you have an opportunity to find out just how imaginative a child can be. Simply ask, "Who'll be in the story?" If the reply is something other than human—a stuffed snake, let's say—you might suggest that it may do human actions for stuffed-animal reasons; perhaps it has to go to Dr. Dolittle because its stuffing is coming out. Story starters like this become cooperative affairs as each of you develops the tale, in this case, of a stuffed snake slipping into a human context. What could be more metaphorical than that?

I've often observed (and I've done it myself) the futile effort of an adult trying to teach a young child the difference between *what* and *who.* A *who,* teaches the adult, refers to a person and a *what* refers to a thing. This differentiation may be okay for older youths who have some idea of what's real and what isn't—or maybe we should say who's real and who isn't. To a young child, however, a what can become a who so easily that the comparison has no hook on which to hang in the child's mind. Flora Flea can run away from the dog's ear and become famous in a circus. Ashley the Ashtray can yearn to become a flower vase. The hollyhock who lives in the barnyard can be jealous of the morning glory who lives by the kitchen door. All of these whats become whos with the flip of a story sentence. The real difference need not get in the way now; it can come much later.

Seven-year-old Wayne once told me a fully detailed story about a lonely asteroid. One day the asteroid saw a spaceship coming his way, and he hoped that the spaceship might become his friend. But the spaceship smiled, waved, and went on by, leaving the asteroid alone again. In conclusion, Wayne decided that the asteroid should make friends with another asteroid going his way. I once saw an assembly program by a third-grade class about a rock who had pains in her stomach, and "When you're a rock, a stomach's the biggest thing you've got."

The time comes when a child begins to question and doubt the wonderful powers which one class of things borrows from another, and he begins to say, "That's only a story, isn't it . . . You're making that up . . . It didn't really happen, did it." The Tooth Fairy loses credibility, and Santa Claus becomes the

Oh, the cookie isn't for ME, Mom. FLUFFY asked me to get him one!

Spirit of Giving. The metaphorical times may be giving way to reality, and the more realistic forms of fiction. But those powers that turn a what into an exciting, lively who are good while they last. And you can make the most of them in the stories you share with a young child. You'll both be happier for them, I promise.

Clap your hands if you think Tinkerbell should live!

Who? Did What?

Answers to these two questions may form a story sentence. It may be as brief as two words—naturally, the doer and the act.

Man fell.

The same story may be embroidered with particulars.

The little old *man* in the tattered raincoat *fell* on the front steps of the Plaza Hotel.

The two answers to the important questions, however, remain the same, and the necessary ingredients—the doer and the act—can still be found in there. "Ya gotta have it both," or you have less than a story sentence. Answers to other questions help the young storyteller to add length, interest, and details, but answers to these two questions build the necessary framework for the story sentence.

Young children who grow in a verbal atmosphere will be busy acquiring the words they need to name and to tell about what they perceive, but they will encounter blanks in their language which you can help to fill. As an example, Michael pointed to a noisy puppy fidgeting around a large palmetto bug (I've often considered a palmetto bug to be a euphemism for a cockroach, but my Southern friends say 'tisn't so!). However, Michael said, "Bug," not "puppy." Doug wisely concluded it was a moment for sentence-making and replied, "Yes, the puppy barked at the bug." Michael did not repeat the whole sentence but, instead, said, "Barked," and then said it again. The name of the action had been supplied and the language blank had evidently been filled. I could almost see *barked* being filed away in Michael's mental retrieval system.

Young children begin to form sentences when they have a

sufficient input of words to name the things and the actions they perceive. The words must come from others, but the ability to frame sentences seems to be something that the mind can do with little experience or perhaps with no experience at all. When a child needs a word to name his perception, be reasonably sure in your own mind that he hears the word clearly, says the word clearly a time or two, and unmistakably associates the word as the name of the perceived thing, action, or quality. It's not always necessary for him to repeat the sentence in which you used the word. Names are the verbal gems to be collected; with them, the child's creation of new, unheard sentences is almost beyond limit. The child must imitate the words of a language, but he will undoubtedly be able to frame new sentences for himself. In no way can we demean the sentence, for it's the most important unit of communication; but we'll remember that children cannot talk about things which they cannot first name.

Time for Actions

Think about it.

First, actions take time. The time it takes to blink an eye may seem like a week compared to a flash of lightning or one of the even quicker events within the science of electronics. A person's lifetime is a tick in the clock of the universe. Nevertheless, whether it be shorter than an instant or longer than an eon, an act requires the passage of some period of time.

Second, the future becomes the present became the past faster than you can read this sentence. Didn't we all at some age ponder one of childhood's greatest theorems on time? "Today is tomorrow's yesterday, today is yesterday's tomorrow." From that point we tested statement after statement— "Tomorrow is yesterday's today, yesterday is tomorrow's yesterday"—and then discussed them to philosophic fragments. Another impressive statement that never failed to bring me abruptly face to face with the fact of time was "Today is the first day of the rest of your life."

We seem to be skimming along on some kind of time ribbon

45

that moves very quickly before us to us behind us. Its beginning is far too far behind us in the dust of the past, and its end
is somewhere before us. Some people claim emphatically that
the "end is in sight" (a fascinating perception!), while others
judge that this time ribbon is anchored at both ends in more
sturdy stuff. Some linger and languish in the nostalgia of the
past almost to the point of neurosis, and others live for now,
one day—today—at a time, on the premise that "this is it, baby,
this is all we've got." Some say the past offers us the lessons to
be learned and the pitfalls to be sidestepped. Each of us, now
and then, is made to face the brutal facts of his own individual
time ribbon.

There is one point in all this hoohah about time, and it's a
whopper. If actions require time (and they do), and if we are
expected to cope with time (and we must), then the language
must enable us to talk about time to each other.

A story sentence reveals time of an action. The name of that
action may indicate one of two major time zones, the past or
the present. Young children don't have your sense of the measures of time. Lisa may not be able to compute how much time
has passed since her last birthday, but she may know she was
four. Charlie can't read a clock or a calendar, but he understands today, tomorrow, yesterday, and the time chunks into
which he can divide them—this morning, last night, supper-
time, among others. "Once upon a time" may be when Mom
was a little girl. But children who use story sentences freely and
fluently have some concept of the present and the past, even if
they do not always know the correct form of the word that
names the time of an action.

The present is now, and the names of present actions answer
the questions Does what? or Is doing what? The past, as far as a
child is concerned, is all that time which is not now any more;
and, as you know, the names of actions in the past answer the
question Did what? When you're encouraging a child to use
narrative by asking him questions, keep the two-part time
period separate by asking What is it doing? for those actions
perceived to be currently in progress, and What did it do? for
those actions that are not "now" any more. When an action

46

you've perceived and talked about ceases—when the siren stops screeching or the hail stops falling—you can use a story sentence to tell the child what it did, giving him a chance to hear and, possibly, to file away another name for a past action.

Future actions don't have special forms like those for the present and the past, because, strictly speaking, they are not yet actions. An action in the future may be predicted, threatened, promised, suspected, anticipated, but it cannot be perceived. You can, if you wish, think of sentences about the future as opinions, since only time will tell if those opinions become perceived, provable facts. The weather forecaster, for example, issues opinions about tomorrow's weather and the five-day forecast after reporting the facts on yesterday's weather.

Help the child, when and as needed, to add word clues which indicate actions in the future.

Greg flies to Phoenix *tomorrow.*

Bess *will* meet him at the airport.

Michelle plays with the Minnows *on Saturday.*

Each of these sentences contains the name of an action which cannot by itself indicate future. Word clues such as *tomorrow, will,* and *on Saturday* are needed to turn each of these sentences into predictions about the future. *Will* is a commonly used clue but it is by no means the exclusive one. The English language users, at one time, were very clearly divided between the "willists" and the "shallists," when the use of *shall* with *I* or *we* became an impressive mark of the educated, the verbally "correct." The shallists have been so outnumbered by the willists in America, however, that *shall* is rarely heard these days. The distinction is very difficult to explain to children; don't feel that you need to try.

A child may now and then become entangled in meanings when he tries to crowd more than one thing and more than one action into the same sentence. It's possible but not frequent that the child may say, "Jill ate and eats her hamburger and her french fries." It's more common and certainly more reasonable for him to handle one action at a time, "Jill ate her hamburger. Now she's eating her french fries." The passing of time reflected in these story sentences becomes clear, and they're

47

helped further, you'll notice, by including the time clue *now*. If children scramble times and sequences in their story sentences, help them to say one thing at a time by simply offering the correctly ordered sentence as a normal reply in your conversation.

MOLLY: I planted and watered the beans and tomatoes.

DAD: First, you planted the beans, and then you watered the tomatoes.

MOLLY: Yep, sure did! Now what?

The answers to the questions Who? and Did what? provide the young sentence maker with the basic parts of a one-sentence story. With keen perception and an interested, active listener—you—the child's story is started. One good story sentence deserves another, and another, and another.

5

Questions—The Third Degree?

The questions that you see written in this chapter will be somewhat misleading. A question looks pretty "straight" when it appears in print. But look out.

Many linguists define written language as a visual representation of spoken language. Speech may be encoded into written letters and symbols; and then, at another time and place, it may be decoded for its original meaning and again turned into speech, if desired. You may have heard of a fairly common explanation that reading is "talk written down." The transmission of meaning from one time and place to another requires that the language be preserved, canned, or dried in some retrievable form.

Missing, however, and it's a formidable however, is some provision in our language for recording in print the way the speaker talks the words and projects the meanings of the sentences, especially questions. Which words need to be marked with some kind of emphasis and shading? The volume, the intensity, or the speed with which the speaker says certain words can color the meaning as well as imply any specific intentions. We've been through enough trouble with secretly taped conversations in the last few years to know how important both the words and the voice are to help us determine the deeper meaning behind the surface meanings of spoken words. Written language is very quiet, and we may look for clues of intent which, though they'd be obvious if we heard the speaker, are excluded when the talk is written down.

Perhaps the closest relationship of oral and written language exists in informal letters. You can think of your letter as a substitute for your side of a conversation if you and the "writee" were within chatting distance. For many people, talking on the phone is the next best thing to being there; writing a letter is the next-to-the-next best thing. But the warm and friendly sounds of the voice you hear on the phone are missing in the letter you read.

To compensate, we often invent marks and manners of making certain words more noticable in an attempt to approximate stress in our informal writing. A row of exclamation marks (!!!!) makes a comment more angry or surprising. Similarly, a parade of question marks (?????) turns a simple query into a major puzzlement. An <u>underlined</u> word seems to say, "Look at me, I'm <u>important.</u>" Some writers try to make words "louder" by printing them fully in CAPITAL letters. We even insert our own laughter by adding HA HA!, intending to tell the reader that our comment was meant to be frivolous or funny. Highly individual, creative writers resort even more to dots, dashes, arrows, extra spaces, and glyphs to bring their oral and written languages more closely together, often to the point where they confuse the intention rather than clarify it.

Linguists generally frown on all these extra, excessive flourishes in standard written language. They can't blame us, though, for attempting to approximate the sound of our voices, since those silent words we write cannot speak for themselves.

ESPECIALLY when we come to a *very slithery* (wow!) part of the language, *questions!!!!* See all those visual STRESSES???

Confrontation, Interrogation

School was out, and the long hot summer began. Julie and her son Lyle were not accustomed to spending so much time with each other. Julie's comings and goings were impeded somewhat by the presence of Lyle, and Lyle was having difficulty coping with Julie's excessive nagging.

After a couple of hours at the Central Park Zoo, not without some strife between them, they stood facing the outdoor cage of Pattycake, the famous baby gorilla. For the first few moments, there was nothing to be seen in the cage. Suddenly, Pattycake came screeching through the opening from the indoor side, climbed the bars directly in front of the viewers, grabbed the branch of the dead tree in the cage, leaped to the crotch of the limb, and sat there whimpering for several minutes.

Julie asked, "Why did Pattycake do that?"

Lyle replied, "Well, Mom, this time it's not my fault!"

Startled, Julie looked down at her son, who quickly managed a wry smile. She sensed the humor of the remark immediately, and she stooped down to give Lyle a big hug. They laughed together out loud. I had the feeling that the summer might go better for both of them after that.

A question can begin a discussion, or it can be the rumbling of thunder before a verbal storm. These questions seem harmless enough in print:

Why did the dog bark?

Where are my scissors?

Why did the rabbit run?

How did the gerbil's cage door get opened?

When did you talk to Daddy?

What's in the package on your bed?

When spoken, these questions may be expressed in at least two ways. They may be asked in a straight, nonaccusatory way as conversation starters which can indicate your curiosity or interest. Or they can be asked in such a way that you seem to want to "start something," by the very subtle way in which you raise your voice, emphasize certain words, project a certain intensity behind the questions you ask, or take a physical posture that seems to project trouble coming. Sometimes, there may be a nuance in your voice or manner, perhaps so slight or offhand that the meaning behind your question confuses the child. The child's reply, offered sincerely, may be, "Why do you want to know?" or "What do you mean?" If you're not careful, the fight begins. If the intention of your question is not unmistakably

51

projected, the child has the right to clear the air, so to speak, so that she knows in which direction the following comments may go—toward a conversation or a storm.

Certain kinds of questions, especially if they are clumsily asked, tend to reduce the likelihood of a following conversation. The wording of the question you ask may be at fault. On the other hand, you may be asking a perfectly harmless question with the added tone, pitch, intensity, weight, or stress that puts a suspicious something into the question, whether you intended it or not.

1. Right-wrong: Children don't like to be wrong any more than you do. The gamble between the right and the wrong answer can be even more crucial to a child who feels that he is at the bottom of the family's totem pole. The child may decide that a simple "I don't know" or even silence is an answer preferable to being wrong and the ensuing criticism. Many children, both at home and at school, seem to prefer being indecisive rather than being labeled ignorant. Read your child's scene carefully. If he seems to prefer silence or "I don't know," then phrase your questions more carefully so that there are a number of acceptable answers, giving the child a multiple choice of responses within the realm of right.

2. Personal wounds within questions: Some questions seem to contain weapons which draw blood, and an acceptable answer is practically impossible for them.

> "Who do you think you are, anyhow, the Queen of Sheba?"
>
> "What kind of an idiot would want to see that stupid movie?"
>
> "Syrup on your french fries? Are you crazy?"
>
> "Why would anybody want a raccoon for a pet?"
>
> "Where on earth did you get those ugly shoes?"

These questions will probably not start conversations, but they'll start fights. Words and phrases like *Queen of Sheba, idiot, stupid movie, crazy, ugly* have almost no place in questions intended to be conversation starters. These questions cannot be revised acceptably; instead, new questions have to be asked after you've revised your own frame of mind. Besides, have you ever tried syrup on your french fries? And raccoons can be very winning creatures!

3. *Invasion of privacy:* Even when some questions are asked out of genuine curiosity and sincere interest, the answers may be none of your business.

"What do you do all afternoon in your treehouse?"

"What's in that red box on the floor of your closet?"

"What are you reading about?"

"Why do you spend so much of your time making model boats?"

You and the children are all entitled to some privacy in the way you spend your time and in the place where you keep your prized possessions. As a general rule, treehouses, pup tents, and refrigerator-crate shacks are off limits to adults, and you're probably dying to know what goes on in there. Probably nothing. If you suspect skullduggery, you must think of softer ways to find out and plan your approach very carefully. You want to be assured, but respect and a soft approach will accomplish more than hard-core accusations.

For the same reasons, reading is a very private thing. The exchange between the characters in a book and an active reader do not necessarily include a kibitzer. When the child is reading, one good rule of thumb is not to interrupt. If you suspect the suitability of the reading matter, plan your soft approach carefully; also, read the child's scene while the child is reading, and note whether the child leaves the reading matter where others may pick it up.

4. *Question behind the question:* Some questions may be too nebulous to stand on their own as discussion starters. The child needs to know more explicitly what you are driving at before she can frame a reply. A puzzled look or a question from the child like one of these gives you the clue to get more directly to the real question behind your opening gambit.

"What do you mean?"

"Why are you asking?"

"What are you driving at?"

"What did you say?"

These questions can threaten you. Be careful. You must not

conclude that the child is either deaf or dense. Instead, look at the nature of your own questioning. Become more specific in rephrasing your question, and offer an explanation on what it is you want to know and why you're asking. And keep your voice soft, even though you may be tempted to raise it if you're piqued or impatient.

5. *The "test":* Some questions force a child to confirm something that you both already know. These questions introduce a confrontation, since almost any reply will lead to an entrapment.

"Who nibbled on peanuts between meals?"

"And where do you think I saw you when I went to pick up your father?"

"We know where you hid Harry's new watch, don't we?"

"What somebody around here was listening on the extension telephone?"

The questions attempt to place blame within the asking, because the blamer and the young "convict" both seem to know that the crime in question has been perpetrated. In a situation like this where the child and the adult are both aware of the behavior referred to in the question, the child psychologists tell us that we don't ask the questions when we already know the answers.

After what we do to children, sometimes unintentionally but quite often very deliberately, using questions as weapons, invasions, and examinations, it's a wonder that children speak to us at all.

Child, protect yourself!

Implication and Inference

This may not be any big thing, but let's get it straight. The person who asks the questions can do two things. First, the asker can project an explicit request for information. That request may be thought of as the direct inquiry carried with no hanky-panky about anything other than that which is exactly the nature of the question.

Second, the asker can also imply something more than what was asked, something more indirectly or even deviously suggested. The order of the words in the question may be either carefully or carelessly planned, and the results may imply more than the direct question. The asker may add words that are emotionally laden. The asker's voice and physical accompaniments—raised eyebrow, arms akimbo or folded, special gesture, tapping foot—undoubtedly project something more than the question itself.

The asker implies an addition to the direct question. The question may be explicit, since the request of the asker is "unfolded" to the other person. Something more may be implicit if it is "folded into" or entangled within the whole question—words, the voice, the body posture, and movement.

The listener gets this whole explicit-implicit, jumbled-up question. First, the direct inquiry was there for interpreting and replying. But, if there's more, it also has to be sorted out. And it's here that trouble may start. Within the mind of the listener, a conclusion is formed regarding the inquiry and the words, the asker's voice, and any perceived stance and motion of the asker's body.

The listener infers. He decides whether to reply and, if so, the words, the voice, and the movement that will constitute a response. Within that very response, the listener becomes the speaker and, in turn, may imply within the reply.

And so it goes. The speaker will undoubtedly imply something, since it is virtually impossible to ask or talk entirely without addition. And the listener may infer before his turn comes to be the speaker.

Ask yourself sometime, "What's in this question I'm asking?" You become aware perhaps of the implications you project with your direct inquiry. You'll be somewhere pretty close to the motivations in your own questions. Are your intentions clear? Figuratively speaking, do the implications in your questions place you side by side or face to face with the listening child?

Threat, Non-Threat

I sit in awe as I watch adults in the more popular television families approach the children and talk so easily and earnestly with them about the situations which arise in this week's conflict. It all goes so amicably, so well . . . then, poof! I realize that it's all so scripted and directed. The TV adults and children know what they're to say and how they're to express and imply the written lines. Can't adults and children in real life talk to each other in exchanges which lack disagreeable implications? It's all so possible, and yet, I wish the lines for some of the conversations I overhear could be written for the adult and the child, so that their conversation might be pleasant for them.

Let's assume that you want to ask a child anything, any question at all, without the specter of threat foreshadowing your conversation. If you can get a good start, the conversation will have a better chance of taking care of itself. You needn't worry so much about what you're going to say; think carefully, instead, on how you begin.

Once more, read the child's scene. Is now a good time to interrupt, or can you wait for a better time?

Will you enter the scene facing the child or beside the child? Keep in mind that face to face invites the posture for a confrontation; on the other hand, being beside your child may suggest that you are buddies rather than enemies.

Does your touch imply (there's that word again) warmth? Is it soft and soothing? Bodies do "talk" to each other.

What about your own height and stance? Do you tower over a child who's sitting in a small chair or on the floor? You needn't raise the child; lower yourself.

What do you have in your hand? A cooking spoon? A folded newspaper? A garden tool? A golf club? Could the object in your hand be construed as a weapon or a device for possible punishment? Sounds silly, doesn't it, until you think of yourself as three feet high faced by a person six feet high (and looking much higher than that!) with a possible wound-maker in his hand.

How's your own emotional "set?" How has your own day gone in the last fifteen or twenty minutes? Has the child been reprimanded within the last hour? Do you have any hurdle to overcome from your last conversation with the child—or with anybody else?

Give the child time to read your scene as you approach. She

can perceive all of your signs and infer (there's that word, too!) a purpose for your entering her scene.

When you open your mouth, does the sound of your voice carry the question plus positive implications? Your words, your voice, and your physical manner should say, "I'm a friend this time."

It may not always have been friendly between you and the child. She may remember some previous experiences when she was approached by you before the questions, the implications, and the accusations began. As a result, your most difficult task right now may be to assure the child of your desire for togethering rather than for confronting.

With apologies to Solomon, let's rewrite one of his proverbs: "A soft question turns away wrath, but harsh questions cause quarrels."

An Invitation to Share

You'll remember that the two questions Who? and Did what? invite the answerer to create a story sentence.

Tyree saw a red bird on the fire escape ten minutes ago. This sentence answers the two sentence makers and more:

Who?
Did what?
What did he see?
What color was it?
Where?
When?
Exactly when?

If every living man, woman, and child had been provided with some marvelous preset mental system capable of knowing everything about everything from the instant of birth, the language would have no need or provision for questioning, because inquiry would be unnecessary. And wouldn't it be a damn bore to live a life without saying at least once, "Ahah! So that's it! Now I know!" As it is, the language provides the questions, and the human mind has within it the ability to perceive and understand the answer. The question and the answer provide the tools for one of the child's greatest pasttimes—feeding a curious mind.

A question invites an answer which fills in the mental blanks with information.

How fast?

Where in Iowa?

Who coughed?

What's your middle name?

Why is it called a hush puppy?

When is your birthday?

A question invites the answer which teaches something the questioner would like to learn.

How does it fly?

What's the difference between rhubarb and a pieplant?

Where does rain come from?

How long do elephants take to get born?

When will you teach me to play the ukulele?

Questions invite answers which tell a story in one or more sentences.

Who? Did what?

Then what happened?

In its least complicated form, perhaps, a question invites an answer which shares perceptions of things, actions, and qualities.

The Question Words

Note that every one of those "invitations" listed above includes one of the basic question words, Who? What? Where? When? Why? How?

The answers to these questions create story sentences and add details to the things, the actions, and the qualities. The young storyteller doesn't get very far by mumbling "Uh-huh" and "Huh-uh" to a series of yes-no questions (coming in the next section). On the other hand, the child can be boosted along nicely in the real or fictional story. Your active listening and your skill in asking the questions help fill in the needed information and the interesting details.

For years journalists have known these story-making question words as the "Five W's," and they have been somewhat generous, although the generosity is to their own advantage for the sake of a better story, in letting *How?* tag along with the "W's." So, although there are neither five nor are they all W's, they are all basic to good news reporting as well as narration.

Think, if you can bear it for a moment, of an airplane crash, which seems to be the news media's favorite reportable gore, usually vying with government secrets and political corruptions for the preferred front-page spaces and the top TV news spots.

1. Who? And there are plenty! The pilot, the crew, the live passengers, the dead passengers, the rescue teams, the on-lookers, the pilferers, and the relatives. And, of course, the plane and thousands of pieces of related wreckage. No short-age of *Who?* here. Perhaps that's the best clue we have to why such a tragedy makes such good reporting.

2. Did What? We can almost write the story before it hap-pens, if we think that each of the whos did more than one or two actions. You can also see where the actions help to divide the reporting between direct news (those who-did-what's in-volved in the direct tragedy) and the features (the actions of others who provide sidelights and human-interest details to other stories).

3. When? This is, naturally, the question that cannot be an-swered in advance. If it could, we would all stay off planes at that moment. Try to remember the last crash you read about, and recall how the news dwelt upon the minute-by-minute re-port of the progress of the plane during its last moments. Keep in mind also how one network or paper strives to "scoop" an-other by presenting the news first.

4. Where? We're all interested in where the air tragedy oc-curred, because we tend to make a mental check of our friends and relatives to see if they might possibly have been in the air at that place at the wrong time. Proximity also lends immediacy to an air crash. Although it may be every bit as gory and serious, an air tragedy in Asia hasn't a chance for as much TV time or news space as a crash within your state and near your city. On-the-spot coverage also tends to depend upon the prox-imity of the accident.

59

5. *How?* Answers to this question by itself help the reporters to add quantity, detail, and interest to the actions of the accident and the rescue work. More details are added to the story if this question is combined with degrees, speeds, amounts or extents, such as "How low? How many? How fast? How far? How soon?"

6. *Why?* Probably the most interesting question of all. The voice recorder, the traffic control tower, witnesses, weather conditions, and past experiences are all combined into both short-term and long-term studies of the cause. This kind of reporting provides for the next week to six months of follow-up reporting.

Your child is not likely to tell a gory story including all the details of an airplane crash. Nevertheless, these six words, when skillfully included in your own questions, help the child to tell better stories, which describe perceptions in greater detail, and explain an incident or difficulty more fully for you.

The Yes-No Question

Unless it is embellished with additional actions and complicated details, almost any sentence may become a yes-no question.

The Yankees lost last night.

The Yankees lost last night?

Imagine saying each of these sentences to a child. Since the words are exactly the same, something in your voice or your physical movements has to suggest that the second sentence is a question. Sometimes the pitch of the voice turns up at the end of the sentence; sometimes the voice seems to go up over a hill without coming all of the way back down again; sometimes the voice doesn't seem to change at all. Raised eyebrows, rounded eyes and mouth, hunched shoulders, palms turned upward and moved outward in a supplicatory manner, or some other body clues often accompany the yes-no question. Think, then, of all of the sounds and sights a child must perceive in order to infer that you are asking him something which requests a mere yes or no. So much more complicated than one of the simple five W's.

Clive went off to school one morning with an empty coffee can and a large empty vegetable can, the two materials he was to use in making his instrument for the nursery school rhythm band. Near noon he came home looking like quite a different child, moping, quiet, downcast. Tina, his mother, entered Clive's scene softly. She pulled him close to her for a moment, then said, "School didn't go very well this morning?"

"No."

"It had something to do with the rhythm band?"

"Yes."

"You wanted to be the leader?"

"Yes."

"Somebody else was chosen?"

"Yes."

"Maybe Ms. Hoover will give everybody a turn?"

"Maybe."

Who got the work-out here? And who said practically nothing? And yet, it was just the right thing for Tina to do. She read the child's scene, entered it, guessed the trouble, and gave Clive both verbal and physical signals to indicate that she understood. The five W's don't work very well when you want to show a child compassion and understanding, since they demand narrative answers when a child may not feel like talking. Tina confirmed the difficulty and indicated a togetherness with Clive. Needless to say, Clive came home in a much better mood several days later . . . after he'd led the rhythm band.

A yes-no question offers you a polite way to ask a child for assistance or to do a task. In this way, the child may infer that his help is requested rather than demanded. It certainly helps for you to stick in a *please* or some other appreciative word.

Did you ever play twenty questions? That's the game where "it" keeps in mind a thing from the animal, vegetable, or mineral category, and the questioners must identify that thing by asking no more than twenty yes-no questions. Skillful questioners learn to rule out large groups of categories and to ask more and more descriptive questions, so that the name of the thing is probably known before the identifying question is asked, much like moving through the concentric circles of a target on the way to the bull's-eye. When your child is old

61

enough for that type of deduction, never hesitate to start a game or two when you have a few spare minutes. The limited purpose of yes-no questions is to confirm or to negate the inquiry. Yes-no questions are useful in eliciting testimony, playing games of deduction, surmising difficulties, and requesting assistance, but they are not very useful in language experiences intended for sharing.

Pursuing Maybe

"There are many shades of gray between black and white," my dad, the country doctor and "manure philosopher," often repeated. *Maybe* seems to be a name for those shades of gray. *Maybe* is a child's safety zone, a temporary refuge where the child can still maneuver verbally when subjected to an adult's grilling.

Mr. Bradley and his son Harv were batching while Mrs. Bradley took a vacation alone from her home and family. Before supper one evening, the conversation in the kitchen went something like this. Mr. Bradley started it.

"Do you want tomatoes with your supper?"

"Will they be raw or cooked?"

"Do you want them raw?"

"No."

"Will you eat cooked tomatoes?"

"That depends on whether they're stewed or not."

"Do you want stewed tomatoes?" Dad's temperature definitely up by now.

"Will you put Ritz crackers in 'em?"

"Is that the way you like them?"

"That depends on whether you'll put sugar in 'em."

"Aw, hell—no tomatoes for supper!"

Harv knew that he would have to eat the tomatoes, and he was undoubtedly staying within the safety of maybe until he was sure that Dad could fix them the way he liked them.

My eavesdroppings confirm that children want to hang on to their maybes long enough to explore the alternatives (and to exhaust the adults, perhaps) as they weigh what they'll miss

No way! Absolutely not! You hear me? NO!

That means maybe.

before they choose what they want. The tenacious grasp of maybe seems to lie within all of us, possibly from our childhood conditioning. Haven't we all worked for bosses who seem to prefer sitting on the fence when the decisions seem so clear to us? So much dickering goes on before two parties may sign a contract. Even then, the so-called agreement is endorsed cautiously after it seems to contain more conditions than commitments.

The difficult questions about life are not usually answered by a simple yes or no. The maybes, the perhaps, and the hedgings somewhere between the absolute yeses and the absolute noes far outnumber the times when a simple uh-huh or huh-uh may suffice. Think about it. How easy do the answers to yes-no questions come for you? Do you find yourself often seeking a spot in maybe country? If you're about to ask a yes-no question, think for a moment if the child is likely to give a maybe answer.

The absolute, final sounds of yes and no don't provide much leeway for a child to change his mind. Maybe leaves plenty of room for maneuvering toward one way or the other. It also provides more opportunities for discussions, since the decision closes the issue. An adult-child relationship, I suppose, is somewhat like the detente-style diplomacy between nations, because each must be free to operate within the agreed limits and, except when clearly and finally necessary, neither must be nailed to an untenable, irreversible commitment.

If you want to avoid maybe, don't ask a yes-no question.

It also seems pointless to ask a child a yes-no question when the reply is of little consequence. "Do you want to go to bed now?" when asked earlier than bedtime sounds like a threat. The same question, when asked at the child's bedtime, seems useless, since the adult knows it's bedtime anyhow. A resounding *"No!"* from the child fuels the fight, but the question from the adult actually starts it. The child is merely taking advantage of an opportunity that shouldn't have been offered. We're back to the advice suggested earlier; if you know the answer, you needn't ask the question.

The Double-Barreled Question

With the exception of the five W's (plus How, remember?), the best question makers in the language, the double-barreled question helps me to get replies that just aren't possible with yes-no questions. I've learned to rely on double-barreled questions for getting responses, preferences, and opinions from people, and I enjoy thoroughly that moment or two before I ask something when I say to myself, "Now, how's the best way to load this one?"

Simply stated, a double-barreled question consists of a couple of yes-no questions that have been blended together.

"Do you want to go to the Burger King?

Do you want to have Chinese food at home?"

The answers could be "No" twice, and you may have started another difficulty. Blended, they present choices within limits.

"Do you want to eat at the Burger King, or

would you rather eat Chinese food at home?"

There are two pairs of choices here for the child to mull. First, the child can eat out or in, the preference determining the food. Second, the child can ponder over burgers or egg rolls, and that choice decides the location.

You can set the requirements, if you wish, then glue together two alternatives for satisfying it.

"It's time for you to rest at least thirty minutes.

Would you like to snooze in your bed, or

would you rather stay on your blanket outdoors in the shade?"

So, it's a thirty-minute minimum sentence, which the child may serve in bed or within the confines of the blanket. If the child says, "No," you can remind her you made an offer she can't refuse, but she can decide where . . . and that's fair.

"Do you like the red or the blue shirt better?"

The adult has selected the price and the quality of the purchase; the child can choose the color.

"I need your help this afternoon. Would you rather fold the laundry or sweep the garage and sidewalk?"

"You may watch TV for a total of an hour after dinner.

Do you want to see an hour program or two shorter ones?"

"Would you prefer pudding, jello, or an apple with your snack?"

The double-barreled question works not only in preferences for food, purchases, and the assignment of tasks, but it's also helpful when you're listening to a young storyteller who's running out of creative steam.

"Did the bear cub hide behind the tree, or did it sneak into the cave?"

"Could the strange duck swim, or was he afraid of the water?"

"Did the horse buck before or after it saw the rattlesnake?"

If you want to try your luck a bit, you can put your own preference as the second part of the double-barreled question, but only if either choice suits you from the beginning. If you really prefer one response from the child to the virtual exclusion of the other, then you're using the wrong question. You'd better come clean, then, and tell the child your preference, explaining if you can. There's nothing wrong with requesting that the child do what you want her to do; just don't give her what she thinks is a choice, only to find out later that she's been made the pawn of your own preference.

Otherwise, get to know and like the double-barreled question. You'll find it useful, and the child will learn to assume the responsibilities and the consequences of valid decision making.

The Question Sandwich

The Central Park Zoo is a great place for eavesdropping. I overheard this scene there, although it could happen in almost any public complex in the country. The very tired father, standing slumped but upright with some assistance from an overloaded trash basket, confronted his son.

DAD: Whadda you want to do? You wanna see the chimps?

SON: Umf—

DAD: You wanta see the polar bears? Whadda you wanna do now? Go on the pony ride?

SON: I yuh—

DAD: Whadda ya want? An ice cream? What?

son: Um, fum—

dad: C'mon, let's go home, you don' know what you want.

Who really wanted to go home? Who dominated the language experience? And who didn't get much of a chance to decide anything? And for whom do you think the language experience at the zoo was really intended?

However, I saw a child standing in front of his father, befuddled by a barrage of questions, trying to sort out his choices, and confused by a man who didn't seem to want to be there anyhow. I wish I could report that the scene ended pleasantly, but it didn't—the man grabbed the son's hand, and they left the zoo.

The father could have sustained what may have been a pleasant experience for just one more brief moment. I hoped that he might find a bench or a step to sit down on with the child, summarize briefly what they had done together, and then offer one last choice, saying perhaps, "We'll have time to do one more thing before we go home. And you can choose." Then father could keep still and rest long enough for the child to think through the alternatives and make a decision. So simple.

This confrontation offers us several good examples of "the question sandwich," a series of different types of questions which make it almost impossible for a child to frame reasonable answers. In order to answer one question, the child has to muddle through the others. That son wasn't speechless; he was just trying to decide how to tackle the questions in order to come up with replies. Unfortunately, he found himself at home before he could decide what he wanted to do.

The rule of thumb here is to ask one question at a time and to give the child an opportunity to think and then answer. Question sandwiches aren't very palatable, and they're sure to cause verbal indigestion.

Interviewing Children

You can use questions to imply blame, to induce a threat, to wound an ego, to invade a privacy, and to test some knowledge or behavior.

You can also use questions to encourage a story, to learn

something, to discover that which you didn't know you needed to know, to begin a discussion, to imply love, to help along a faltering conversation, to ferret out a problem, and to express your understanding and compassion.

Your questions can put you by a child's side or before the child as his adversary.

Two of your questions can help a child to tell a story sentence. The five W's-and-an-H can help her to fulfill that story.

You can turn almost any sentence into a question by the sound in your voice and your physical accompaniment.

You can avoid or create a quarrel with either carefully or carelessly chosen questions. Either will do either.

You can use questions to play games. The games may be bright, quick, and exciting; or they may be neurotic, dark, and perverse.

Questions assist you in providing a leeway of choices within your selections or limits.

Above all, skillful questions and thoughtful answers provide an adult and a child with the language tools to share the perceptions around them, to narrate the richness of the culture which preceded them, and to ruminate on the future which lies before them.

6

Rubbing Words Together

If everything had a name, just one name, there'd be so many fewer names to learn. If an animal, any animal in the world, were called *animal,* that would be that.

If *walk* named every action that meant going forward—heel down first, toe up last, heel-toe—no other names would be needed.

Tall could name the quality of anything over five feet high, period. No tall*er* or tall*est,* and no favoritism, either. More than five feet? Man, that's tall. Less than five feet? We'll really simplify this, and call that *not tall. Short* is out. And that eliminates a lot of qualities.

We could make our language even simpler. Children may pick their favorite colors on their seventh birthdays. Instead of a birthday that year, children celebrate "Favorite Color Day." Sometime during the party, the name of the child's favorite color is tattooed on his right thumb. Green, for example, on one newly turned seven-year-old. And, for the rest of that child's life, colors are so simple—they're either green or not green. No changing of favorite colors allowed; when that thumb is marked, that's it for life, kid.

There's a fringe benefit to this thumb tattooing. By marking the right thumb, the child doesn't ever need to be confused about which hand is which. He has one right hand and one not-right hand. If he has the misfortune to be left-handed, then society will definitely mark him as "not right."

Just these few innovations would cut our need for words down to the bare minimal essentials. We'd also be left without a useful language. Language can't exist by naming only what things are not.

Our language maintains its power, convenience, and interest by its resource of names for slightly varied things, actions, and qualities. Except for the most specifically detailed things, almost everything in our daily lives has more than one name. And I, for one, am grateful to the language makers, whoever they are, for the number and the variety.

What Do You See? What Else?

A group of about eight children, looking as if they might enter first grade that fall, were standing in a small park overlooking the East River. They came from a neighborhood "City Camp," a far cry from the kind of camp with tents and woods and baked beans; nevertheless, the city camp undoubtedly filled their days, which can hang quite heavily on children in the city summertime. They were looking through the wrought-iron fence at the activities surrounding the river. The counselor asked, "What do you see?" Needless to say, it was a wonderful start to encourage the children's perceptions. But the counselor's intentions soon fell apart, because he insisted that each child have a "turn."

Each child made a single response, in turn: "Tugboat . . . helicopter . . . bridge . . . river . . . factory . . . people on a boat . . ."

The child who'd already mentioned the helicopter said out of turn, unfortunately, "Look, the helicopter's going to land by the river!"

"Hush, Allan," the counselor reprimanded. "You've already told what you saw, and I have to give everybody a chance."

Well, Allan didn't tell what he saw, he told only one thing that he saw. He seemed to be tuned in to the helicopter and was ready to give a report on its movement. Too bad for him;

he'd had his turn. Children's perception systems don't turn off after one response, but adults do turn off children's responses, unintentionally, or in this case, in a bid for fair treatment to all of the children.

"What do you see?" can be answered with one name. Be grateful if a child can say one name. "What else?" urges the child to respond to additional perceptions. A number of answers to the second question broadens and deepens the child's perceptive powers. There can be a "what else-ness" already going in the child's perceptive scanning of his surroundings. Your question merely invites the child to share his responses by naming more and more of his perceptions. Be greedy for a number of responses from the child.

Try to avoid saying "That's right," "Good," or other types of judgment regarding the child's responses. At this time, the right answer is not nearly as important as the quantity of possible responses. It won't take long for the child to realize that her chances of being right far outnumber her risks of being wrong, and the responses may come more easily.

Feel free to perceive with your child, and, together, to lengthen the list of things you perceive, rather than to imply by either your silence or your judgments that the child is performing. Your participation may call the child's attention to things which he has not previously perceived or which he cannot name himself.

The "What else?" game may be honed to rather sophisticated lists of responses. Not only can you talk about all of the sensory perceptions, but you can combine them in interesting ways.

"What do you see that you can eat?" "What else?"

"What do you see that can make a noise?" "What else?"

"What animal would you like in your own private zoo?" "What else?"

"What do you think is kept in an ambulance?" "What else?"

The Uh Place

Try it for yourself when you are in the subway, your living room, the haircutter's chair, waiting room, behind your desk, waiting for a stoplight, wherever you are. Simply name the things you see as quickly as you perceive them. After about four to six names, you're likely to pause, perhaps with an audible "uh." Then you must literally look again, think for a moment, and perceive more carefully to name things that were not on the tip of your tongue when you began.

Try the experiment with your memory as well as your perception. Quickly now, how many flowers can you name? Try the twelve signs of the Zodiac or the players' positions on a baseball team. How about the names of the seven dwarfs? The twelve Apostles? For each listing, you probably got off to a good start with three or four names, but then you paused and gave out a vocal or at least a mental "uh." You quickly reviewed your list, and then proceeded much more thoughtfully, trying to pick up the elusive names which don't come so easily.

In short, we need thinking time at some point. So does your child. There is a point in this "What else?" game when a child's perceptions or memory falter for a moment, and he has reached the "uh" place. If the two of you are sharing the experiment, it's your turn to add to the list. If not, then please don't be impatient or annoyed at the child's silence, because thinking is a quiet thing, and thoughts often disappear when the thinker is interrupted. Keep calm physically and remain interested. Don't talk unnecessarily, ending perhaps the child's very act of deeper perception and recall for which you had hoped.

More Than One Name for a Thing

Certain names refer to closely related things within a group. Suppose for a moment that "something" is in the air. One whiff of a sniff (there are two words to play around with!) and you can call it an odor, scent, smell, stink, perfume, aroma, bouquet; if you want to be really fancy, call it a pungency. That something in the air may be called by a couple of these names, but probably not all of them. The perceiver must select the best name for the sniff by mentally rubbing the meanings of the words together and deciding which meaning, according to the user, is most appropriate for the perception.

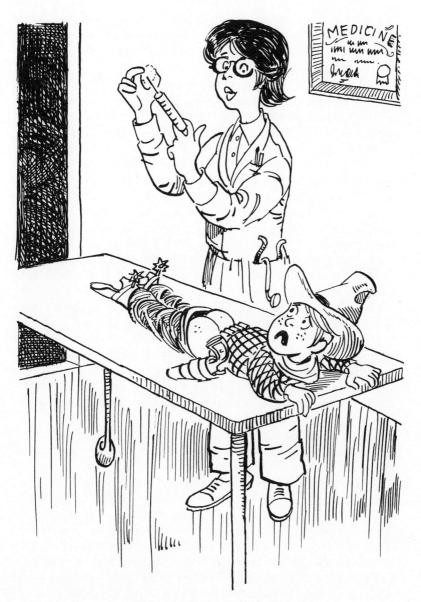

Is that your sick shooter, Doc?

We are referring now to synonyms, words that have almost the same meaning. Almost, but not quite, and that's an important difference as the child accumulates names for closely related perceptions.

You can think that synonyms name related things within a group, and yet, at the same time, those names may be used to denote the differences of the things within the group. Think of names for things within the general class called *boat*. Perhaps your list includes *ship, canoe, skiff, frigate, dinghy, rowboat, sternwheeler*. A landlubber may not discern a dinghy from a skiff, but an old salt will probably be glad to explain the differences. As a growing child becomes more interested or active in a particular hobby, sport, or profession, the differences among names previously considered to be synonyms become increasingly greater.

Let's go back to that frigate for a minute. That's its common name (noun, if you wish). But almost any boat you've ever seen has another, very special name, that refers to just that one. We'll call this frigate the *War Lord*. That's its proper name. After we've referred to it specifically, we can also call it an *it* or refer to it more lovingly as *she* or *her,* a common conversational practice when talking about ships. Those are pronouns, if you care. It may also be called a *vessel,* a *warship,* an *escort,* and in certain circumstances a *target* and a *wreck.* There are ten names for that ship, and in a related conversation, there may even be more.

Many, many things may be called by more than one name. The names fall into three categories: common names (nouns); proper names; and pronouns.

When you're talking together sometime, try to list all of the names that you or the child may be called. A girl may be also a daughter, sister, niece, cousin, grandchild, for starters; you'll think of others. She may also be called Susan, Sue, Susie, Twinky, Nerp, as well as a collection of other monikers, assigned by her family and friends. *She* and *her* are used by people talking about her, *you* is spoken to her, and she uses *I* and *me* to talk about herself. She may be a pupil, a shortstop, a gardener; she can be a passenger as well as a pedestrian, but not at the same time. And those names are only the beginning. The list as well as your discussion can be quite long and quite interesting. The main point of all of this is to help the child to keep in mind that she does not have merely one name. And that when talking about herself, or you, or anything, the more specific the name, the better.

Children can give two or more names to things in sentences without having to tell what they did, but sentences like these are not story sentences.

Ms. Markova is our neighbor.

She is the lady in apartment 5-E.

He was the first boy into the nurse's office.

Dad is Uncle Cecil's brother. He's a Met fan.

Different names may refer to lumpy objects as well as to living animals and people. Keep in mind, especially when you're starting an interesting story, that an object can very quickly assume a proper name when it is given the actions borrowed from another category of things.

Rubbing Qualities Together

"Pink? Whadda ya mean, pink?" says one little word-keeper to another in a child's mental retrieval system. "That's gotta be red, 'cause that's the only word we have for that color."

"I dunno much about it," the other one replies. "I figured it was red, too. But the word the kid's ears brought in to us was pink. This new color's lighter and milkier than the red we know."

"Yeah, I guess so," the first word-keeper says after giving the two colors some thought. "Okay, we'll just move red over a little and make room for pink. But somebody's gotta remember the difference."

"I'll try to keep 'em straight," says number two, "but how many more words for red do you think we're gonna get?"

Quite a few, I'd say, if the child has what we call an eye for color. To the young eye there may not be much difference between burnt sienna and umber, let alone knowing their names, but if the child grows up to be a painter, beautician, or photog-

75

rapher, the colors will surely be named and their differences will become quite apparent.

Children can name the qualities of a perceived thing in sentences without having to tell what it did. These questions will help both of you to give qualities to things. The answers are not story sentences.

What can it be?	A pizza can be round or square.
What is it?	The chinch bug is tiny. The June bug is bigger.
What are they?	Roses are red. Violets are blue.
What was it?	The soup was hot and salty.
What were they?	The firecrackers were loud.

Since a perceived thing may have more than one quality at the same time, the child selects one or two of the qualities which he'll name. Generally, a sentence becomes overloaded when the child names the size, shape, color, and too many other qualities of a thing. Therefore, the child responds to one or two qualities which sufficiently identify the thing or set it apart from nearby things having several similar qualities. In this way, the child mentally rubs the qualities of a thing together in order to choose which one he'll name.

A child may compare the qualities of things. Dana, for example, rubs the tallness of several buildings together and names one taller than another and one that is tallest of the three. Naturally, the shorter and shortest are implied in Dana's comparisons, but they need not be named. Whenever the conversation permits, take an opportunity to rub the qualities of things together. Which seems heavier, a stick or a pole? Which seems wilder, a hedge or a thicket? Which seems spookier, a hole or a cave? And which seems quicker, a second or a moment?

What can be green? Sorting things by one quality can combine quite an interesting group—a leaf, tomato worm, T-shirt, sunglasses, soap—things that would be quite dissimilar if some other quality were used in the grouping. You and the child can also rub the quality of green together by jumping the fence from one group to another. Do these green sentences make sense? Bananas can be green when they're green, and yellow when they're ripe. A player can be green on a team until she gets more experience. The green is the green area around the golf cup. Zoe is a good gardener with a green hat and a green thumb. Jealousy has green eyes. Some sick or frightened faces may be green. Green is the color of "go."

Pursuing almost any common quality in the same manner is a fine way for you to explore a dictionary with an older child. Just look at the "green" list and rub one meaning against another.

> happy   pink   blue   ————

Vida, a dark Puerto Rican second-grader, faced these three words during a test. The task was to "pick the word which does not fit and write it in the blank." The answer key indicated that the correct response was "happy," since it was not a color. But Vida wrote "pink" in the blank. When her paper was returned, Vida had the courage to ask her teacher why the answer was wrong. The teacher asked, "Vida, why did you write 'pink'?"

"Because it didn't fit," Vida said confidently. "I can be happy, and I can be blue, but I can't very well be pink." She got credit for a correct answer.

A famous television superstar and her daughter played this game before millions of viewers. First, mother closed her eyes and described her daughter's size, shape, age, hair color, eyes, weight, and other qualities. She did it pretty straight; that is, she tried not to exaggerate. Second, the daughter, who was about four at the time, closed her eyes and described her mother's qualities in a like manner.

Try this with a child you know. I did. I guarantee that you'll be pretty surprised with the child's concepts of size, shape, color, and age (especially age!). You'll be softer and more understanding when you insist on descriptions from children whose ages and experience give them so little to go on when they're comparing things.

Specific Names for Actions

You'll remember that most things have the power to do actions, and the power depends on the category—object, plant, animal, human. There is a what-elseness to perceiving actions just as there is to perceiving things and qualities. But actions also take time, so the more actions you and the child perceive that a thing did or is doing, the more you imply the passing of time. No action? Or only one action per thing? Not much story. What did it do? What else? What is it doing? What else? It's that "What Else" game that lays the actions in a row in order to get a story together.

Help the child to give actions specific names. Suppose a child says, for example, "I looked for my toad." You can offer a more specific name without much fuss before continuing the exchange, "You searched for your toad. Where did you find it?" No need to grind in a vocabulary lesson, risking fewer exchanges in the future, when it's so easy to deposit a specific name in the child's ears before moving on.

Synonyms may name similar actions. And *similar,* as you know, means *almost like;* and *almost* means *not quite.* Synonyms may name actions which are very different to the participant or insider, even though the differences are not necessarily discernible to the onlooker or outsider. If you think that *jog* and *sprint* aren't much different, try running each way. It's the little difference that wins the race. Children will tend to name actions in gross ways when they are beginning to talk sentences. You're needed to supply those hundreds of specific words which help the child to acquire a vocabulary. When Lainie watched a wild rabbit race across the lawn, she said, "The rabbit ran back and forth." Gram took the suggestion above and offered, "Yes, the rabbit zigzagged across the lawn. Where do you think it went?" Lainie ignored Gram's question but rephrased her own story sentence, "Yep, that rabbit zigzagged back and forth across the lawn." And Gram got the clue that Lainie didn't understand zigzag, so they talked about zigzag a bit more till Lainie realized that *back and forth* is part of the action named in *zigzag* and that she didn't need to say those words with that name. Children and adults are unnecessarily redundant in adding qualities that are already expressed in the action. A child may say *go fast,* which is okay; but *hurry fast* is redundant, since *fast* is already expressed in *hurry.* When you and your child are rubbing qualities against actions, opt for the

78

name that already includes the action and then omit the quality.

A Word About Learning

There are more psychologies on learning than you'll ever be able to count or comprehend. Educators flock by the thousands to annual conventions where they ponder over learning theories and stroll among the latest books, machines, and assorted gadgets purported but rarely guaranteed to cause effective learning. The best way to become instantly known in educational circles is to develop a "new" theory for learning, not that you will suddenly be mobbed by believers, but you will more than likely gain the attention of detractors and skeptics.

Keep in mind one important, irrefutable thought on this subject: *If learning were so difficult and so complicated, almost no child on earth would be able to do it.* There would be no such thing as curiosity, no padiddling with things to see how they work or how they're made . . . and no language, because children would have very little use for it and probably couldn't even master it, anyway. But, and it's a but to remember, children everywhere learn, so it's an effort that's possible, reasonable, satisfying, fairly easy, and not especially painful for children to do.

Learning is making things go clang. It's rubbing words and meanings together. It's getting a hold on a couple of concepts, then banging them together to test their relationship, their usefulness, and their permanence. Learning is discovering something that seems to make sense. It's finding words, ideas, preferences, and attitudes that are worth knowing because they work.

Learning is looking at a filly and knowing that it's a filly and not a colt, a gelding, or a stallion. Learning is knowing how to put the flour into the gravy so that it won't be lumpy. Learning is knowing how to read a word, but it's also knowing that you'll know all of the words on the next page, too. Learning is knowing how to put thirty-nine cents equally into three different coin banks. Learning is coping with your context, but, more than that, it's knowing that you'll do okay, and that you'll stay "cool" no matter what may happen to you.

79

The real clang comes from making generalizations, from figuring out things for yourself. It comes at that moment after you say, "Aha, so that's how it goes! Got it!" It comes from going clang when you discover that somebody likes you, talks the way you talk, and wants to share with you.

Children aren't all that complicated. We're the complicated ones. Children have more to cope with in us than we do in the children. Surely, we can talk freely, easily, and pleasantly with almost any child who speaks the words we speak. All it takes is a little forethought, a little scene reading, and a soft start.

So don't bid for your fame with a new thingamajig at some convention, just turn to any child and get the language going. That's where your immortality lies.

7

Bossy Sentences

"Hurry back!"
"Come again."
"Get well soon."
"Enjoy yourself!"
"Have a good day."
"Wear it in good health."
"Join us for dinner on Friday."
"Come in, sit down, make yourself at home."
"Tell us where you went on your trip."

You undoubtedly hope that children will say some of these and other courtesies as they learn to cultivate friends. The ones listed here are pleasantries of a very special kind. Within the context of friendship, the speaker is telling the listener what to do. These are friendly orders designed to solicit another's company, comfort, and conversation.

Sentences like these are good soldiers. They make their commander the boss. They also indicate rather clearly to whom the commander is issuing the order. Unfortunately, between adults and child, if my eavesdropping is any indication, not enough of these soldiers march off to make children at ease, welcome, and free to converse.

In this chapter we'll give our attention primarily to sentences which command or imply some action for the listener or the listeners to do. The subject of these orders in their most direct, familiar form is you. Since the commander usually is issuing these bossy sentences directly to a listener or a reader, the subject is quite often missing in a bossy sentence because you know who the *you* is.

Some of the more subtle bossings may be expressed in the form of questions. They may also be accompanied by words or phrases which act as softening agents—*please* is the usual softener. Food handlers in restaurants are very familiar with orders which are softened by phrases such as *if you have the time, when you come back, when you get a chance,* and *if it's not too much trouble.* Directives may also be couched in even more subtle remarks about what "good children" do.

Direct commands tend to strain, inhibit, or stop a conversation between an adult and a child. Conversation may follow a command, but it tends to shift from the talk of two people who equally share language. Instead, the one who's been commanded must try to talk of details, of the fairness or the appropriateness of the command, of limiting or amending it. But the commander knows who he is, and the other—undoubtedly the child, who must comply, finagle, defy, or ignore the command—knows who he is.

Children, Adults, Parents

Let me take you on a quick guided tour of people in a public place—a park, a shopping mall, an instant-food restaurant, any amusement area designed for children—so that you can amuse yourself by doing some perceiving of your own. The bus stop at any busy street corner is a good place, especially when restless, moving children in the crowd are combined with the suspense of an arriving bus.

The children are the younger, littler ones. They're generally more active, and they can be suddenly underfoot; if so, stop. The children probably don't see you, and even if they do, their ability to work out the trigonometry of collision courses is not yet well developed. At any rate, the children are the ones who move around quickly, or want to, unless they're strollered, harnessed, or otherwise impeded.

Children come in an assortment of colors and in all imaginable shapes from pumpkins to twigs. My favorite is the pregnant string bean.

There are little kids and big kids. A big kid is any child noticeably larger than a smaller kid; however, a smaller kid may not necessarily be a little kid if he's about the same age as the bigger kid. The size does matter somewhat, but it doesn't seem to matter quite as much as age; if a kid is younger, he's definitely a little kid. Age is the great dividing line among children. Perhaps that's one reason why it's so important for a child to say that he's six and a half going on seven, because it sounds so much older than a mere six.

All in all, it's not difficult to spot the children in crowds; they don't have to keep announcing that they're the kids.

The adults are the bigger ones. However, there is a gray area where it's difficult to decide if they're adults or children. Some members of the crowd are big enough to be adults and they act like adults some of the time, but they also act like children some of the time. Our social structure seems to label this gray area adolescence, the teenagers. Many adults lump them generally into a group with the phrase "those young kids," spoken in a derogatory way. The word *young* in this case is probably employed to widen the social space between those kids and the complaining, no-longer-young adults.

Adults also come in varied colors and all imaginable shapes. Generally speaking, they don't have to keep announcing that they're adults.

The parents can be the most interesting group of people in the area to watch, because they keep having to announce that they're parents. They have only one distinguishing characteristic—one or more children. It seems that the only way for adults to indicate that they're parents is to keep one or more of those children close at hand, or try to. After all, a grown-up person without a child nearby may be labeled merely an adult. Now, if the child or children are not nearby, the adult who's also a parent seems continually compelled to make parent noises. Those noises must project for the child, and for the other adults in the area, some command for action. It may be

83

implied and accompanied by a softening agent, but it is more often explicit in the form of a raw, naked, bossy shout.

From observing and eavesdropping on American and on European parents, I have noticed one big difference. The European parent seems to prefer going to the child, entering the child's scene, perceiving and discussing what the child perceives, and guiding the child more personally and privately. The American parent seems to prefer sitting in the center of concentric rings, allowing the child to play and wander not too close as to be underfoot in a series of widening arcs until the child goes too far by the parent's measurement. At that time the child is commanded to return to the parent before again being allowed to wander. Naturally, the parent must make a noticeably loud noise to shout the command to a wandering child, who must return to the "bull's-eye" each time. It's also an enticing game, the child soon discovers, to see how far he can wander or run before the command is sent for him to return to ground zero. Irresistible, too, must be the urge to discover how long the order may be ignored or how many times the order must be given before it becomes too threatening to remain unheeded.

Early on, we proposed that one goal of parents is to provide those conditions which will eventually permit the children to have homes of their own, incomes of their own, children of their own, and minds of their own. In short, independence is the name of the game. Do you want a series of relationships with your child, each one on a more and more mature basis, so that the ultimate relationship of an adult parent and an adult-aged son or daughter is comfortable and satisfying for both?

Or do you want a relationship of dominance which will surely and inevitably weaken as you attempt to maintain a dwindling power over a maturing son or daughter who learns and yearns for independence on his or her course toward adulthood?

Your relationship with your child probably lies somewhere on a balance between independence and dominance. Tending toward one or the other, however, is your choice every single time you read your child's scene and determine what you'll say as you enter it.

I can't read it, either, but it probably says don't do something.

The Old Power Play

"Don't run your boat across the coffee table."
"Don't stir the mashed potatoes into your chocolate milk."
"Don't lift your skirt and show your panties like that!"
"Don't play with the car radio when the motor's off."
"And don't slam the screen door when you go out!"

Don't! is one of the most-used commands, and apparently one of the most popular adult noises. Children learn it early in life. *Don't!* is an unmistakable play for power by an adult, and yet its power diminishes to practically nothing with overuse. Unfortunately, *Don't!* doesn't tell the child what to do; it only tells the child what to don't.

I have counted and yet I just can't believe the number of don'ts, together with other commands, that I hear adults issue to children in the name of conversation. Listen for yourself; other comments from adults don't come close. We all realize that a certain number of commands must guide children to avoid danger and to think about safety. Understandably, when a child is unknowingly threatened, we must boss now and explain later. Keep in mind, though, that the excessive use of command erodes the power of the commander.

An adult who continually engages in command can make conversation with a child unlikely if not impossible. We've already seen that conversation involves a sharing between an adult and a child. How can a child assume any attitude of equality in a conversation if she is expected mostly to do this and don't do that, proving again and again that she is the object of the power play and not the wielder of the power?

How are you on the inside when you hear a command intended for you? Do you prickle with the feelings of subservience? What responses to commands form in your throat? "Yes sir"? "No sir"? "Who do you think you are, anyhow"? or "Go to hell"? Perhaps some of your own responses are better left unsaid, depending upon whether the commander is one of the more powerful bosses in your life. It's often been said that everybody works for somebody. Undoubtedly, you assess the power of the commanding person before you voice a response.

86

Unfortunately, the child very seldom has the same opportunity to make the same choice.

On a gray, drizzly, low-barometer day I was shopping at a local food chain. The next checkout line was at the mercy of an officious cashier. But the customers weren't taking his orders well.

"Pick up your groceries, lady," the cashier ordered.

"As soon as I put away my money, young man," she said, and I caught the edge she ground on the word *young*. "I have two hands, just like yours."

"Move up your cart, mister," the cashier said. "Put your groceries where I can reach them."

"I'll put them where there's room; you can move them from there," the man said. Each word was measured.

"Watch your back, lady. Don't stand near the empty carts," the cashier said to another customer. That lady grumbled an unintelligible reply.

The cashier, unaware of how his words and manner were grating his customers, said, "My God, what's the matter with all you people today?"

A fourth customer, who'd missed nothing, said, "People like *you* are what's the matter with people like us today."

The silence of mutual anger prevailed until that checkout line renewed itself.

You may hear the echoes of subservience to your own parents and the adults in your life when you were young. I often do. Those days are gone forever, and you're the powerful adult now. Yes? Do you think it's possible for one to "get even" with excessively bossy parents by passing it on, so to speak, to the young when you gain your own adult power?

One evening I was having a pleasant drink with my friend Dwight. Without realizing it, Dwight stood for a moment between the television set and his daughter Margaret at a time when the action on the TV was particularly rousing. Margaret shouted to her father, "Don't stand in front of the TV, Dad!"

"Don't tell me what to do," Dwight said, "I'm your father!" With that, he whirled around and turned off the television set. Dwight's action seemed to be a move designed to protect the power of his fatherdom, his subservient feelings countering with a bid to regain power. Who said the wrong word? They both did. But whose behavior provoked the incident?

Raise your level of consciousness about the orders you issue to children. Hear yourself when you say them. Count them. A moment later decide if your command was really necessary. If it wasn't, why not explain that you didn't really mean it, and say what you did really mean? Also, maybe you can determine the number and the need for the orders before you give them until you can actually hear them before you say them, reflect a moment whether the scene you're in warrants the power play you are about to make. If it doesn't, bite your tongue.

Pleas and Requests

"Help!" is also a bossy sentence, but in a very different way, because the user admits the weaker position. The command becomes, in fact, a plea, and the pleader is commanding rescue, assistance, or support. The word *Help!* could be the ultimate plea. Children must be taught to use it in earnest and never in jest. You can use Aesop's famous fable of the boy who cried "wolf" to help you make your point.

The use of *please* softens a command to a request, since a request is merely a command offered politely. The goal of a request may be assistance rather than obedience. You can double-barrel the request by adding the softening agent as well as by turning the command into a question.

Command:	"Pick up your toys."
Request:	"Please wash your hands now."
Double-barreled plea:	"Will you please get the paper for me?"

Point out, if the child can read, the word *plea* in *please*—no coincidence, either; the words have a common derivation.

Pleas and requests are exchanged in an atmosphere of mutual respect, compassion, and love between an adult and a child. My dad, the country doctor and manure philosopher with whom you are acquainted by now, taught me, "The best way to make a friend is to let him do you a favor." For which, of course, you make your appreciation unmistakably known.

Directions

Children probably learned their first set of directions from adults who taught them to play patty-cake and helped them to learn the rhyme all the way through.

> Roll It,
> Pat It,
> Mark it with T,
> And put it in the oven . . .

Directions are given to tell a listener or a reader how to proceed, how to act, or how to make something. They consist of a sequence of command sentences, usually two or more, any one of which might be considered to be a very bossy sentence. It would seem quite likely that some children (and adults) hear only the bossy orders given in a set of directions, until they realize that directions are intended to lead the listener to a place, a finished product, or some other anticipated behavior or outcome.

When you're giving directions to a child, don't flood her with too many bossy parts. If the directions seem complex, offer them in segments of two or perhaps three parts each. More than three parts? Don't try. Write the directions down as you discuss them, or use glyphs as reminders for the children to check off later. If you have to buy a number of grocery items, you can't always remember them all; similarly, directions with a number of parts are difficult to remember. Test yourself; count the number of things you can keep in mind before you have to say to yourself, "I'd better make a list."

A rule of thumb, when in doubt, is to write down the directions, word clues, or a set of glyphs to follow, marking each checkpoint that you or the child reaches. Not only will this save you from having to rely on an unreliable memory, but it will also help you both to keep your place if you are called away from your work by unforeseen distractions.

Getting children to follow directions is a real accomplishment, and, very often, quite a problem. It's entirely possible that those old feelings of subservience crop up here as you or the child react negatively to one or two of the bossy sentences and forget the expected behavior or outcome which is intended by the whole sequence of directions.

I'm fond of do-it-yourself kits. Opening a kit one time, expecting to build a small electronic gadget, I found a slip of paper underneath the flap that read, "As a last resort, read the directions." Could it be that we seem to hate receiving directions because of our conditioning to dislike do-don'ts when we ourselves were children? Take note sometime of the stranger who asks you for directions, then stops listening before you complete your sequence, and leaves you without saying thank you. Perhaps that stranger feels that being in the need of assistance is, in itself, a position of subservience, and the stranger forgets your offer of assistance in an effort to regain personal control of the situation.

Games come with directions. After a game or two, your child often likes to change the directions. Rules are fixed directions which determine how the actions in any game will go. Some children make some of the rules, other children follow them, still others break them. Change the rules, and change the game.

A recipe includes a set of directions especially sequenced for making a food. The recipe implies that the same dish will be produced each time the receipe is precisely followed. Change the ingredients or the sequence of directions, change the dish.

The code of law, taken as a whole, comprises a set of directions regulating how children and adults shall live together in a social group. These collections of laws differ from community to community and from state to state. For example, it may be legal to carry a gun in one state, but quite illegal in another. Change the law, and change the nature of the social group.

Respect for directions, rules, recipes, and laws begins in your conversations with a child. You help to determine whether the child will be a lawmaker, law abider, lawchanger, or lawbreaker.

More Subtle Directives

"A Scout is friendly, courteous, kind."

"Courteous children say thank you when they receive a gift."

"Thoughtful children chew gum with their lips closed."

"A helpful child does his part by taking care of his room."

Sentences like these, when reasonably proposed and thoughtfully discussed, help a child to evaluate his own behavior, and to assess the expectations of the adult who wishes to guide him.

"Good children hug their mamas before they go to school."

"Clean-minded boys sleep with their hands on top of the covers."

"Good little girls get A's in school."

"Grown-up children (!) don't wet the bed."

"Children who eat liver grow up to be big and strong."

You hold a strange and potentially dangerous weapon when you wield one of these subtle directives. It is not as overt as a command, it is not as polite as a request, it is not softened by *please*, and it can be very pushy. Sentences like these might as well be followed by three dots instead of a period, because they are elliptic. The real honest direction from the adult is missing. It's as if the adult were pointing to an invisible "good child" and saying to the child before him, "Well, kid, how about you?"

"Okay, how about me?" The child may reply, either out loud or silently. "If I did it I'm good . . . If I didn't do it, I'm not good (or I'm bad, which is worse than merely not good) . . . If I want to do it, I'm good . . . But if I can't do it, am I bad? . . . I couldn't do it, so was I bad? . . . At least, I tried, so isn't that sort of good? . . . But if I almost did it, why does that have to be bad? . . . Can't I be almost good? . . . I meant to do it, so is that good or bad?" The ellipses become mental convolutions. And, for a child, that's bad!

I'm reminded of a slogan used to advertise a national brand of egg noodles: "Get to know what good is!" And it's very good advice to the child at this point. If the child hasn't yet learned what "good" is and mistakes your directives for a rejection of herself rather than her behavior, the child may conclude, much

91

to your surprise and horror, "If I have to eat liver to be big and strong, then the hell with being big and strong." Another child, perhaps without your knowing about it, has said to himself, "I'm not much good anyway, so I don't have to keep my hands on top of the covers." Conclusions like these from children may generate an unnecessary and difficult chain of events. Maybe not.

When slung like rocks, however, to recriminate a child for his behavior, without explanation and without any consistency of your overall expectations, miscellaneous directives become adult thrusts for which the child may feel that some retaliation is due. The child's resulting behavior may present a problem, but keep in mind that your zinger may have started it.

Careless directives generally result from a whim or pique of the moment. They are often inconsistently derived standards for behavior from time to time and from child to child. A child can go crackers trying to remember the combination of shalts and shalt-nots that make a "good child." Fortunately, these hasty and inconsiderate directives, when laid on the child, are rather easy to retract, countermand, and apologize for, when you have gained control of yourself, are able to discuss your expectations calmly, and know what you want from the child.

Better yet, define, define your expectations clearly when you talk with the child, avoiding bossy sentences. You can then invoke them on obvious, more serious infractions of behavior. When you must, attack the behavior itself, but stay off the kid's back.

Someplace along the way, you surely began to see through the directives of those who wielded the adult power over your younger years. Child psychologists and educators have all weighed the advantages of implied power against the dangers of the unspoken threats within these kinds of directives. Think how you can offer any child real, reasonable guidance.

Is This Hassle Necessary?

Mother, waiting in line to board a bus, called to her daughter, who was standing by a picture window no more than fifteen feet away, "Get over here, Diane."

"I'm right here, Mama."

"Diane, I told you to get yourself over here."

Diane moved, quite belligerently, to about six inches from Mother's face and said, "Now, what do you want?"

"Nothing. I just want to know where you are."

Diane moved away. "Well, Mama, I'm going to be by that window. And if you want me, all you have to do is look over there to know where I am, because that's where I'm going to be."

The anger showed on both their faces. Both boarded the bus together, of course. I won't tell you the struggle they had about who would sit where.

What a tough, unpleasant way to travel together—and so unnecessary.

At no time in your language experiences together must you read the child and the scene more astutely than the moment when you decide whether to enter the scene to issue a command, what command to make, how to make it, and how you intend to make it stick. The moment is so important that you must have all of your good senses with you, and you must make sure that you are not entering the child's scene emotionally overheated.

As you enter the scene, will you confront the child face to face, or will you manage the situation and the behavior side by side? If your directives are to have any effect, you must assume that the child is well intentioned and that the child places some value upon your concern and your guidance. Your mutual feelings, each for the other, must include respect.

If you're in doubt, ask the child something that can be answered with explanations rather than yes or no. Get the words from your child going. Reserve your judgment for a while. Listen to what the child has to say. Don't be too quick to display your adult power. Determine the nature of the child's behavior and the child's own point of view toward it. It will be easier for you to direct your statements toward the behavior and the situation that caused it rather than toward your child.

Making something go clang against a past directive, experience, or discussion is preferable to a raw display of your power. If you agreed on any previous shalts and shalt-nots, invoke an appropriate one rather than creating a new, perhaps inconsistent shower of commands and directives. Think a moment. If you were your own child at this very moment, what would you want or need? Direction? Comfort? Condemnation? An arm around the shoulder?

Above all, continue to ask yourself, "Is this hassle necessary?" After all, you and the child may have to spend the rest of the day together. Is the nature of your command or directive going to make the rest of that day difficult or better? In plain words, is what you are about to do going to be worth it?

I saw a parent sitting on a bench in a neighborhood playground. A noisy son, clacking a noisy rat-tat-tat on a noisy plastic motorcycle, was zooming back and forth on the noisy brick area. He was obviously aiming to graze mother's feet, but he never managed to touch them. The mother seemed to become increasingly annoyed by both the noise and the prospect of being run over. She broke first.

"Stop that! Get off that bike! Come here!"

The child blurted, "I hate you!"

Mother stopped a moment, visibly pulled herself together, waited one more moment, and said, "I don't like myself much, either." Another moment or two passed while she gained control. "Can you ride to China and back?"

The child, a winning smile on his face, was off to the opposite corner of the playground and back.

"Now go to the South Pole, but be sure to come home again."

The child was off again, and the crisis passed.

"Buy Me!"

Imagine sitting with a child in the open bay window of your London townhouse (okay, you're really wealthy!). The year is 1763, give or take a decade. You're both listening to the hawkers singing their street cries as they peddle their products and services back and forth below your window—newly laid eggs, curds and whey, jemmy sticks (canes), hot dumplings, cherries, washballs of soap, shoeshines, chairs and bellows mended. Each of the peddlers, both men and women, has a distinctive cry. One of the best of the plaintive tunes comes from the match man.

> Come buy me fine matches, come buy 'em of me;
> They are the best matches that e'er you see.
> Me mother she lives in Rosemary-Lane.
> She makes all me matches, and I sells the same.
> For lighting of candles, or kindling the fire,
> They are the best matches that you can desire.
> All you that has money, and I that have none.
> Come buy all me matches, and let me go home.

Remember Andersen's "The Little Match Girl," by the way? She was a street peddler. You might try reading it to your child; add this street cry for authenticity, but sing it—c'mon, try!

Anyhow, back to London, the open window, and 1763. You

tire of listening to the street cries, but the child does not. You leave the open window, but the child stays. You try to coax the child away from the window, but the child insists on remaining there to hear the peddlers' commercials. Finally, a bit annoyed, you walk to the window and close it. The child follows you to another room in your townhouse, half-humming lightly. "And stop singing that stupid dumpling song!" you insist. End of the scene in 1763—back to now.

The medium by which we hear the sweet-voiced cry has changed in ways that would astonish the street peddler of two hundred years ago. It would even astonish the vendor of no more than forty years ago.

The hawkers' appeal to buy, however, has changed very little.

Cries and Commercials

Advertising isn't so new.

The golden ages of Babylonia, the Nile civilizations, Athens, and Rome both saw and heard advertisements—to identify special shops, to offer services, to announce the arrival of cargoes, to sell slaves and livestock, and to promise rewards for the return of runaways and the capture of criminals. Later, the cries of peddlers and roving vendors were commonly heard in the Middle Ages.

As printing became more common and as more people learned to read, ads on posters and handouts were the usual kinds of advertisements. The increased production of salable items intended for the common man and woman resulted from the Industrial Revolution, and the need for advertising those mass-produced wares became more and more apparent to venturesome businessmen. Magazine and newspaper advertising became more and more competitive, especially during the early years of this century. Current interest has been revived in framed advertisements and catalogs reprinted from the turn of the century. In those days, however, children were largely overlooked by the advertisers. Not only were children considered to have very little buying power, but also they had to be old enough to read in order to be subjected to the pressures of commercial persuasion.

The popularity of radio in the '30s and television in the '50s changed all that. Children did not have to read in order to hear the exciting adventures—and the commercials—on *The Shadow,* *Captain Midnight,* and *I Love a Mystery* (remember Jack, Doc, and Reggie, swinging back and forth on a fraying rope over a pit of deadly snakes in some deserted temple?). I don't remember much about the adventures of Jack Armstrong, "The All-American Boy," but I do remember that he helped to sell Wheaties. I didn't care much for Ovaltine, so I wasn't much of an Orphan-Annie-button message decoder. But I pushed my mother to buy Post Toasties, so that I could send for my Melvin Purvis detective paraphernalia—I must have been a Commissioner, or whatever the highest rank, and I didn't even know who Melvin Purvis was.

Television, especially in color, with the fast, splashy, cartoonish ads accompanied by bodiless voices, frosted the advertising cake; and there were millions of children, sitting right there in front of those millions of TV sets. Advertising agencies were well aware of children's susceptibilities to color, action, pacing, and sound. They have researched children's perceptions to a fine detail, not only for the commercials but also for the kind of entertainment to sandwich, perhaps too briefly at times, between the appeals.

You may be annoyed, but surely you can't be surprised when the appeal, the action, and the color offered by your television set are stronger for the child than your own appeal to the child to spend time in other ways. It's no wonder at all that many parents complain about TV's competition for the time and the attention of their children. It's quite understandable, isn't it, that some parents feel a loss of power to the TV? Perhaps without admitting it, some parents are jealous of their children's love for television.

Come clean, now, and think honestly about it. How do you feel?

A Word About TV

I try, when I can, to avoid talking about television viewing when I speak at conventions, workshops, and programs for parents and teachers. Especially when I speak before combined groups, and *especially* when I know that thousands of classrooms rely greatly on television programs as part of the daily curriculum. Discussions about TV seem to cause bad feelings between parents and teachers and to make parents who are feeling guilty enough about the television crises in their homes feel even worse. Personally, I find television a rather dull discussion topic, but not a dull activity.

I'm puzzled by the people I meet who say that they hate television and vow that they never watch it. If they don't watch it, as they say they don't, then they have no basis or right to hate it. If what they say is true, they don't know anything about what they're missing. I ask these people if they own TV sets; if they do not, then I assume they mean what they say, and I don't continue the point. Some people, particularly those who own television sets, may temper their negative stands to admit that they watch the news, a very special special, and an occasional old movie. Then, it quickly becomes confession time as they tell how guilty they feel watching those "occasional" shows when they should be doing something else, which is usually defined in very nebulous terms. Who makes them feel guilty? I certainly don't.

I'd be less than honest with you if I knocked television, either for you or for children. I love TV! Television provides me with the sights and sounds within the real world that I can't see and hear for myself. And that, I think, is my main criterion. I'd rather go skimming through a Norwegian fjord on a hydrofoil myself; but if I can't, I'll watch, intent and entertained, as the villages and the glaciers skim by on my TV screen. I'm not about to go sloshing through the Everglades to chase alligators, but I enjoy joining the hunt as long as there is a television screen between me and the swamp. I'd rather follow the famous golfers through the Masters Tournament, but I admit that there's a special sense of immediacy and drama that comes in a close-up of the ball dropping in, or just missing the rim of the cup. In fact, watching many historical events on TV is really better than being there. Also, I've promised myself to see the Rose Parade in person on some New Year's Day, but I'd also be tempted to take along a belly telly in order to have the TV host there to tell me the features of the floats.

I especially value NET, the Network for Educational Television, and I contribute annually to its support. NET is surely one place where I can see what I'm getting for my money. I watch plenty of television; in turn, I recommend to you and your children many of its programs.

But here's an important point: those TV sets turn off as easily as they turn on. There's no law that requires you or your child to watch television for a prescribed number of hours per day. Television viewing is by choice and by habit only. If you've found the on button, you've also found the off button. Is it possible that some people hesitate to turn off the television, fearing that it may insult or otherwise be inhospitable to the performer? Although you can see all the way through to the TV studio, the TV personalities cannot see all the way through to your viewing area, although they would have you believe by their manner and their warm words that they can. They're not maimed or whipped when you stop watching.

Shop for suitable programs in the television guide as you would look for attractive bargains in the supermarket ads. It only takes a moment to mark those stations and times which you feel would be appropriate for your child, provided that the child wishes to view television. Don't force television upon the child.

Television viewing can easily become a habit to children (and adults, too). And the habit may grow from a feeling of boredom at a certain time of day. It's quite possible that children and adults watch television at a certain time because "there isn't anything else to do" at that time. If you are trying to woo the child away from the set, realize your alternatives, and plan ahead. If children don't watch TV, then what will you do with them? Well, you're "on" to make puppets, take a walk, play games, assemble a jigsaw puzzle, share a hobby or a do-it-yourself activity, teach the child how to make prune whip or peanut clusters. Is it too old-fashioned to go to the library? Thousands of people think not.

You may find yourself in competition with TV for the attention and company of your child, but keep in mind that you have the tremendous advantage of appearing "in person."

You don't have time to share language and companionship with your child? Then you have no right to call a television set a "boob tube." And you mustn't feel rejected or jealous when the child prefers the company of the TV. After all, many of the programs and the commercial messages are aimed directly at the child, as if the performers had no one else in the world to spend time with. It must be a wonderful feeling in the child's mind to be the recipient of so much colorful, active attention.

If you can't fight *it,* join *them.* Make TV serve your interests, your curiosities, and those of your children. Know it for what it is. With the exception of NET and subscription TV (for which you've already paid), the commerical stations intersperse times during which you are informed, enlightened, or entertained with times during which you are asked to buy, to believe, or to contribute.

The TV Message

Television is a young pre-reader's first confrontation with the pressure of hard-core commercial persuasion. The child is influenced not necessarily to buy himself but rather to ask or force you to buy in order to satisfy the child and, of course, the advertiser. With a dazzling bombardment—dizzying color, frantic action, talking animals, hyped-up humans, and overenergetic voices reminiscent of evangelism's greatest day—the television commercial makes its pitch. When you join the children to watch television, discuss together the messages, not for what they sell but for the tactics employed in their persuasions. Here are some commercial checkpoints to look for; they don't all appear in all commercials, which only makes your hunt and your discussion more interesting when you perceive them.

1. Some visual and oral expression of the child's need or desire for the product. Usually, some statement or picture tells what the child wants to be, to do, or to avoid.

2. Some oral and visual expression of how the product will please, soothe, and satisfy the child.

3. Some reassurance of the quality or durability of the product. A promise, but rarely a guarantee, offers the manufacturer's claims. The law does require that anything sold directly to the consumer by television commercial must make a clear statement of satisfaction guaranteed or money refunded. I've heard of the discontented viewer who asked for her money back, on the grounds that the advertisement had said, "Your money cheerfully refunded if not satisfactory." She received this reply: "But your money is entirely satisfactory and will not be refunded."

4. An oral and visual appeal to the child to buy or plead for the product. You may see and hear a command or a more subtle directive. Infrequently, you'll hear a request in a question almost never softened with anything as servile as "please."

A television commercial is quite an impressive effort and an expensive little show when you view it for its ingredients and its intentions. But one showing is not usually enough. Television advertising agencies would quickly agree that one added factor in an effective appeal to children is repetition. Chances are that you and the child probably didn't attend all of the message the first time; so, TV time must be purchased to show the commercial to you again and again. That explains one reason why there are so many surveys to find out when certain-age children and perhaps their parents watch TV. The advertisers pay to show their commercials at times when the same viewers are expected to be facing their sets.

The effect must be cumulative in order for it to become memorable. The children must be able to identify the desired package when they see it on the store shelf. They must be able to identify or describe the wrapping and the brand name when they make their own commercial appeals to the purchasing adults.

There are slogans for the child to memorize and the words and tunes of jingles to be learned. For this reason if no other, the modern TV commercial is a direct descendant of the street cries of centuries past. Visualize yourself and your child sitting once more in that window of the London townhouse. The cries weren't spoken; they were sung. Say this one several times, and you'll discover its rhythm.

Hot cross buns, hot cross buns,
Onefa penny, Twofa penny,
Butt'ry hot cross buns.

Like today's TV jingles, the cries were meant to be catchy, instantly recognizable, and memorable. They were not necessarily meant to be intelligible.

Mieu (milk), mieu, mieu below,
Buy mieu below, below.

Floun, floun, flounder,
Buy my live floun, flounder-r-r-r-r

The sound had to go with the tune, since it was the tune that became the peddler's "theme song." Different milk peddlers, for example, sang different catchy tunes, so that you could identify and buy from your favorite. TV jingles today? Just the same. Competing cereal makers wouldn't dream of using the same jingle! The times haven't changed much for peddling, have they?

Beverly Sills, the great soprano, and Danny Kaye, the entertainer loved by the world, once stood together on the stage of the Metropolitan Opera House before almost four thousand children, and they sang "The Meow, Meow, Meow, Meow Song," a television jingle for an often-advertised cat mix. The uproar of approval from the young audience must have gratified the advertising agency for weeks. Imagine their joy if each of those children owned only one very hungry cat!

There's no way that you can force your children to hide their eyes and cover their ears when the television commercials appear. Those ads will always be there on the commercial stations. Keep in mind that our American system of commercial television networks requires the participation of advertisers who are willing to buy TV time in order to keep the station's programs on the air. Rather than trying to avoid the TV pitches, you may find these questions useful in discussing the commercial messages.

1. Who's talking? Real, unpaid people? Or professional actors?

2. Who wrote the words that the people say?

3. Who's paying to put this commercial on TV? Why?

4. Is this commercial "live," or has it been filmed in scenes until the most desirable scene is used?

5. Would you ever expect to see a dog that didn't like the dogfood? Why not?

6. How many breakfast foods can you name that you've seen on TV this week? How many breakfasts can you eat in a week? Then why are so many breakfast foods advertised?

Another way, more subtle and more interesting for older children, to get them aware of the "rigged world" of the family in the TV ads is to ask them if that's the way things are in real life, always will be, or should be. Do the TV ads show us real people in a real world? Do fathers wander through real bathrooms murmuring the name of a beloved mouthwash? Do children in real homes generally get stripped to the buff in front of the automatic washers? It seems that only the boys in TV ads get dirty—don't the girls get dirty, too? Perhaps you've noticed that only baby girls get their diapers changed in TV ads. Why? Perhaps baby boys don't soil their diapers! Do only women buy laundry detergent and wash dishes? Do white tornadoes really go whistling through kitchen windows? When's the last time you saw a covered wagon and horses disappear under the sink?

If you've discussed bossy sentences before now, you might ask the child to identify commands in commercials: "Buy three and save!" "Send for your free copy today!" "Compare, if you care!" With discussions and practice, you and the child will be able to determine commands, requests couched in questions and softened with courtesy words, and the more subtle directives—but this is not an overnight accomplishment.

Dishonesty was not rewarded in the street markets of three and four hundred years ago. Dishonest peddlers were punished immediately and publicly. For example, one peddler might be locked in a pillory over a smoldering fire of his own rotten meat. A baker caught cheating on the weight of his bread might have been hung by the heels with his dishonest bread tied around his waist. From then on, consumers avoided these dishonest peddlers or watched their weights and measures very closely.

It's an intriguing thought to consider an "Honesty in Advertising" law which might stipulate that deceptive television advertisers must be punished on the same station and time as when they committed the fraud—and they should even have to buy the TV time for the punishment! Wouldn't that be an effective lesson for your children?

Reach Out

The public-service message is constructed in many ways like the TV commercial. It pleads with you to contribute money, service, or materials (old clothes, furniture, eyeglasses, perhaps your own body's blood or organs) to a nonprofit or community organization. The commands, you'll notice, are softened with words as well as by the voice and the manner of the person making the appeal.

Compare the similarities and the differences of commercial and public-service messages. Help the child to understand, when appropriate, the goal of the organization and the aim of its appeal. Be objective. Note that public-service appeals are also written and directed by TV pros; the emotional plea is very carefully planned. The child must learn compassion for the misfortune of others and sympathy for organizations that help the needy, alleviate pain and illness, and prolong life. But as the child matures, she must listen and make choices regarding how and through what services she will assist, just as she must choose the products and services she buys after seeing and hearing commercial advertising.

When the Child Can Read

How many commercials do you see on signboards, posters, colorful cartons, food wrappers, sides of cars and trucks, store-window paste-ups, placards, and other hurry-hurry-get'em-while-they-last notices in your neighborhood shopping area? Some estimates indicate that your school-age child may see up to one thousand ads, perhaps even fifteen hundred in more concentrated commercial areas, each day. It might be interesting for you to check this out for yourself. Simply dedicate one day's perception to noticing all of those printed "hawkers" that are out there competing for your dollar and the child's allowance. Although most of the ads may be aimed toward that big dollar in the consumer's pocket, there are hundreds of appeals on wrappings and packages designed to attract the child's eye.

The commands, pleas, requests, and subtle directives in printed advertising are very much the same as those in television messages. As a matter of fact, advertising agencies deliberately plan media packages relating design, color, and message. Printed ads provide you with the same opportunities for language as television commercials, but with one added advantage: the message does not disappear in thirty seconds or a minute, and you have more time to study the appeal.

A number of the more reputable children's magazines control the integrity of their advertisers, because they do not want to risk offending the adults who pay for the copies or subscriptions. However, it's "buyer beware" for many of the stray publications on the drugstore magazine racks.

I studied three full-page ads in a monthly issue of one of the country's best-known magazines for children from five to twelve years old. The first ad offered the child a two-dollar "reward" for every subscription to the magazine that the child could sell to friends—a fair offer, since the child did not have to send for any kit or prepay for the product to be sold. The second ad offered a selection of eight activity books at one dollar each—cookbook, jokebook, coloring and puzzle books. The coupon provided space for the adult's credit-card number, presuming that the child would ask the parent to send for a collection of the books. Also a fair offer, assuming that the size and the content of the activity books makes them worth a dollar each.

The third ad on the back cover was more tricky. Twenty-four attractive prizes were pictured in color. The ad stated that most of the prizes shown could be obtained free for selling forty-five packs of vegetable and flower seeds. Without thinking carefully, a child could easily conclude, "Oh boy, I can get a bike just for selling eighteen dollars worth of seeds." Not true. The kicker in this ad lay in the word *most*, which means the majority or any quantity more than half. The ad could be true if only thirteen of those pictured prizes could be had for selling forty-five packets of seeds, *not* including, I'm sure, the bike, the watch, the skates, and the typewriter. The ad did not seem unfair, but the details were in the small print, and the nitty-gritty was in the even smaller print on the return coupon. Children can be persuaded by pictures and large, splashy headlines, but they (and adults) must learn to read the fine print carefully. If your child wants to earn money selling subscriptions, seeds, or whatever (and who isn't attracted by the prospect of a prize or an income?), discuss each of the details of any offer so that the child unmistakably understands the conditions and the responsibilities which he must assume as his part of the scheme. Read most carefully the return coupon, which contains all the conditions and hookers in the proposal.

Who enjoys receiving mail? I certainly do. When I was a child, I used to go through the old magazines in the house, cutting out the coupons for free brochures and sample materials. This was an especially fine summer pastime. For four to six weeks I must have been the curse of the local mailman, who had to drag all of the junk mail to the door. However, Dad and I had quite a talk about mailing coupons after a traveling salesman came to the door one day with an offer to sell storm windows that we found very difficult to refuse. Many of those coupons are direct leads by which salesmen earn a living. Both their time and yours can be wasted if the child is not careful. It's better for you and the child to agree on some conditions about what may and may not be requested through the mail.

Possession

The concept of possession precedes the concept of value, but the concept of value is essential if the growing child is to become a wise consumer. To a young child the words "It's mine!" can mean only that it may not belong to or be played with by anybody else; later, the child will learn with your help that possession means getting one's money's worth not only at the time of purchase but also during the period of use. Also, a responsibility may develop as the child learns to keep track of things and provides a space in which to keep them.

Many child-development specialists recommend that a room, a bookshelf, a box with a lock, or a drawer be set aside to hold treasures that children can call their own. You can put your child's name on a drawer or box—with a suitable ceremony— mark it PRIVATE, and keep it private. If you are sewing or marking the child's name in clothes, use the opportunity to talk about the rights and responsibilities of ownership. When the child can write his own name, ask him to mark each of his own possessions. A place or space that satisfies a child's need for separateness, individuality, and privacy will help the child learn the concept of possession.

What about your own desire for a private place, considered off limits to anyone without your specific permission or special invitation? If you grant the child a private space or place, you may feel free in turn to insist upon one of your own. On a rare occasion, you may wish to invite the child to see and talk with you about a treasure you keep in your private place. Family pictures, a piece of your grandmother's jewelry, the garter or special cufflinks that you wore at your marriage, an old shilling or other souvenir given to you as a remembrance. If keeping old things like family pieces and antiques is important to you, talk about your pride in owning special things during those quieter moments in private you share with a child.

Trading and Borrowing

Bugs, stamps, baseball cards, shells, record albums—almost anything collectible has been valued somewhere sometime as a practical currency by young traders. The relative value of each thing in a child's pocket goes on the block as it is determined tradable for another thing in another child's hand. And children *will* trade. Their experiences at trading and bartering seem to reflect in a curious way the history of any cultural group before it agrees upon a medium of exchange. "What'll you take for those skate wheels?" or "What'll you give for this cat's jaw?" help to develop a child's concept of value.

Calvin was not so experienced as John at trading comic books. Those were the days when Wonder Woman was worth five Archies and a Captain Marvel traded even for a Batman. John kept his comics stashed out of sight under the sofa, but Calvin held his inventory in his hands. John insisted that Calvin's comics were not worth what John had. John always seemed to bargain in his own favor. Calvin finally learned to show only a sample or two and keep a little supply out of sight in order to improve his own dickering power.

Children's trading on relative values are okay; it's been done for centuries. Occasionally, a child makes an error in judging value, perhaps when trading with an older child who may be more experienced in bargaining and more mature in associating a money value to the trade.

When you see children trading, stay on the far edge of the scene, and watch unobtrusively to see that your child is not outrageously cheated. Between trades, if you can, help your child by discussing relative and money values of the traded items, but never the stupidity of your young trader. If the trade does not affect you crucially, even if your trader has received the slightly poorer end of a bargain, consider the trade as an experience from which the child can learn and be done with it.

Within reason, value must relate one thing with another or with money. Value is learned through a collection of trading and purchasing experiences—going clang with two bartered things or with a thing and money.

Before children learn sharing and trading, they're sure to grab each other's toys and possessions. You can help by explaining whose toys belong to whom. You might suggest that the children may trade toys, then trade back; or one child may use a toy for five minutes, then return it with a thank you.

Help your child to learn that borrowing is only half of a trade transaction. The other half of borrowing is lending. One condition of the lender in this agreement is unquestionably the return of the borrowed item. If you must borrow some minor item from a neighbor, you might ask the child to borrow it for

Yes, I know it's a great turtle! Now return it to Janie Pierson and get your little sister back!

you. Use the opportunity to discuss the meaning of borrowing and lending. There is a great lesson in value to be learned through the possession without ownership of a thing—*to borrow means to return.* Otherwise, it may be construed as stealing.

When you lend your comb or anything to a child, mention in some way that you expect its return. Teach the child the words of a borrower, including *please,* and add when you expect the return of that thing if the child asks to keep it for more than a few moments.

The concept of value may lead to the concept of values. It's possible for a teenager to know the value of a TV set, steal it, and sell it without having a sense of values. But don't think that one learns values without some sense of value. A word play, perhaps, but an important one.

Change, Exchange, and Choices

Children will sense the importance of money before they learn its worth. They must have a sense of numbers, primarily from one to ten and from one to one hundred, before they can understand the mechanics of money and making change.

If you're opposed to having children play with dice, cards, and play money, then perhaps you can use other counting games in suitable ways. In any case, play easy-to-learn number games. Card games or counting games that add to ten. Dime-store games—the bossy kind that say "Go ahead free" or "Lose one turn"—that use only markers and some kind of counter. Play any kind of put-and-take game. For example, one red die is the put marker, and one green die is the take marker. Use ones, fives, and tens in play bills from another game. Each player begins with ten dollars, and after five, seven, or ten rolls, the winner has the most money. The reverse game, called "Throwaway," is just as much fun; play it the same way, except the winner ends up with the least money. Mrs. Hodgson and Bonnie played "Count Your Change," by making change in coins for each other, sometimes making inaccurate change, on purpose. For years after, Bonnie pointed out count-your-change signs at cashiers in grocery stores and restaurants.

Grocers know about children. They put goodies where children riding in grocery carts can see and reach them. Follow an adult and a child at a supermarket sometime. Do they go up and down the aisle in face-to-face confrontation or side by side as fellow consumers? When you go shopping, does the child have any idea at all of your budget, your food planning that precedes the trip to the store? Children are not born with the knack of clever shopping. The art of being a consumer is learned. Quite likely from TV. At the supermarket the child's experiences with TV may result in a number of face-to-face confrontations as you pass the peanut butter with the blue label or the cereal that the talking tiger eats, especially if the picture of the talking tiger is prominent on the front of the box and at the child's eye level. However (sigh), leaving your child at home in front of the television set while you do the shopping seems only to postpone the day when the child can be helpful to you and, eventually, lead his own life as an intelligent consumer. We won't even talk about the dishonesty of adults who open packages and snack with children, then throw away the bag before they check out!

Kathy Bowden very cleverly chatters while her child sits with her in the kitchen. She shows Arnold the shopping list and, even if he's too young to read it, she talks with him about one or two things that he may shop for and bring home. If Arnold sees a product on television that he wants, she says to him, "I'll put it on your shopping list." When it's time to go shopping, she checks the list with Arnold and says, "Now, your list is as long as mine, and we just can't bring everything home." Arnold may have one or two things from his list, including toothpaste and other necessities, without going over his "budget."

Nobody but nobody in a book can tell you how much allowance your child should have. But most of the child experts will agree that some arrangement between you and your child seems sensible after she has learned the mechanics and the value of money. Keep in mind, however, that an allowance is another form of power. The child will perennially struggle to get that allowance raised or to find a way of earning money independently (and independence is a goal for children, remember?). We're back now to the talks about selling magazine sub-scriptions and flower seeds, aren't we?

It's possible that you will continually struggle to keep from being overly bossy about the child's allowance, since strict shalts and shalt-nots defeat the purpose of the child's efforts to man-age his "income." Discuss and agree on what the allowance is expected to cover, and write down those agreements—you'll be very glad you did. Each may take a copy as if it were a contract, or you can keep the agreement in a prominent, public place for referral. Emergencies, of course, are numerous. You'll proba-bly always be willing to discuss the child's extra needs to deter-mine if they're beyond the allowance expectations. Assist the child in making choices, if needed, and revise the budgeting if the wants are within the allowance agreement and expectations.

Mistakes in managing that allowance are inevitable; you can help, but cautiously, by reviewing the child's choices, making an in-out cash-flow record. Don't be too quick to indict the child for stupidity, thoughtlessness, or lack of foresight; instead, keep your discussion on the money and the spending. "Keep it simple" is the adult's rule of thumb. Although an allowance makes the child's management of money important and, at times, open to your comment, limit the topics to listing wants and needs, accounting money, and discussing choices. And, of course, any extra allowance is for the child to have as his own.

Humans are the recipients of a most unusual gift—the pres-ence of a will, the ability to choose, whether it be between turn-ing the TV on or off or between spending and saving part of the allowance. Choices like these and thousands of others are bound to cause you and the child some problems. But in a bur-den of problems, said a world-famous thinker, lies sanity.

9

In the Eye of the Beholder

During the silver screen's silent days, a tear as big as a quart jar could be squeezed out of a talented eye as big as your living-room wall. Lillian Gish knitted her five-foot eyebrows, and a sympathetic audience hoped prayerfully for the alleviation of her suffering. When Valentino, his eyes bleary with sexual smoldering, extended his hand, half the women (and some of the men) in the audience would gladly have traded places with Vilma Banky.

In one of her famous screen roles, Gloria Swanson, speaking of the silent film's great personalities, said, "They had faces then!" We perceived something in the silent star's manner, added up all of the movements and qualities, named the combination "restrained desperation," then longed to help her through the awful moment. Well, audience, that wasn't re-strained desperation inside that star at all, that was acting. The carefully portrayed and timed action put the restrained desper-ation as a conclusion in our own minds, so that the desire to help a star came from our own reactions after perceiving a wonderfully talented person earn a living. And we loved it . . . and love it.

Skip this chapter for now, if you wish. If you and the child are busy pursuing names, actions, and qualities that you per-ceive, you need not confuse the investigation with naming things and actions that you can't see. One day, though, when it will occur to the child that you can't see things like hope, friendship, patriotism, and grief, it will be time to check on what's in this part.

Naming Reactions

Betty and her grandson Ryan play this riddle game often. It's "their game." Ryan doesn't cooperate well with others who wish to initiate the game without Betty. One of them is allowed to list only the qualities of a thing; the player may not name it or tell what it can do. The other one, of course, guesses its name. They're experienced at this riddling business, and the game is played with much more "far-out" things than this, but here's an idea from Betty.

Small, red, heart-shaped,
covered with tiny seeds, green stem.

This combination of perceivable qualities is intended to hit something familiar in Ryan's mental retrieval system that will help him to go "clang" and to give that combination a name— Betty had strawberry in mind. However, if Ryan had never seen a strawberry and heard its name, Betty might still be struggling for qualities. Their game is not scored; it may be without points, but it is far from useless.

Suppose, though, that Ryan hits the right combination and something goes "clang" in his mind. But, instead of naming the berry, perhaps Ryan says, "I hate 'em, they're itchy." Now, *itchy* is not a commonly perceivable quality of a strawberry. Ryan, though, could have responded in quite a different way, since he's allergic to fresh strawberries. *Itchy* names how Ryan feels toward the strawberries, based on several uncomfortable eating experiences.

Three children watched a large, sleek, brown Doberman making a mess (as the euphemism goes) in the street. Since dogs' messes in the city streets are so common, the children didn't notice the dog's action; instead, they commented upon the dog's appearance.

Bianca said, "That's a pretty brown dog!"

Kristyn said, "It's not so pretty. It's tail and ears have been cut off. Floppy dogs are pretty."

Wait till you taste my chili. The cookbook says it's absolutely delicious.

Carter remarked, "I think little fluffy dogs are pretty."

The children had quite different ideas about what was *pretty*. Even though they used the same name for their reactions, they had in mind quite different thoughts, based upon their feelings about combinations of qualities they perceived in "pretty dogs." You and the child may also disagree about what makes a dog or anything else pretty, regardless of a thing's perceivable qualities. Several people looking at an emerald may agree that it is both green and square-cut, but they may quickly disagree on its value and beauty. *Beautiful* truly lies within the mind of the beholder.

When you're talking with a child and you react to something by calling it *funny*—a dressed-up cat, for example—continue to say in a sentence or two how the cat looks and what it does. Detail a bit the combination of the action and the qualities that go "clang" in your own mind so that you react by saying, "That funny cat." You'll help the child to realize that you're using *funny* as a one-word opinion, and that the child may perceive with you that combination of action and qualities that elicits *funny* as your reaction to the cat. A short time later, perhaps, when your child calls a clown in a TV commercial funny, pursue the child's reaction a bit by asking, "What did the clown do? What happened? How did the clown look?" Later, perhaps the time will be ripe to ask, "What are some other funny things? What do funny things do?" Your role is both to elicit the child's reaction verbally and to contribute in the language exchange.

Words like *goofy, bad, noisy, afraid,* and *best* become increasingly useful as the child reacts to his perceptions. These words become one-word opinions about things and actions. The one-word opinion is learned at first from you, from adults, from children, and, of course, from television. You can increase the child's vocabulary of reactions when you use and discuss those one-word opinions (better make them clean, yes?) for the experiences you share.

In addition, you can always take an interest in the new words the child uses to react to his perceptions. Continue a conversation around his one-word opinion by asking how a thing looks and what it does in order for him to react with his chosen words. Let the child hear your own reactions.

Be careful not to act as a judge to the child's words. It is tempting, when a child uses an outlandish or inappropriate word, to turn face to face to a child and judge the expression; instead, share the experience side by side as you offer more appropriate words for the child's use. Remember, when the child says opinion words that you find cutesy and oh-so-clever, that she's probably using a word inaccurately. You aren't doing the child a favor by leaving inaccurate or rude opinion words uncorrected.

"Oh hell!" or worse may conveniently express your own opinion about a dead battery, the alarm that didn't go off, the smoking skillet you left on the stove when the phone rang, or a flooded motor on the lawn mower. Earlier, we said that although children don't need to imitate your generation of sentence structures, they must have the input of meaningful words in a language. If they hear adults spewing a string of expletives frequently and in the emotional tone that generally accompanies these expressions, the children will naturally file the words as well as the conditions which surround them, and say them later in contexts they believe to be suitable. Hearing the words and using the words are a reasonable part of the language acquisition process. And there you are with a cusser on your hands!

The child's words didn't start the problem; she got them from somebody somewhere. If reactions within earshot of your child are profane or obscene, you can pretty well expect to hear the child try them out when reacting to something similar. To the child, profanities and obscenities are not objectionable, and you may be unfair in punishing a child for repeating what you or another member of the family has said. The two rules of thumb here are to express for the child other, more acceptable reaction words, and to eliminate the source of the unsuitable language. Does this mean *you?*

Rubbing Reactions Together

I'm not at all enthusiastic about antonyms, which explains why I don't see much point in making a big thing about them with children. *Sweet* doesn't have to be the opposite of *sour;*

salty, spicy, bitter, bland, oniony, and a list of other tastes have to be reckoned in the comparison. *Not sweet at all* seems suited to be the opposite of *sweet,* but it's too many words to be considered an antonym. *Left* doesn't work out too well in my mind as the opposite of *right,* because one of each works well when walking or playing cards; and you can go around the house to the left, or you can go around the house to the right, and you will get to the back of the house either way. Why can't the opposite of intelligence be ecnegilletni? See what I mean?

Woman is certainly not the opposite of *man. Boy* is not the opposite, either. Nor is *beast.* With wars and abrasions the world over—those "opposing forces"—the most obvious opposite to man seems to be man himself. *Opposite of* may be used in questionable ways to imply *inferior to.* And who wants to think of themselves as *opposite of* if that means *less than.* I don't.

Pairs of reaction words like *happy-sad, mad-glad, wise-foolish,* and *kind-cruel* may, I suppose, name some fairly distant checkpoints on a range of meanings. However, overemphasis on opposing pairs seems to place those words and their meanings not at the ends, but side by side in the verbal spectrum of meaning. As children become aware of a more far-reaching range of meaning, and if they've learned that so-called opposites are very close together on the range, then they seem forced to lengthen the range of meaning with what they themselves may call the far-out words like *super, fantastic, terrific, out of sight,* and surely one of the ultimate in the range, *fabulousest.*

Rather than emphasizing opposites, why not use and discuss the numbers of words which lie between the limits? Express degrees of meanings along the spectrum of reactions. Real vocabulary growth lies in the child's abilities to express reactions finitely within a choice of specific meanings rather than having to reach beyond the verbal limits.

Clever, silly, reckless, tricky, smart, sensible, and *intelligent* are a few of the many words that may be used somewhere between wise and foolish. *Friendly, gentle,* and *tender* may be used as synonyms for *kind. Mean, brutal,* and *hostile* may fit as synonyms for *cruel.* All six of those words with a number of others lie somewhere on the range from *kind* to *cruel.* Synonyms are often mismatched as reaction words, because the users tend to think of them as having identical meanings. But, in fact, they rarely do. It's much more useful for you and the child to think of synonyms as words having *similar* meanings, the differences depending upon the way you use them in language. Otherwise, when several words are considered to have identical meanings, your child could easily and reasonably choose to overuse one of them in preference to the others. Therefore, the child without your help could tend to limit rather than enlarge his own vocabulary of reactions.

Derek came home and told his dad that he was unhappy because he wasn't chosen for the student traffic patrol that week. Dad replied, "You were disappointed that you weren't chosen."

"Yes, I guess I was disappointed instead of unhappy," Derek said. And that's about all there was to the conversation. But two understandings came from the exchange. First, Derek felt that his dad sympathized with his feelings. And second, his dad had given him a word which more specifically described his reaction.

Adding words to the child's vocabulary in this manner is no big thing, but every little word helps. As the child's word usage matures, you may both enjoy pursuing the more subtle differences of reaction-word pairs and their meanings, such as *wasteful-generous*, *silly-humorous*, *stingy-thrifty*, *expensive-priceless*, *beautiful-attractive*, *heavy-serious*, and *thoughtless-dishonest*.

Marge Clark, discussing questions with her third-grade class, gave us something unexpected to think about. She asked, "How do you feel when you're asked a question you know?" The replies from nineteen of her children boiled down to *bad, super, smart, OK, good, glad, wonderful, dumb—happy* was the predominating reply. One boy, perhaps unaccustomed to knowing a question's correct answer, replied *weird*. One girl, who seemed well aware of her ability, answered, "I feel the same as I usually do."

Marge then asked the same group, "How do you feel when you're asked a question you don't know?" The self-confident girl replied, "Not so great," a step or two down on her ability-inability spectrum. Other replies from the children were *mad, dumb, scared, funny, sad, sorry, unhappy.* Several children replied *bad,* and several others qualified their bad feelings with *kind of bad* and *real bad.* One child was quite frank to reply, "I say puddin'." In lieu of a more descriptive one-word opinion, no doubt! Another admitted to being *in berist,* perhaps a place in the child's mind more preferable than *embarrassed.* I might have enjoyed playing with that child a bit about *berist* to find out where the place is, how people get there, and what they do when they're in berist. Another day, though, and with older children.

There are only nineteen third-graders in Marge Clark's discussion group, not enough to make a generalization. However, we can say that this particular group had a few more reaction words for their inabilities than they used to respond to their strengths. It is an unfair summary. A question arises, though, and a caution. Is your child learning more words to name reactions to his shortcomings than to his abilities? From whom?

Naming Behaviors

Simon had a dog named Cyrano. Simon's dog finally walked by his heel for the first time after a number of coachings and coaxings. "If Cyrano can heel once, he can do it twice," Simon said to himself, and sure enough ol' Cyrano did it again. Simon tested Cyrano's ability to heel several times during each training session and for several sessions each day. Soon, Cyrano could sit and lie as well as heel. Cyrano was rewarded with a biscuit each time and a brisk rub between the ears; in addition, Simon could proudly tell his friends that Cyrano was obedient. *Obedient* expressed Simon's opinion of Cyrano's ability to sit, lie, and heel—actually, to obey Simon's commands. *Obedience* was the word Simon used to name the consistency of Cyrano's actions. That is, until ol' Cyrano blew it a couple of times by doing disobedient actions, a new opinion word from Simon—and no more rubs between Cyrano's ears for a while.

Now, here comes the fine line of a crucial difference. Simon used *obedient* to give his opinion of Cyrano's actions, and he used *obedience* to name the consistency of Cyrano's conduct. When Cyrano's actions became disobedient, Simon preferred to change Cyrano's conduct rather than to change dogs. Simon used the words to talk about Cyrano's behavior and the consistency of that behavior; he was not talking about Cyrano himself. Simon reacted verbally to Cyrano's behavior. He also responded physically to Cyrano's behavior with the behavior of his own, a rub between the ears.

There's a saying in the conservative breadbasket of the country, "Long acquaintances make lasting friendships," which brings up a set of interesting questions: What do friendly people do? What is a friend? What is friendship?

Let's suppose a series of actions and reactions between two children, Ellen and Rita. Ellen does several actions which Rita perceives. Rita goes "clang" with that combination of perceptions, and her one-word reaction is *friendly*. Rita thinks or even says, "That was friendly of you, Ellen." However, Rita may feel a bit distrustful and aloof, thinking, "That may be friendly, but I'll wait and see."

Another set of actions by Ellen. Again, Rita goes "clang" with the combination of perceptions. "Hm-m-m, friendly again," she says or thinks. "That was also friendly of you, Ellen." Distrust? Perhaps, but less aloof. "I'll wait a bit longer and see what she does," thinks Rita, however.

Another action from Ellen. Another clang by Rita. Rita says, "Friendly." Clang again. Those clangs are beginning to add up. "I think I like her," thinks Rita, "I'll do some friendly action for her."

This time, Ellen goes "clang." They both say, "Friendly." Both say, in action or words, "Let's be friends."

Friendly actions make friends. Friends are very special kinds of people. They like, need, and want each other's time, ideas, reactions. They share. There is a consistency, a kind of time pattern to the relationship between two friends, which we may call friendship. *Friendship* is also a kind of one-word opinion we use when we react to the conditions between two friends. That condition can last as long as the behavior of each person toward the other may be called consistent. You'd best add that a child's thoughtless or heartless reactions can jeopardize or sever a relationship.

You can ask the same questions which define the relationship between children and their countries: What do patriotic children do? What is a patriot? What is patriotism?

Your discussions with a child may approach words like *courage, loyalty, faith, honesty, love, hope, grief, boredom, strength, charity,* and hundreds of other conditions. Ask for the child's ideas on the behavior that leads one to react with a one-word opinion. For example, "What do honest people do?" From there, it's a fairly easy move to talk about the words we use to name our one-word reactions to the behavior, the appropriate name we give a person, and the consistency of a relationship. These names are to be given by both children and adults to behaviors thoughtfully and never in haste.

Getting Pushy with Words

When Simon named Cyrano's behavior *obedient,* he had evidently perceived enough of the dog's actions to merit this one-word opinion, and Simon could reasonably expect Cyrano's future actions to be obedient.

In a similar way, a child's actions may merit this reaction from you: "That child is obedient." The child's obedient behavior over a period of time may both prove to be consistent and also to engender your future expectations, which may be named *obedience.* From then on, you rather expect the child to be obedient again and again and again, based on the child's growing list of past actions. Oddly enough, an expectation can work in both constructive and destructive ways. We've just mentioned one of the constructive ways. On the other hand, if the child acts disobediently with some consistency, you may, sometimes too quickly, shout "Disobedience!" or even a profane reaction. The child could feel quite reasonably that the reputation for disobedience must be upheld; or, the child could consider that the adult reaction was either unfair or hasty, and the child could enter a period of excessive personal struggle in feeling that "You don't care about me any more."

Let's create a brief scenario to illustrate the point. You arrive at your front door one day and discover Richard sitting on the front steps, crying. Meaning to be helpful, you sit by Richard on the step and out of you comes a pushy directive: "Manly boys don't cry."

Richard sniffs once or twice and then replies, "OK, I'll stop crying."

We'll move Richard out and move Steve in; otherwise, the scene is the same. Steve replies, "Oh, yes they do! I'm manly, and I'm crying."

Same scene, different boy. This time it's Jerry, who says to you, "Then I must not be manly, and there's no further point in acting like somebody I'm not."

Clay, replacing Jerry in the scene this time, says, "And you wish you had a manly boy—right?"

Play the scene once more, this time with Eddie, who turns to you a bit defiantly and says, "Humph, that tells me what manly boys don't, but what do they do? Rape? Fight? Murder?"

If you meant what you said, then Richard probably behaved according to your expectations. Steve included himself in both sides of your directive. Your comment to Jerry backfired. Clay interpreted your remarks about his behavior personally and felt that you desired a replacement. Eddie very logically put your pushy directives to the most severe test by asking what to do rather than having your opinion on what to don't.

This pushy kind of directive has gone "clang" in the minds of our five young characters, causing five quite different reactions. But let's not question the five behaviors. Instead, let's doubt the value of your directive, spoken both hastily and unnecessarily in our brief drama. If this scene occurs in your real life, instead of attacking the child's behavior, you might try changing the conditions which caused it. It seems logical to say, as a rule of thumb, that you can change a behavior in two ways. First, provide the conditions which make the desired actions as easy as possible to do. Second, reward the desired behavior with your own physical and verbal reactions.

We can be immediate and sensible in reacting to the behavior we want to encourage in a child.

That was a thoughtful thing for you to do.

You were helpful by going to the bakery for me.

I'm glad you told me that you were sorry about spilling the orange juice.

Thank you for getting the mail.

Your best reaction when talking with the child is to associate closely your reaction word with the child's behavior. Your message will get through when the child's kind and positive act is met with your own kind and appreciative words.

We can be just as immediate and sensible when we seek changes in the child's behavior. The child must be assured, though, that we wish for different actions and not for a different child. A very successful executive once gave me advice which you may find helpful: "Praise your praises and handle your successes in public, but make your changes and handle your problems in private."

Proverbs

Worthless said the buyer as he argued the price;
Bargain he boasted later to his friends.

Here is an interpretation of one of the Proverbs (20:14) of Solomon. It can provide you with plenty to talk about when you and the child feel like rubbing a couple of words together.

Who called the item worthless?

Suppose that he were the seller—what would he then call the item?

How did the argument between the buyer and the seller determine the price?

What did the buyer think of the price when he talked to his friends?

How do you think the seller felt later?

Ancient and modern proverbs are filled with reactions and one-word opinions. They make fine conversation starters for you and your child. Caution! The answers to questions about proverbs are not always clear-cut. Instead of laying proverbs on your child as indisputable truths, the two of you may examine them together to determine their truth and to consider their applications, if any, to your own experiences.

Here's another one of Solomon's Proverbs (16:21), para-
phrased a bit in order to offer a point.

Wise parents are known by their common sense,
Pleasant parents are best.

Do you agree? Would your child say it's true?

10

The Big I

I, me, my, mine, myself—

I do, I will, I have, I want, I think, I am. So many of the sentences we say begin with these words! *I* is the ninth letter of the alphabet. *I* is the symbol or abbreviation for iodine, an electric current, an imaginary unit of math, an island or isle, an isospin (betcha didn't know that!), the Roman numeral for one, and the ninth anything in an outline. But relatively few people in the world care fervently about knowing all that.

We all care much more that *I* is *me*. *I* is the favorite topic of concern and conversation for almost all of us. I am the only person in the whole world who can call myself *I*. *I* is unisexual. Every man and woman, without regard to sex or sexism, can call themselves *I* and mean exclusively themselves.

One *I* can do fine until it gets lonely for the company and the understanding of another *I*. Then *I* has a way of becoming *we* in the language. But *we* consists of two or more *I*'s, each with separate wills, needs, desires, thoughts, goals. If two *I*'s, which have combined to be a *we*, choose to create a family, the resulting family group may still be called *we*, although the *I*'s continue to increase, one for each family member. Each *I* wants to have a voice in the family *we*. It is the give and take of the *I*'s within the *we* that may strengthen, balance, strain, or even break the family unit.

Giving a child the freedom to find her or his place and to tell personal feelings as one *I* in the family or social unit may be one of the major things that this chapter and this book are all about.

Opinions, Compliments, Insults

John was invited to speak at the banquet sponsored by one of the town's prestigious community organizations. The invitation also included Imogene, and both had honored positions at the speaker's table.

After his slick after-dinner speech, many of the attending diners gathered around John and said, "That was one of the finest speeches we've ever heard. You are certainly a great man."

Gloating over his success and the following praise, John asked Imogene as they were driving home, "Honey, how many great men and women are there living in the world today?"

"Quite a few, I suppose," Imogene said, "Maybe the Pope, and Queen Elizabeth, the President . . . and, I guess, Barbara Jordan, and Makarios . . . and Billy Graham."

"But just how many, do you think?"

Imogene replied, "Oh, John, I don't know exactly, but I'm certain there's one *less* than you think."

You and your child use opinion words to tell what you believe about something or someone. When you talk together, even when you think you're sticking closely to the facts based on your perceptions, those opinions invariably slide into your conversation to tell another person of your conclusions, predictions, reactions, or impressions.

We noted earlier that sentences about the future constitute a kind of opinion, since future actions are not yet perceivable.

I think we'll have snow tonight.

Flying Carpet will win in the third at Belmont.

That stock will double by the first of next month.

Sheila will buy that new rug when she gets paid.

Even though these opinions may be based, quite reasonably, on perceptions of the present and experiences in the past, any statement about the future implies some risk. The word *predict* means to tell something beforehand, and *predictors* always take some gamble on being wrong. So do stockbrokers and handicappers (and, boy, can they be wrong!). In addition, circumstances can alter future events. People can also change their minds about their intentions.

Opinions don't have to begin with *I think*. "Snoopy is more intelligent than Charlie Brown" stands as an opinion with or without *I think*. Certainly, nobody feels the urge to document this opinion with truth. Besides, who would dispute it?

An opinion doesn't have to be true, and it doesn't need to be proved one way or the other, although it may be modified or doubted by another opinion.

> That's the best picture of Peedie you've drawn yet. (Except, maybe, for the picture you gave me.)
>
> This chili is too peppery. (Not for me—I like it *hot!*)
>
> Karen is too little to go skating with us. (Karen probably has a different opinion about that.)

Now and then, an opinion can be fairly noncommittal, making it difficult for us to decide whether the opinion-maker likes or doesn't like something. Here are two classic examples.

> Man, that *is* a set of wheels!
>
> Of all the Easter outfits I've ever seen in my life, that certainly is one of them.

More often, though, opinions absorb from their makers a kind of plusness or minusness. An opinion which leans toward the plus side may be considered a compliment, depending upon the listener's reactions to one or more of the opinion words within the sentence.

> Tyree plays a mighty powerful game of basketball.
>
> Great, Matt! I've never eaten your homemade ice cream before. All right!
>
> I think your new haircut looks attractive . . . really pretty around your ears.

When the opinion-makers stop talking side by side and square off to talk face to face at each other or about each other, their opinions may absorb varying degrees of minusness. An opinion which leans toward the minus side may be called an insult.

I'm tired of talking about me. Let's talk about you for awhile. What do you think of me?

Man, you are so damn clumsy when you get a tennis racket
in your hand.
She (He) certainly married an ugly duckling.
What are you, deaf or something? Or are you too dumb to
know when your name is called?
You're a liar!

In each of these sets of opinions notice that a word or two
may be removed from the context of a sentence and hurled all
by itself as a compliment or an insult—*best picture, peppery, too
little, powerful game, homemade, attractive, damn clumsy, ugly duckling, deaf, dumb.* These words by themselves may project a
plusness or minusness. In addition, just think how a vocal manner and physical movements by the speaker can intensify these
opinion words! It's not easy for you or the child to stay calm or
objective when you must sort out the plus or minus intentions
of such emotionally loaded opinion words. When Audrey says
to Lucie, "I think you are stupid," Audrey is no longer talking
about an absent or distant perceived thing. Audrey is talking
straight into Lucie. The opinion as it stands, without vocal or
physical softeners, hurls at Lucie a minusness which may be
identified as an insult. If you were Lucie, what would you say
and do?

Brody and Bart were young players on a league team under
pressure to win a local championship. Brody said, as they
waited on the bench for their first times at bat, "I think we'll
win today."

Bart shot back, "Not if you goof off in the field and screw up
at third like you did yesterday!"

Brody made an opinion about the future action of the team.
Bart directed a minusness—two insults, actually—at Brody.
Brody could ignore Bart's zingers and talk some more about
the abilities of the team. He could ask Bart how he goofed off
and how to improve his game today. He could return with an
insult to Bart's behavior in yesterday's game. He could offer to
fight Bart, substituting physical actions for words. Brody could
withdraw from Bart, perhaps even to cry. At any rate, it's a
lousy way for Brody to start a high-pressure game.

Children are entitled to every one of their opinions. If you try to restrict a child's opinions, you'll only drive them into the child, where they'll remain silently unsaid, but not unconsidered. It's better to hear and deal with opinions from children, especially the minus kind—but you yourself have to be "old enough" to handle them calmly and objectively without flying off your own handle. Although you must resist any unsuitable actions which result from the child's feelings, you and the child can talk out your opinions so that you each understand the other's feelings, and so that you are better equipped to deal with the child's behavior. That's what language is for.

Keep in mind that you have opinions, too, and that you're entitled to share them. Learn to identify your opinions and those of the child, those minus opinions which approach insults, and those plus opinions which go toward compliments. Spot the words which operate toward plusness or minusness, whether you say them in sentences or by themselves.

Ask for your child's opinion about things. Feel free to express your own in reasonable ways. After all, you are the two *I*'s that make a language exchange within the *we* possible.

Respect

When you ask the child for opinions, real opinions about important things, you are asking for admittance to a very private place of personal feelings. Think carefully about how you will behave in this carefully guarded scene. The child will decide how to receive you on the basis of your first question. "What makes you think that's such a cool bike?" is likely to leave you well outside the fence around the child's private thoughts. A calm, fairly intimate voice, slow to doubt, eye-to-eye level, a feeling of togetherness rather than confrontation, genuine sincerity, a desire to listen—these considerations on your side of the discussion may gain for you many more satisfying exchanges of inner feelings about things. Listen. Make it easy for your child to use opinion words. You might help to supply them now and then. Try to offer the child's most needed word of the moment and not your own ("Could you say . . . ?"). Use the child's most communicative words and offer others to the child's vocabulary when you express your own opinions.

Express yourself in a fair exchange, but don't be in a big fat hurry to impress the child with your own opinion. Consider your feelings for now to be less important than helping the child to express his opinions. Stick to talking about the something or the someone, the topic of the exchange. Bite your tongue when you feel your own judgment toward the child's opinions trying to get out of you. Show your child verbally and physically that you really care about his personal, inner reactions.

As your child describes perceptions and reacts with opinion words, be slow to judge and careful when you feel the need to amend or negate them. Let the child talk first and often, and react gently to gentle feelings. One nasty or arbitrary zinger of your own, and you may be out. And, in the case of a child's mind, once you're out it's damn difficult or impossible to get back in. Talks change opinions—one big blast from you stops them.

And that, dear friends, is respect.

In New York we have a useful household vehicle called a shopping cart, a wire or canvas basket on two wheels for lugging groceries, laundry, trash. I have one that I call Homer. They're not seen much outside of cities, where residents rely more on cars than on their feet.

Anyway, about five one afternoon the city bus stopped at a corner where a woman attempted to board with a child about six and a heavily loaded shopping cart.

"I'm sorry, lady," said the driver in a flat but not unkind voice, "no shopping carts allowed on the bus during rush hour." Rough on the lady, maybe, but a well-intentioned regulation.

She turned it all on for the bus driver. "But I have my son and we have to get home."

"You and the son are welcome, but the cart must stay on the corner," replied the driver.

The lady lifted herself in a huff and said as a curse, "Irish Mick!"

"And I thank my God every day, madam, that I was chosen to be Irish," the driver said, not allowing himself to show anger.

The woman, realizing that her first volley had not wounded deeply enough, hissed, "Nazi bastard!"

The driver said with a hint of irony, "And a good day to you, madam," closed the doors, and drove away from the curb.

The six-year-old boy (and the rest of us near the door) heard every word.

A sad experience. And, for the son, a poor lesson in respect.

Another day, if she'd sprawled over somebody else's cart as she tried to exit a crowded rush-hour bus, don't you wonder what sizzlers she'd have burned us with? Wow!

Please may express the child's respect and appreciation for somebody who's in a position to contribute, assist, or alleviate. *Thank you* may convey the child's respect and appreciation for one who has contributed, assisted, or alleviated. *Sorry* may project a respect and appreciation for the inconvenience, misfortune, sorrow, or regret for others. Courtesy words, spoken immediately and sincerely, indicate in one way or another a person's respect for some other person.

On the other hand, these same words may be spoken and accompanied by physical movements to express a kind of disdain. The next time you find yourself holding the main door to a supermarket or post office, trying to enter as several people are leaving, notice how some may smile and express a sincerely meant courtesy word, others may utter the words as if they're speaking to a clay statue, and still others may say nothing, as if you were paid to hold the door open. A basis for comparing vocal and physical expressions of courtesy has occurred right there at the door.

Notice, too, how a person on the street may ask you for directions, or how another in a store may ask you where to find something. Does the person walk away from you without a word of thanks, often leaving you in the middle of your directions? It's easy to infer that the person who requested your assistance had no genuine respect for either the help or the helper.

Explain, discuss examples and circumstances, and practice with your child on how to request directions or assistance from any person, how to listen carefully to the reply, and how to express a courtesy which shows respect for the help.

Needless to say, be free with the courtesy words to your child. Life's not too short to take time for being genuinely pleasant with each other.

Child's Work

Think of play as a form of self-employment for children. Perceiving things and actions, learning language, comparing the qualities of things, learning one's strengths. It's a full-time job. Add to that the monumental tasks of finding a place in the family unit, learning the expectations and limits imposed by others, managing and being managed by people. Well, that's heavy work in itself, to be put on top of the other full-time job of perceiving and discovering things for oneself. Several years later, when the child is old enough to enter the classroom, there are three big jobs to keep going—personal play, family, and school. It's a bit like having three different offices and three different sets of fellow employees to deal with. If we adults had to cope with three separate jobs, three different sets of co-workers, and three different social structures, in a similar manner, we might go bananas trying to keep it all sorted out. You've got to hand it to children for managing themselves, their families, and their schools as well as they do. No wonder they get cross and short-tempered when things go out of whack!

As you read a child's scene, you may wonder for a moment at its complexity before you enter it. Think first. When the child chooses to tell you her troubles, decide how you may be able to help side by side rather than add more problems to the present difficulties. If there's trouble in the back yard or in school and the child is seeking a helping hand from you, you have two choices. Will you alleviate some of the strain? Or will you complicate the problem by causing an additional strain from the family front as well?

When the child comes to you needing help, try to help—it's that simple. Try to be reasonable, fair, immediate, calm, firm, and positive in your actions and words. You can run off a mental checklist of possible difficulties—hunger, fatigue, overlong exposure to others, in the house too long, out of the house too long, possible illness. Experts differ on the physical and emotional effects of the weather, but I insist that I am not at my best, and often at my worst, on low-barometer days. Others who pooh-pooh their reactions to the weather nevertheless often tell me that they feel down, sluggish, or out of sorts on days when I notice that the barometer is also down. It's only another thought for you to add to the checklist concerning the child. If you find a clue that will help, then help.

Surprisingly, your child may present a difficulty to you for which your help isn't actually necessary. The child may present a problem, hoping mostly for your reassurance that the one corner of the child's "working world" where you are remains stable and securely in place, giving the child enough confidence to deal with one or both of the other full-time jobs. That which seems unsolvable to an inexperienced child may seem a great deal simpler to you. Perhaps you need only to give the child an idea or a boost which will help in his attempt to solve his own problem. Use your question words, avoid questions that can be answered by yes or no, and listen until you know how you can help.

Also, the child may be testing your control of the limit within which he may operate. Children often need to be assured that the adult controls remain firm.

Conflict and Control

The family, whether it consists of one or more parents and their children or any group of people related by some common circumstance, exists somewhere in the balance of the actions, the wills, the wants, the thoughts, and the beliefs of all of its members. A family is established by its members for the protection, education, and well-being of those who have a place in the family unit. Each member of the family has the responsibility of giving and taking in order to maintain or regain balance in the family. This is beginning to sound like a cross between the Gettysburg Address and the Preamble to the Constitution, but its all here to make one major point: The use of language by the members can strengthen, strain, or destroy the family unit.

Do you hear yourself saying the following comment often? Have you heard others say it? "I just live for my kids, that's all, only for my kids." Really? I wonder if you mean it. Look at all of this wonderful adult life that you're giving up. If you mean what you say, you're putting your own family unit perilously out of balance by letting family life revolve only around the kids instead of the family unit. Besides, there's something rather selfish about saying "my kids"—*my* kids. Whether you wish to or not, you will share those children with other school and social units as they grow older. Will you hang on to those kids more tightly in years to come, as you continue your efforts to prove that they are still yours? When your adult sons and daughters have lives and perhaps families of their own, and the realization comes to you that they are not really yours any more, will your favorite cry become, "To think what I gave up and this is the thanks I get"? It's guaranteed to wound, but not to regain your children.

Here's another comment you can say often, if you wish to throw the family unit out of balance: "I'm only the mother (father) around here, and nobody seems to care how I feel, but . . ." You might as well throw garbage over your head in the middle of the living-room floor. This opinion-starter gives you two minus opinions about yourself. Your family unit is not in balance if you continue to subdue yourself in front of your family. Balance is achieved through the confidence and the contribution of its members. Of course, a statement like the one above is very useful if you wish to control your family by a form of self-humiliation. But the effects are not everlasting.

Frequently, it's quite true that "Mother (Father) knows best." You are expected to be experienced adults, and your opinions should count in the final decision. Keep in mind, however, that children have had more recent experience in being children, and their opinions should count for something, too. Really try to understand what the children want and believe, so that decisions consider the well-being for all. Sometimes, you'll discover that your family has become bipartisan on some issues—dad and child vs. mother and child or dad and mother vs. children. It's generally better for the adults to settle their own differences in private. Also, you can handle private problems privately, if the difficulties do not involve all of the children. Family discussion should be able to settle other family differences. A caution: be careful not to wound anyone, even unintentionally, with your own opinion words about the issue and the opposing family members.

Decisions on family matters can be made when all of the opinions have been heard and understood. A child's own feelings of place and responsibility within the family unit and his relationship with other family members depend upon how much giving and how much taking he can manage to do. Young children are not always experienced at offering opinions and participating in decisions. They don't know and can't predict how their feelings and actions will affect the others in the family. As you discuss difficulties that arise from differences, also talk with your children about how respect grows from understanding and how thoughtfulness grows from respect. After all, independence, the name of this growing-up game, is learned from independence-oriented people. Otherwise, if independence is to be grabbed from adults, isn't it then called escape?

The Sorensens have what they call the "repair shop" for discussing and settling family differences. When a problem is considered weighty enough to be taken to the "repair shop," each family member, in a way appropriate for his or her age, is informed about the issue. Any established rules or regulations which are considered to be pertinent to the difference are reviewed. All opinions receive time for their expression. Any commands or bossy sentences designed to be played for power are not considered opinions, and they are not allowed. Any angers which arise are given time to subside. All members of the family remain for the family decision, and all must agree that they can abide by it. One parent is the moderator; the parents may share the leadership of the discussion, depending upon the nature of the difference. Even the younger children witness the "repair shop" and may participate if the issue is pertinent to them. Each member is assured that it's OK to be wrong when they are wrong. The power of the family to make the decisions rises from reason and not from the doggedness of one or more of its members.

The Sorensens don't talk about discipline, which is generally the business of the adults; instead, they discuss family business.

In your family one alternative to some version of the "repair shop" is silence, aloofness, and a growing resentment. It would be tragic if, for the lack of a language exchange, a child in your family said to herself, "I can't wait till I'm old enough to get my Big I out of here."

Entering Children's Arguments

Suppose for a moment that you are having a disagreement with another adult, a minor issue but relatively vocal. Suppose further that a child walked into your argument and started to take sides in favor of the other adult and against your side of the issue. How quickly would you be tempted to say, "Go away, this doesn't concern you"? As we talk about entering arguments between children, the first question that you should ask yourself: "Does this concern me?"

Shelley and Beth were having a noisy difference of opinion in the family room of Shelley's home. Shelley's mother, two split-levels away in another room, yelled to them in a more-than-shrill voice, "Girls, stop fighting!"

Shelley turned to Beth and said, "Let's go outside where we can argue in peace."

From an inconspicuous distance, listen for a while to the difference two children may be having. Decide, if you can, on a name for that difference along the spectrum of differences—discussion, altercation, disagreement, argument, quarrel, dispute, fight, fracas, skirmish, tiff, conflict, or battle. Some of these differences may not require your entrance; others may indicate that you'll be needed rather soon.

When you enter an argument between children, what is it that you want? Silence or settlement? Is it more important to you that the children drop the argument or resolve it? If your child is one of the opponents, is it important to you that you help your child to win, whether or not the child is right? Do you wish to enter the argument just to make powerful adult noises?

Teaching children how to settle an issue is more important than halting this particular difference between the children. Yelling down the battlers may quiet things for you a bit and relieve a negative situation. But it may not leave anything positive or memorable in the way of language experiences for the children to use next time.

If the children happen to be quarreling about family duties, rely on whatever regulations have previously been established for sharing the work. Take a cue from well-organized teachers, who chart duties for a week or two. When the wailings begin on who's supposed to do what, they patiently ask the students to consult the chart. So easy.

Otherwise, if the children remain verbal and their opinions differ about an issue, you probably won't enter the fracas, at least immediately. Discussions between children (and between adults, too!) sometimes seem to turn to arguments, and no one seems to know when the shift takes place. The heat of a disagreement, however, can often be charted as children turn from an outside issue toward hurling opinions about each other. Experienced adults can sometimes draw the line at this point, but children who are inexperienced at using language can turn surprisingly quickly from hurling opinions to hurling fists. When a verbal exchange becomes a physical exchange, then you must, of course, enter the dispute. It's much better, though, if you can handle words with words, so you must try to foresee the direction of the children's differences.

"Can you settle this between yourselves, or do you want me to help you?" A double-barreled question, designed to help. Avoid, if you can, questions that can be answered by yes or no, since yes-no is already too evident in the verbal exchange. Stick to questions that start with your question words: "Why is this a difficulty for you? How will you settle?" Insisting that the children sit down, perhaps with milk and brownies, is a wise move on your part, since seated positions restrict physical movements. From the beginning, teach the children how to substitute words for physical exchanges, to reduce the confrontation from battle to issue, from disagreement to discussion.

If you are to settle the difference, hear both sides. Actually, you can help each child to state her case and to offer her opinion. You are being quite fair as the judge when you help each child to verbalize the differences and the issue. Then, restate the argument in your own words, and ask each child if you restated it fairly. Be willing to make amendments in your restatement. For either way the issue seems to be going, make sure that all opinions have been made clearly known, the argument reviewed, and the settlement, when reached, clearly stated and agreed to by both children.

In the end, feel free to state clearly your own wishes that the children's disputes are to be settled rather than battled. Battling is for board games, where rules must be followed and strategies must be designed. Battling is not the way to resolve anger, nor is it a reasonable substitute for language when resolving differences.

Ethics

There are numerous legal, social, and religious agencies that set down for us codes of acceptable behavior (which often differ from agency to agency, unfortunately), so we don't have to list standards of conduct here. You'll find a passel of books and articles on store and library shelves, written by child psychiatrists and other guidance experts, on how to achieve positive and change negative moral behaviors. If we mention the language of ethics briefly here, please don't feel that teaching moral conduct to children is as brief or as easy as it may sound. It continues year after year, and requires large portions of your hope and prayers.

The concept of acceptable and unacceptable conduct comes from perceiving, naming, and discussing that which, as you compare your opinions, may be labeled right or wrong, thoughtful or thoughtless, moral or immoral. Remember, however, as we've said before, there are many shades of gray between black and white. It is rather difficult to find actions which are completely wrong or completely right. Those actions that lie somewhere within the shades of gray are the ones for which personal opinion must be formed and discussed during your language experiences. As the two of you collect perceptions and reactions, the child will undoubtedly rub together those opinions you share, and make conclusions based not only on perceptions and past experiences but also on the relationship he shares with you.

The shalts and the shalt-nots best come from within the child's own reactions to perceptions mixed with the memory of any past experiences and their consequences. Conclusions on conduct often follow a series of "clangs" which rub a behavior and your reaction with the outcome. The shalts and the shalt-nots also come from following examples of conduct. Some of the most difficult discussions on ethics that will pester you for years often follow comments like these: "I did it because you did it." "If you can, I can, too." "I had to go along with the gang."

Besides hoping and praying, here are some suggestions that may help you.

1. Keep children busy. "What shall I do?" can be an indirect announcement that the child is heading for trouble without your attention, direction, and inventiveness to provide constructive, interesting time-fillers and companionship.

2. Have some reasonable, fairly imposed regulations which all members of the family are expected to follow. Children (adults, too) live with greater security and self-confidence when they are well aware of the limits beyond which they cannot go.

3. On the other hand, avoid making your home so tightly regulated that the children cannot remember all of the complicated shalts and shalt-nots.

4. Make it easier for a child to behave acceptably than to behave unacceptably. Be sincere, kind, and appreciative when the child conducts herself in ways that you admire. Associate complimentary opinion words with acceptable behaviors.

5. Set an example of the kind of behavior you want the child

to emulate. Help the child to understand what you do, how you feel, and how you feel about the child's personal values. By example and with language, discuss your expectations in positive ways and, when the child is away, trust that the child is conducting herself admirably. Nothing erodes moral conduct like suspicion.

6. Spend time with the child. Share perceptions, reactions, and experiences with the child. *Talk* with the child.

11

In Another's Place

There's a newspaper and whatnot store across the street on the corner called, not unimaginatively, the Corner. I was about to enter the Corner when a boy came out the door, shucked a candy bar, and dropped the wrapper on the sidewalk.

I was too much the civic-minded teacher to let that pass. I said to the boy, in an attempt to be both polite and directive, "Won't you please care enough to put that wrapper in the trash basket?" I indicated a wire receptacle less than four feet away.

The boy never slowed down, but said, "What the hell do I care? This ain't my neighborhood."

For him, it was someplace else, both geographically and mentally. It was my place, though; I picked up that wrapper, the big civic gesture, angry as I did it, and dropped it into the basket.

You're the mark by which the child measures the thoughtfulness of others. Whether you're the parent, grandparent, aunt or uncle, neighbor, teacher, babysitter, or passerby—you're the mark. The concept of thoughtfulness is gauged by perceiving and registering the actions of others. The child may perceive both thoughtful and thoughtless actions, and with any one action, the child may conclude, "That's important to her; she's important to me; therefore, that's important to me, too."

The child decides the way the world works by the actions of the people who surround him, since for a time those are the people of the child's world. Where do you suppose the boy who dropped the candy wrapper got the idea about the area that "ain't my neighborhood"?

Spozing

You won't find *spoze* in the dictionary; nevertheless, it's in the oral vocabulary of thousands of children. It's like *plack,* a word Ralph used as a child, as in, "Plack you're the engineer of a train, and plack my car is stopped across the tracks." With the flip of a *spoze* or a *plack,* children somehow beam themselves out of this real world and into another time and place. They materialize as other beings, sometimes human, but, just as easily, they become something else.

Spozing alters reality for a few moments. Projecting oneself imaginatively into roles helps a child to test and extend the reality of other times, places, and situations. In turn, spozing helps to confirm one's own reality. To some extent, we all fantasize "what it's like." We sit behind the wheel of a new car in the auto showroom. We throw a sample of material over the sofa to see if it would look good as a slipcover. We imagine a youthful, attractive stranger as a sex partner panting for a good time. We freeze on the street and, at the same time, imagine the warm sand by the blue water in the Caribbean. We try to picture how the meeting in the boss's office will go tomorrow morning.

Spozing need not be a deliberately planned language game that you play with the child. It can be a few moments now and then that come easily and naturally as you talk together about almost anything. For example, as you drive along the highway, you may see a truck full of new cars. After you and the child share what you've perceived, spozing may start with almost any question similar to these.

Where do you think the truck came from?

Where's it going?

Which car do you want to buy?

What's a good name for the driver?

What do you think the driver of that heavy truck thinks about?

How do you think the driver will feel to get those cars off there?

Suppose those cars belong to you, and you want to sell one to me. Let's make a deal.

You can spoze with very young children. For example, during the child's bath you might say, "Spoze you are a great big pelican. Flap your great big wings and fly. Now you see a juicy little fish in the water. Scoop him up and eat him!"

In reality, the time is now, and the place is here. Spozings help you to be somewhere else or somebody else in another time. After you've had several of these experiences, and the child discovers that there's no threat in your "setup," you can become a great deal more elaborate in your imaginings.

Try, if you can, to avoid using *would,* as in, "What would you do? What would you say? Where would you be?" The use of *would* sets an almost impossible frame and inhibits the imagining, the telling, the drawing, or the writing. Instead, be more straightforward in your setup, such as: "Spoze the driveway is an ice rink and we can go skating. I'll put skates on you, you put skates on me, and we're off!"

"Spoze you're a dragon right here in the middle of the street. How did you get here? Where did you come from? What are you doing? What are you thinking? Spoze, Mr. Dragon, you met me right here on this spot. Maybe I'm afraid of you, and maybe I'm not. Say something in dragon talk to me."

With a mirror in your hand: "This is a magic mirror. You can look into this mirror and see any land you wish to see. What do you see in there? Spoze we step through this mirror to be in another world. Let's go!" Don't laugh—Alice did it!

Guard against employing your amateur psychotherapy. These are language experiences for giving a child an opportunity to be in another time, place, or another person. They are not visits to the psychiatrist. You and the child are only testing and extending reality for a few moments.

Depending upon the age of the child and the child's experience in using imagination, your efforts to spoze may not go too far at first. A younger child is likely to react and respond to your efforts, but you will definitely be the leader in the spozing. An older child will contribute and perhaps initiate a word or two or a situation or two after she understands clearly that there is no threat involved in the experience. Spozing is a year-after-year thing which becomes more elaborately constructed as a language experience of its own, in addition to being a positive support for role-playing, reading, and writing.

You can talk out without acting out the consequences of spozings, such as if the moon were shaped like a donut instead of a globe. You also can create some unusual dialogues by spozing that you're another class of things—two rocks sitting together in the hot sun, two trees in a wild thunderstorm, two hungry mice in the kitchen (that conversation may result in a raid on the refrigerator).

In teaching reading and writing, I have met entirely too few imaginative children. Many adults seem to stereotype children as highly creative, undeniably imaginative, and adorably resourceful, but my experience tells me that it isn't quite so, for most children. Children's misconceptions of reality are not to be construed as cute or imaginative. Experiences with you in creating other times, places, people, and situations help a child to become imaginative in reading and writing. Cloris Leachman, the actress, attributes a major share of her dramatic abilities to her Iowa childhood when her mother helped her and her sisters to plan imaginative activities during meetings of the "Leachman Each Week Club."

Reading both requires and also provides opportunities for children to visit other times, places, and characters; to identify with characters in conflict; to experience empathy with the emotional burden of others; and to create a needed atmosphere within which a story can be set. The ability to spoze is a highly valued attribute, but it's not simply "there." The child must become aware of the ability to imagine, and you can help a child to develop it. You'll also be pleased to discover that spozing is contagious, so save some for yourself.

Bodies "Talk"

I was sitting in the waiting room of Dr. Ramsey's office. Dr. Ramsey shares that crowded waiting room with several other

146

dentists, and for a while every seat was taken. I shared a two-cushioned seat with a girl about five years old. After a few minutes, two of the dentists' assistants came to the waiting room, called their next patients, and accompanied them to various examining rooms. This left the five-year-old girl next to me and her mother across the room. The mother's eye met mine for a moment. "Jeannie," the mother said, "sit over there in that chair."

The girl did not mind where she sat, and I did not mind where she sat. But the mother minded. Although the rules differ somewhat between cultures, each cultural group seems to have its own rules about the distances to be maintained between people. These distances also differ between strangers, between acquaintances, between friends, between close members of an immediate family, and, of course, between lovers.

There is a social space which is maintained between two people who are conversing. That distance may differ a bit, depending upon the subject of the conversation and the familiarity of one person with the other. Notice for yourself sometime, when you are talking with another person; as you talk, slowly move a bit closer to the other one, and notice how he or she may either back away a bit or seem increasingly uncomfortable. The other's movement and manner tell you that you are invading that person's space.

Notice, too, when you are conversing with a child, that the nature of your conversation changes when you pull the child closer to you to make a friendly or loving physical gesture. Note how you and a child move slightly closer together if you are about to share a confidence—a deep, dark secret—within your conversation. We've mentioned many times before that side-by-side talks with a child are quite different from face-to-face positions, which suggest a confrontation.

Watch how two children may deliberately divide the table space in half, sometimes sitting so that a noticeable crack or mark in the center of the table becomes the dividing line. If the children are working on separate homework or projects, even if they are stitting together, notice how one's movement across the center may be considered an act of aggression, causing the other to make a countermovement or to become a bit edgy and uncomfortable because his space has been invaded.

Two people on a subway at rush hour play a kind of game called "You're Not There." They may stand somewhat apart when they talk, even though strangers may stand closer to each of them. However, because of the crowded conditions, the strangers aren't really "there." The friends may even feel the body heat of strangers, and yet mentally consider the strangers to be invisible.

Young Ross wanted his mother's attention at a time when she was busy. Ross invaded his mother's body space, moved closer, and touched his mother more insistently as she tried to ignore his invasion. Finally, his mother gave up, turned, and offered Ross a broad smile. At that moment, Ross was no longer invisible; he was "there" and was acknowledged by his mother. He actually backed off a bit from her in order to smile back. Once he was acknowledged, Ross could resume a social distance.

Miss Fox rarely moved from her teacher's desk in front of the classroom. Any of her second-graders who wanted to talk with her had to approach her desk; she remained seated, a child remained standing. This relationship between Miss Fox and one of her pupils seemed so backward. Why bring a child from the learning space in the room to the teaching space? Teachers, in order to be available when needed, can best work side by side with their students in the room's learning space. The use of space and the maintenance of distances relate to the ways in which a person's body "talks" for power—I'm the teacher in the powerful teacher's place, I'm the parent in the powerful parent's position, I'm the adult occupying the towering adult space. These adults' bodies are bidding for a space gap which also may become an age gap.

"Look at me when I'm talking to you" means, kiddo, that you'd better understand me very clearly. When we say this (and what parent hasn't said it at some time or other), it also means that we must put on our sternest, most serious face, because one wink or crack of a smile and our bodies "say" that we don't really mean a word of it. Look in the mirror sometime and check out the face you put on when you're trying to be stern.

My teacher talks to herself. When she talks to me, she thinks I listen—but I don't!

Many adults have their favorite chairs in the living room, their favorite lamps, their established places at the dinner table, and their exclusive towel racks in the bathroom. Does the child in your home have an established place to sit in the living room, a comfortable chair the child's size, a good light for reading, an appropriate-sized table nearby?

Terry, about eleven, was playing rock music in the family room while his father Eric and I were talking about nothing in particular. Eric is an incessant smoker. Terry and I were both annoyed by the blue air in the room, but I was "company" and had to mute my discomforts. Terry, on the other hand, was competing for the air space in the family room. It was quite obvious to me that Terry would raise the volume of his rock music each time Eric lit a cigarette or exhaled a large quantity of smoke. Without a word, Terry and Dad were both battling, Terry offending Eric's ears while Eric annoyed Terry's lungs. The situation was resolved when Eric insisted that the music be turned down, and Terry agreed only if the glass doors could be opened to let in some fresh air. Eric got the point.

In recent years a number of writers are suggesting to both adults and children how messages may be sensed by people using their bodies instead of or in addition to spoken words. You can find a number of moments to talk with the child about the meaning of body movements. What does a smile say from the smiler? What can an arm around your shoulder mean, a wave from a distance, a snapping of the fingers? How does a person say *go away, stay put, come here,* or other common commands with the body instead of with words? Applause is a way in which the people in an audience talk back to a performer with their bodies.

When you're helping a child to become interested in watching football, baseball, basketball, or other games, you'll discuss the game's scoring system and the basic rules that govern the play. And you can have an enjoyable time learning the body signals of the referee or umpire. When an official in a game makes a move, ask the child what the official's gesture means. The games become increasingly interesting when you and the child can perceive both the official body talk and the movements of a player or players who initiated the official's action.

How does a traffic officer use physical movements on a busy street corner? How does a rock group know when to start and end at the same time? If you're watching a "pops" conductor on television, discuss what some of the arm movements may mean to one of the orchestra's musicians.

You might try learning the alphabet and both your names in the manual signs for the deaf, not only to perceive one more way in which bodies talk, but also to understand the point of view a deaf person has toward language. Notice, too, that your language may be readable, even without the sounds, when a deaf person reads the speech on your lips and face. With your child, say words and phrases without the sound to see if one can perceive the silent "talk" of the other. Turn the sound off during TV commercials and try to repeat some of the words or phrases you "see" on the lips of the performers.

Assume a body posture such as lifting a big, big box, or pushing a car—and then ask the child, "What does your body say when it is doing this?"

We read gestures that accompany the language we hear. A person's movements often tell us more of that person's intentions (implications, if you wish) than the words themselves. You can help a child to become aware of a body's language by asking, "How can you show me without words that you're hungry (thirsty, tired, injured, frightened)?" Watch people. Discuss the inferences and reactions that each of you get by another person's movements or gestures. Discuss the people that you see in pictures as you look at magazines together, "Suppose that person talked to you. What does he say?" You need not limit your supposing to people; you can also ask what dogs, cars, birds, snakes, and any class of things might say. When you're reading together or when your conversation provides an opportunity, note how certain words like *slumped, downfallen, forlorn, wary, weary, energetic, sheepish, impatient,* or *sneaky* all project a feeling about the body of the person or animal they describe.

Point of View

Ms. MacGowan stood on one side of the room in her class of third-graders. She asked Casey to stand in the same place on the opposite side of the room. "Can you see what I see?" she asked Casey. And then she named a number of obvious things in the room which they both perceived—Hosea's desk, Corinne's sneakers, and the plaster dog on the reading table. Casey replied that she could see everything that Ms. MacGowan named.

Then Ms. MacGowan named a different kind of perception. "And can you see the patch Arlyce sewed on the sleeve of her T-shirt?"

"No, I can't from here."

"The place where you signed your name on Michael's arm cast?"

"No, it's on the wrong side."

"The bandage on Renee's elbow?"

"No, Ms. MacGowan, you're naming things on your side of the room."

Ms. MacGowan made her point with one more question. "What would you have to do to see what I see?"

Casey replied, "I'd have to be where you are."

"One more thing, Casey. What can you see across the room that I can't see?"

Casey thought a moment, and her answer was brilliant. "You, Ms. MacGowan, I see you."

Where we are, where we stand, physically and emotionally— our point of view—relates very closely to what and who we perceive and how we respond. Everything depends on where we are.

When you ask a child to consider the point of view of another person, or perhaps a hungry cat, or a bike that has been left in the rain, or a tree with a broken branch, or a man who's dropped his wallet into the mail box instead of his letters, encourage the child to think as the other would think and to talk as if he were actually the other person, animal, or thing. Encourage the child to change the pronoun names from *she, him,* or *it* to *I, me,* and *mine.* And you'll also try to use *you* as if the child were actually the other thing. In this way, supposing takes on the cloak of role-playing.

Understanding a point of view seems dependent on one person's being able physically, mentally, or emotionally to occupy the space of another. Assuming another's point of view is not only useful in helping a child to develop attitudes, it is also essential if one is going to learn that there's more than one side to an argument.

To see another's point of view in a difference of opinion depends, first, on the child's position in the discussion and, second, on his willingness to abandon that position long enough to move mentally to the position of the opponent. If you are the opponent, and yet getting the child to understand both sides of the difference is more important to you than winning that difference, you must not mistake the child's willingness to understand your point for the impression that you've won your point. If the child is willing to vacate his side of the difference for a moment, you must not allow yourself to attack the child's abandoned position. Instead, you must elucidate your opinion in order to help the child to understand it. You cannot besiege the child's argument while he's trying to understand yours; just as important, you cannot leave your own point when the child is trying to view it.

Point of view, like so many hundreds of other things in the language, has several names. Among them are *manner of thinking, standpoint, attitude, feeling, position.* Whatever the name, for all of us—adults and children alike—there's a tremendous advantage in the ability and the willingness to understand a point of view other than our own. And to see ourselves as others see us is, of course, the ultimate advantage.

The Truth

The truth, like honesty and beauty, lies in the eye of the beholder. My experiences with children as well as my eavesdroppings on conversations between adults and children lead me to believe that the child's thoughts of others help to determine what is the truth.

Accuracy is one form of truth. Sincerity is another. But accuracy for why? And sincerity to whom? For whom must the child be honest and true? From the standpoint of a child, a true friend is faithful and loyal to the one who calls him *friend* and behaves toward him in a genuinely friendly manner. A child's loyalties may easily lie more closely with a friend, even a pet, than with adults, and especially adults who are parents.

The consideration or fear of others influences a child's (and an adult's) version of the truth. A child tells or distorts the truth according to his need to protect a friend or to blame an opponent. This need is not developed internally as an attitude all by itself. Dozens of the stories on television, including many of those which Disney has made famous, are full of children who can't or won't tell the truth because of their loyalties to a friend or an animal.

The power an adult holds over a child may force a collection of part-truths, but it does not necessarily encourage the full truth. The child is constantly faced with questions he hears from within: "What'll happen if I tell the truth? What'll happen to my friend or pet if I tell? What'll happen if I don't?" You may approach a child with an "I-know-better" attitude which may get you what the child thinks you want to hear or what will most quickly and surely, in the child' view, protect her. The consequences are balanced by the child between points of view versus thoughts of others as she determines what truth or part of it will be revealed. If you hold very little or no adult power, you may get as a reply, "It's none of your business!" A different kind of confrontation may follow if you feel forced to prove your adult power instead of pursuing the truth.

You might take a lesson from doctors, lawyers, and police officers who wisely and calmly ask for "the facts," the whole story, several times in several different ways as they look for that one comment, clue, or other giveaway that reveals the key to the true situation.

The real truth from a child is his attempt to reveal something the way it was, the way he saw it, from his point of view, and not the way he wished it or the way he thinks you wish it. The truth is easier for a child to reveal when you permit the child to tell it. As you listen to the telling, remember that the truth is being revealed to you only as the child perceived and understood it. The better the child's perceptions, the better the child's ability to make things go "clang" in his mind, and the better equipped he is to reveal the truth.

Back to good old quotable Solomon again: "Any story sounds true until someone tells the other side and sets the record straight."

Cooperation, Competition

A child cannot and should not be expected to cooperate to the point of selflessness. On the other hand, the child cannot and certainly should not be expected to compete to the point of cruel, even brutal selfishness. Within each child there seems to be a mixture of cooperative attitudes and competitive attitudes which the child must deal with together, generally at the same time. Competitive actions must temper and be tempered by cooperative actions, and it is a formidable task to expect children to do by themselves. Less fortunate children have to try. More fortunate children learn to balance cooperation and competition with your guidance and understanding.

A child learns cooperative actions by working together with other children, developing a spirit of togetherness as a member of a team or group, recognizing a common goal, striving with others to attain it, and joining with any social group for a recognizable purpose which the child considers worthwhile. A child learns competitive actions when she enters or is placed in a position of rivalry against another person or team, when she works against another for the same achievement, when she expects or is expected to equal or outdo another in some ability. Cooperation and competition rub against each other when a child is expected to cooperate with one team at the same time she is expected to compete with a different team. The attitudes may become even more murky and intricate when a child is expected to compete for excellence within the cooperative actions of a team which, in turn, competes for a score, prize, or recognition with another team. It can be most confusing to a child. Perhaps he must work for the highest batting average on a team. At the same time, he must develop a winning team spirit while competing with another team or league for the honors and the recognition of adults. Is that recognition for the child's accomplished cooperation or competition?

Fair is the name of the reaction we give to the child's lack of self-interest and self-indulgence when behaving with others within a set of rules. *Fair play* and *fairness* are the names we give to the consistency of a child's or team's actions within a set of rules. Very complicated words, since they involve very delicate mixtures of cooperation and competition. You can't expect a child to sort out the attitudes of fairness and fair play without discussion regarding actions within rules. As you talk together, you might also keep well in mind that *cheating* is the name of any action which is not according to agreed-upon rules.

A close friendship with another child is frequently marked by times when a sensitive blend of cooperation and competition affects and even jeopardizes the relationship. Competition is very serious business to a child, as it is very serious business to an adult. But children can't close their shops at five-thirty and resume social friendships with their business competitors. It's all one and the same for children. Rivalry between young friends, without your understanding and help in patching the differences, can often result in quarrels.

Notice how feverishly close friends hope and strive to be in the same class, on the same "side," to ride in the same car, and to be invited to the same parties. They seem to know the pitfalls of separation and, therefore, possible competition.

A concept of cooperation develops over a period of time within the family unit as the child learns to help others. Requests and polite commands, softened with *please* or other courtesies, are exchanged by family members as each considers the well-being of the other. Each member contributes to the welfare of the family by observing its ground rules, the regulations on which the happiness and the security of the family unit depend. The child's concept of cooperation may also embrace obeying the laws of his community and state regulations depend largely upon your own conduct and attitudes regarding the law.

Children aren't born with a concept of competition. However, the need for security and approval is right there and apparent from the first few moments. Parents are very quick to note the various ways in which an infant competes for their time and attention. A friend of mine once put the thought very well: "I love being talked to, I like being talked about, but I hate being ignored."

Always feel free to play games with children appropriate to their ages and developing abilities. Make and agree upon a rule or two for almost any game, and play according to the rules. Rules can become more numerous and more detailed as the child grows more mature in her ability to play the game. Rules set down the conditions for competition. They also set the conditions for cooperation. Games have standards for excellence which a player must attain in order to win. Rules become more and more important as children learn to play games with each other, and a very detailed sense of fairness is developed from the children's cooperative-competitive attitudes.

Children also emulate what they admire. According to their age, they may copy your stance, your speech, your manner, even your very appearance. When you notice that you are being copied and "shadowed," you have an excellent opportunity to talk with the child about attitudes and behaviors which you consider important for a successful and happy adult life. You're cornered somewhat, however, if you talk about one set of attitudes and behaviors, while the child perceives in you quite a different set of actions, reactions, and attitudes. You may be complimented, but you'll sometimes find it far from easy to be the object of a child's emulation.

Ambition is born in some mixture of cooperation and competition. What you want the child to do or to be, how you want the child to succeed, depends largely upon the cooperative and competitive attitudes that you discuss with the child, those attitudes and actions that you expect the child to develop, and the child's own desire to emulate and please you.

A moral code of conduct—ethics, if you wish—must be developed from the inside out by the child's awareness of others and from the outside in from the child's respect for rules, laws, commandments. Both meet somewhere, we hope, on the inside. A feeling for right and wrong is first developed by the child through a thoughtfulness for other people, animals, and things. If the child's behavior is not consistent with the rules and regulations of the community or the state, then right and wrong become subject to the interpretation of the legally powerful and are enforced by threats of fine, restriction, or confinement.

Friendly Actions

What does a friendly child do? Questions about *friend, friendly,* and *friendship* have been raised earlier in this book. *Friend* is the name a child gives to another person who consistently behaves in friendly ways. Friendly children impress other children and adults by their thoughtful actions.

The so-called "popular" child behaves consistently and dependably in ways that we can call outgoing, friendly, affectionate, and pleasant. The "popular" child seems to be balanced toward cooperation rather than competition. However, that child, when competitive, maintains an energetic sense of team and teamwork. The child seems quite well aware of himself or herself when contributing to the team effort.

The manner of the so-called "courteous" child indicates that she is considerate of others and able to place herself in another's position. She is well aware of thoughtful behavior and perceives thoughtlessness. Lee and his dad were shopping at the fresh-fruit and vegetable counter in the grocery store. Lee moved his grocery cart forward to a point where a lady had parked her cart crossways in the aisle, making it impossible for people to pass her from either direction. Dad, noticing Lee's difficulty, turned to him and suggested, "Say 'Excuse me' to the lady, Lee."

"Why, Dad?" questioned Lee. "I'm not the rude one!" And, indeed, he wasn't; neither his behavior nor his comment could be considered thoughtless. Lee had learned (as many adults still have to learn) that "Excuse me" is an apology for thoughtlessness; it is not a license for rudeness.

The so-called "considerate" child is, among other things, giving in his manner of behavior. He knows how to acknowledge friendly actions by returning a "thank you" or other kind re-mark. You might, by the way, encourage a child to acknowl-edge gifts and other kindnesses by a note sometimes, instead of in person or by telephone. A simply drawn picture of the gift in use or the child's feeling toward it captioned by a simple "thank you" will surely be valued more highly than the most expensive message in the greeting card shop.

Tolerance, consolation, pity, clemency, mercy, leniency, under-standing, condolence, leadership—all of these adult words presume an ability to project oneself into another place and to under-stand another's point of view. They are the names of consistent behaviors involving some balance between cooperation and competition. While the child is trying or learning to think about other people, keep in mind that all of those other people are also sizing up the kid. You're not going to get all of the chil-dren in your neighborhood straightened out; but you can hope that your conversation with a child and your actions, which the child perceives and perhaps strives to emulate, may rub off. At the least, the child can learn not to drop candy wrappers in somebody else's neighborhood. And just think what a help that would be!

12

Toward Reading

Reading presumes a familiarity with the sounds of the language. It also depends upon some association between the words a child hears and the ones a child sees. It's possible for you to take a full-semester college course built around one important, memorable theme: Facility in reading is related to a facility in oral language. And therein rests the single-minded purpose for this chapter.

The average child begins to read words somewhere between five years and six and a half years of age. Some read earlier, some later, but that's what makes an average. For our purposes here, the median doesn't matter. However, think of those wonderful five or so beginning years when you and the child have thousands and thousands of opportunities to share and exchange language experiences. Those first five or six years with oral language literally make a lifetime of difference in the child's abilities to read and understand written language.

It's not illegal or immoral for you to be caught reading. It's not illogical to be seen doing what you want the child to do. My mother actually read very few books in her lifetime; she did read newspapers, but not regularly. However, she read and saved magazines for rereading all of her life. And we went to the library—oh boy! did we go to the library! While Mrs. Anderson shuffled me off to the children's corner for my "culture," mother sat on the other side of the library reading the latest copy of *Vogue*. Nevertheless, we both read then. As soon as I was hooked after the first four or five pages of a book, Mrs. Anderson gave mother the high sign, I was yanked out of the book corner, the books were checked out to me, and we were on our way home, where I was generally allowed to read alone and without interruption. The habit became addictive. This seems to prove that it doesn't really matter what you read, if you're seen doing it by the child, and if the reading can at times be shared.

The total experience with reading, as with any language experience, should be more pleasant than unpleasant. Therefore, any language experiences which follow in this chapter (and anywhere else in this book) should be continued with the child for as long as the child is interested. Abandon or postpone the language activity of the moment in favor of something else if you see that the child's interest lags. You don't have to ram reading down a kid's throat, but you don't have to stop carrying on when you're enjoying yourself.

Mostly, have fun!

Carrying On Together

Begin early—from the baby's first day—to talk, sing, chat, chant, laugh, count, wax poetic, clown, chatter, gabble, croon, recite, narrate, and serenade for your child's benefit and amusement. Make happy, pleasant, cheerful, joyful noises! At first, the child won't see you clearly and won't understand you at all, but that doesn't matter. The child will know you're there, that your noises are warm and affectionate. And the child will love it!

Be a loveable fool—it won't hurt a bit.

After the first few months, when the baby can focus his eyes on you and can turn to you when you talk and carry on with all your foolishness, you can also start reading to the baby. It's another way to share words; although the baby can't name things for you, don't underestimate the baby's ability to perceive the book, your voice, your attention, and your own good time during the reading experiences. We're not quite sure when the baby begins to register words as meaningful sounds, so you may not be able to tell when the baby's perceptions combine with reactions, go "clang," and come up with some concepts and feelings about reading. Your good times with a baby and a book can't possibly hurt—provided that you sincerely enjoy the experience, too. One rule of thumb is not to do it when you may risk projecting boredom, duty, or fatigue with the reading activity. Remember that, eventually, if you don't laugh, sing, act, chant, hoot, and carry on with your child, your TV set will. Which is it going to be? Keep in mind, as we said earlier, your distinct advantage in being able to appear before your child "in person."

Fret not about being repetitious. Read Mother Goose or any other Mother that you think the child will enjoy three times each from cover to cover, backward and forward, and then start again. Sing repetitious songs about nose, elbows, knees, and toes. "Old MacDonald." "This is the way we wash the clothes." Anything with repetition which the child may eventually be able to sing or chant with you. Tell all of the rhyming stories you know about little piggies going to market, good ships named *Lollipop,* and what would happen if all the seas were one sea. Don't know any? Then visit the children's rack of the nearest paperback book store or the children's corner at the library. Or make them up. Try your own hand at writing children's stories and poems. Oh yes, don't forget "One potato, two potato." If you were a rope skipper in your younger days, you've got a great repertoire of counting and jumping rhymes.

Children simply don't learn these songs, chants, and rhymes by reading them—they're mouth-to-ear heritage. Unfortunately, by the time children are able to read these rhymes they may be too old for them, or think they are. And without them, children may have difficulty learning to read, anyway. You can't go wrong. So carry on!

Reading Pictures Together

Reading picture books and magazines together is a side-by-side experience. Be sure that you and the child are both facing the pictures from the same point of view as you read. Ask the old faithful questions which help the child to perceive and name things, actions, and qualities: "What do you see? What else?"

A picture is a visual record of the past, just as a story sentence that answers the question "Who did what?" also becomes a record of a past action. When you and the child read a picture together, you can both rather safely assume that the people or animals are not still there at this moment doing exactly those same pictured actions. It's very tempting, for example, to ask, "What is the cowboy doing?" or "Where are the zebras running?" But resist. Instead, you'll want the child to use past actions when telling about what happened in a picture, since sentences with actions in the past are most commonly used to tell stories. In this way, talking about pictures relates more closely to reading stories.

An action picture is also a slice of life. Several pictured slices can be lined up in a sequence. Sentences can put actions in sequence, too. The stories you make up together about pictures can include before and after. For example, ask, "What happened before the picture was taken? What did Ari do? Where did he come from?" or "What happened after the picture? Where did Ari go?" Both perceiving things when the picture was taken and also imagining things and actions before and after the picture are all invaluable preparations toward reading stories.

Keep in mind one important advantage as you read pictures. The odds favor appropriate responses. You can give proper names to the people and the animals, if you wish, and you can add a great deal of imagination to the minimum of things and actions that you perceive together. Creative responses come much more easily as you and the child discover that you can have your story just about any way you want it.

Still life and scenic views without actions are fine pictures to talk about as the child learns to name and compare perceivable qualities of size, shape, and color. Feel free to rub qualities together when the picture presents a good opportunity and when you think the child can respond. For example, "You said the trees are yellow, and you said the flowers are yellow. Are they the same yellow? How are they different?" It's less important, by the way, to speak of still life and scenic views in the past, since it is conceivable that the scene may now be there as it was then pictured. Of course, you can create story sentences of what happened there a few moments before or later.

When you think the child is old enough and can handle it, cut out pairs of pictures or comic strips. Ask the child to arrange them in a sequence and tell a story based on the pictures. Then, as a variation on the basic theme, you and the child may wish to rearrange the panels and retell the story in a different sequence.

Try this sometime. My nephews, Mark and Matthew, and I were watching television one time when the sound went off, leaving us with only the picture. For reasons that none of us could explain, instead of tinkering with the sound, Mark and Matthew took the parts of the "silent" cowboys in the western film. They created dialogue when the cowboys spoke and even provided some of the sound effects, the best being the gassy indigestion suffered by the horses. Our sides ached from our laughing at their nonsense. Sensational!

Making and Captioning Pictures

The child's earliest efforts at scribbling involve the actions of the arm and the process of mark-making rather than the anticipation of a finished product, the picture. For some time, the child does not seem to associate the body movements, the pencil, the paper, and the marks with a finished drawing. The marks don't even need to be on paper, and they don't have to be made with pencils, either, which you probably have discovered as you scrubbed eye liner off the wall and magic marker off the linoleum. Of course, you'll get firm with your bossy don'ts about marking on the floors, walls, windows, and doors. At the same time, you'll want to provide materials, a comfortable place, and some friendly encouragement for scribbling on L-A-R-G-E pieces of paper with blunt pencils or crayons.

The scribbles themselves don't give you much to talk about in terms of pictures, and they don't need to. As long as the child remains interested in the movements that produce marks, take your cue from the child's interest and talk about how the child went "back and forth" and "round and round" instead of asking, "What is it?"

Let's hope that you're out of the child's scene but watching sometime as the child one day goes "clang," discovering that the movements and the marks become related. The child realizes, sometimes in awe, that he can control the scribbling to some extent, and the product which visualizes before him becomes the part to watch. He doesn't do this kind of scribbling with the half-hearted attention that we offer our doodlings while we talk on the telephone. It is for the child a source of intense effort and interest which approaches fascination. The effect may be almost hypnotic as the child discovers a product in the making on the paper. It's probably not a time for togethering during the scribbling, but it's a time for you to watch from beyond the child's private scene. Of course, as you may know, the child now becomes quite enthusiastic about sharing the product rather than the process.

The picture may become the topic of the conversation, although the child may not be able to name what's drawn.

Christine, about three years old, finished one of her controlled scribbles and marched off with the flush of accomplishment to share it with Clare, her mother. Clare had already seen enough scribbles recently to fill a gallery, but she treated each as a new, fresh work of art. But she knew not to ask, "What is it?" because she'd learned that Christine was unable to answer.

"I see grass," Clare said, "tall, t-a-l-l grass." Giggles from Christine.

"And I see something in the grass," Clare added mysteriously. Christine's giggles turned to puzzlement. She looked, then replied, "No."

"Oh yes, I see something in the grass." Clare insisted. "Here it comes, and it's . . . a worm!" And she took a pencil and quickly sketched a small, wiggly worm in one corner of the t-a-l-l grass.

After some more carryings on, the drawing joined a growing pile of tall-grass art.

Your conversations about the child's art will center around what you see and, perhaps, what happened in the picture if it depicts any actions. Words labeling things in the picture are not needed yet; talk is enough for now.

The time is ripe now for experimentation with different kinds and colors of paper, and different kinds of mark makers (dry pencils and crayons are better now than wet-ink markers). Cut up large brown paper bags; save large colored junk-mail envelopes. All of this drawing and color business becomes very serious to the child, and perceptions of line, space, and color are coming a dozen a minute. It's a good time for you to watch the child's efforts from outside the scene of her concentration. You'll be tempted to draw something for her to copy or to suggest something for her to draw. Don't be surprised or miffed, however, if your suggestion and your artwork models are ignored.

The picture will be shown with great enthusiasm and, probably, with an immediate eagerness which will not wait for a minute. So *talk,* even if briefly. The child may not yet be able to offer names or captions for the drawing. Restrain yourself from asking, "What is it?" This question presses the child to prove the validity of his intentions and, as a result, leaves his talent vulnerable to your judgments. Instead, rely on the questions that invite perception: "What do you see? What else? What did it do?" You can also offer without judgment responses to your own perceptions, for example, "I see a big, big rock near some tall bushes. I see a turkey peeking out from behind the rock." Draw a quick suggestion of a frightened turkey, if you wish. "The turkey thought that you wanted him for your Thanksgiving dinner, and he ran to hide behind the rock." All of this is offered in lighthearted narration and conversation. Never a need to get heavy about children's drawings.

There's also no real need to label or caption the child's drawings just yet. The oral language experience which the picture offers to you and the child is the big thing now. You won't injure the child's feelings or thwart her talents when you use a lot

167

of maybes and perhapes, and stick to what you see instead of what it is or what it's supposed to be. Take your cue in conversation from the child, if any description or identification is offered by the young artist. Now is a fine time to begin naming the basic colors and helping the child to remember them.

After a time, a new combination of perceptions and reactions goes "clang" in the child's mind. The child discovers that she can represent on paper the things that she sees—Mother, the dog, the car, the house. When these new types of pictures are delivered to you, the child may now volunteer a name, a label, a sentence, or maybe a whole story about something which you find absolutely unrecognizable.

Now is the time for titles, labels, and captions based on the child's language and your conversations together. Use your five W's to help the child name perceptions. For example, Clyde may say, "I am running," making it very easy for you to ask, "Where do you run?" Clyde may offer, "To the back door." You can print the caption on the drawing using actions in the past, such as, "Clyde ran to the back door." Feel free to print labels near anything the child named in the picture.

With language experiences like these, children realize that their actions may be recorded with a drawing and that perceived things may be pictured. You're using those drawings to help the child learn that perceptions may also be named and that actions may be recorded with words as well as pictures.

I was told the story about seven-year-old Henry, who sat at his desk using paint to create a very simple picture. First, he painted an orange sun in the upper righthand quarter of the sheet. Then he brushed on large blue capital C's across the top of the sheet one way and reversed them for a second row across the page. He made large, bold strokes like capital H's across the middle of the page with thick brown paint in order to create a fence. Long stringy blades of green grass. He was thoroughly consumed in his work.

His father entered Henry's scene with grave doubts about his work. "What in heaven's name is that?" asked Dad gruffly.

"It's a landscape," Henry replied, his manner calm and cool.

Father wasn't convinced. "It doesn't look like a landscape to me."

"But it's after the manner of Van Gogh," Henry said, a keen perception for a seven-year-old.

"I don't give a damn about your friend," his father said. "Paint it right!"

When the child is old enough to copy letters, write words which he can copy as models if he requests your assistance. You can write the needed words on scrap paper and suggest that the child then copy the captions onto his picture. When an older child can write some but not all of the words needed to make a story sentence about the picture, give him the needed words on scratch paper which the child can then include in the caption.

The next developmental step may be to write the story which accompanies the picture. At some time after that, the next step may be to compose the story first, then to illustrate it. Instead of the story supporting the picture, in this last step the picture supports the story.

Stepping into Pictures

Peter Pan and Wendy flew out the window to Never-Never Land. Alice fell into a rabbit hole and found herself in Wonderland. Dorothy stepped out the door of her house into Oz. Gulliver sailed into Lilliput. If they can do it, you and the child can do it. You can fly, fall, step, or sail into any picture that strikes your fancy.

You can step into a picture vocally. You and the child can create the words and the vocal manner of any two things you perceive in pictures—people, animals in a barnyard, fish in a bowl or stream, two mountains (!), the two vultures flying over a carcass . . . anything. Suppose you turn to a colorful picture in an advertisement for an airline; there are two people, a passenger with baggage and an airline employee at the check-in counter. Or you find a cat-food ad in which a cat and a child are sitting before various cans as the cat is trying to decide which mixture she wants to eat. Each of these situations and many others invite conversation. Be satisfied at first with just a line or two before the child melts out of the language exchange and seems unable to continue the vocal charade. The picture has served its language use.

Remember that nonhuman things can borrow human voices simply with a click of the child's imagination. Together, you may sustain only two or three exchanges of dialogue, but you can take the leadership at first and let your young pretender be a vulture who likes to listen more than talk. Rely on your five W's for encouraging the child to perceive in the vocal manner and from the viewpoint of the thing he's chosen to be in the picture. With time, your language experiences will lengthen and fill with detail. Silly? No. Don't knock it till you've tried it a couple dozen times with the child.

Stepping physically into a picture involves a slightly more sophisticated form of *spozing* or *placking,* which we mentioned a few pages ago. When you and the child step into a picture, the past once more becomes the present. The people and the objects in the picture move again; there are sounds and smells around you. Things take on a third dimension. Pictured cakes may then be cut, rabbits may be held in the hand, and snakes may be caught and tamed (!). You may pantomime a scene for a moment, if you wish, but it seems more natural to allow the freedom of words. Again, take some leadership for creating both the roles by talking the child through a characterization and asking her to perceive the sights, sounds, smells, and tastes of pictured things. Take your cue from the child; when the child begins to fade and retire from the experience, end it.

Some children may wish for these scenes to become a bit more formal. If you want to plan a short play, put two straight chairs back to back, six or eight feet apart in the middle of the room, to form the side frames of any selected action picture. You and the child can actually step through the opening between the chairs to enter the live action of the picture. One or two children may choose to wander alone into the picture, or you and a child may plan a short scene together that might be taking place in any part of the picture. Perhaps you'll choose to depict something that happened just before or just after the action that you see.

The space between the two chairs provides a kind of escape

valve. Whenever the child no longer feels that he can sustain the imaginative perception, he can simply step back through the opening between the chairs into his own real life. Many children are willing to enter this kind of spozing only if they are assured how and when they can end it.

The idea of a dress-up box is as old as the hills. It may be an oldie, but it's a goodie. When I was about eight or so, I remember spending Saturday afternoons with the Gholson girls and other assorted kids in the neighborhood when we went to see the Flash Gordon serials at the movies. Afterward, we rushed to the Gholsons' back yard to recreate the scene and the exciting action. I preferred to play the part of Emperor Ming, because I felt that the villain had the most fun. The large box of old clothing, sheets, and discarded dish towels on the Gholsons' back porch prepared us for playing the afternoon's installment. Have you ever seen Flash Gordon played in a blue gingham tablecloth?

Reading Stories with Children

Read something aloud with your child every day, every single day. Reading together is a side-by-side, not a face-to-face operation. Sit comfortably together so the child can easily see the words and the pictures on the page as you read. The child can quickly learn to be the page turner.

Reading together leads the adult and the child to think about something beyond themselves. The biggest and perhaps the most unsung advantage of reading aloud together is the sharing of new ideas and attitudes to talk about, especially when you read adventure, nonfiction, nature and ecology, and how-to-do-it materials.

Reading together helps the child to realize that she's not alone with her difficulties. A child's own feelings can be formidable. Reading together and mulling over the problems of others helps the child to realize that her feelings are not stupid, unique, weird, or far out. Minor difficulties can be introduced for discussion by reading together. Suppose, for example, that you must move to another neighborhood or town. There are "moving stories" which will help you to prepare your child for leaving the security of a known neighborhood and for discovering the adventure of a new address.

Suppose, for example, that you are somewhat worried about the child's telling harmless fibs that, in your mind, may turn to something more serious. Instead of making booming, bossy adult noises, you might try reading stories together and discussing the character's problems involved in telling fibs. The librarian can help you to locate appropriate "problem books." Be sure to read the book first to see that the problem and the solution fit the difficulties you want to discuss with the child. Don't get bossy about the child when you are reading the book together. Stick to the story and its problem; discuss the difficulties of the characters.

Reading together can be in stages or depths. First, you can read the kind of stories that put children to sleep or amuse them without much effort at comprehension. Second, you can discuss what happened, the facts so far, answer questions posed in the reading, and respond to the things, actions, and qualities in the illustrations. Third, you can react to the motives, the humor, the points of view, the feelings of the characters in the story. For a moment, you can vocally step into a picture by asking, "How would you feel if . . ." or "What did (the character) say then?" Fourth, you can forecast the coming events, conflicts, or turns in the story and its characters.

The most appropriate place to pause for forecasting is at the bottom of the righthand page just before you turn it to continue the story. For example, you ask for opinions and predictions: "What do you think will happen? What will Ellie do? Where will Ollie go?" Rely on your five W's to ask about the future of the story, then turn the page to find out if the predictions became events. One of these stages is not necessarily more skillful or sophisticated than the other. Different stories lend themselves to different depths of comprehension and reaction.

If you read a character, become the character. If you ever wanted to be a successful thespian in your life, here's your big break! Pull out all of the stops. . . . and emote. Distortion, to a child, is a sure-fire form of humor when you're reading a story.

Watch the words for clues on how to say them, because that's one way a child learns to associate words with their meanings.

"The giant roared, 'Fee Fie Foe Fum!' " Giants roar, so roar. Roared words are not said quickly, so roar slowly.

"The mosquito gasped in a faraway voice, 'The wind is too strong, I'll never make it!' " How would a gasping mosquito sound? There you go! And in a strong wind, too. You may get applause on this one.

Encourage the child to participate with you in reading, but don't become bossy in your efforts. For example, if you're reading a story about a voice and an echo, urge the child to become the echo, then pad the dialogue a bit with some extra hello-hello-hello. Also, discover the knack and the fun of reading in incomplete phrases.

"And the little scrawny billygoat said, —————."

"And the scary, hairy giant said, —————!" Taking your cue, the child will supply the dialogue, and, we hope, in a vocal manner appropriate to the character.

Don't hesitate to repeat a popular story, and don't worry if the child wants it again and again and again. You can always vary the depth of the reading by forecasting one time and reacting to motives at another time. You can always personalize the reading by suggesting to the child, "This time you be the wolf and say what the wolf said." After a reading or two of almost any story, you and the child can alternate in "reading" the part. Supply a bit of dialogue or a hint or two about the story whenever the child seems to falter.

Needless to say, the child can have a small bookcase or shelf in the family book place for his own books, pictures, magazines, and scrapbooks. Put a label on the shelf to indicate the child's ownership of the space and its contents. Of course, respect the child's privacy of his personal book and picture area.

Preschoolers and early readers can enjoy reading the newspaper with you. Skip the gory news, if you wish, and look at the bottom of the column and in the corners of the pages for strange and humorous stories—the kind of little blurbs about a woman who found an ostrich in her back yard and the man who built a house using soda bottles.

Several weeks before starting kindergarten, Karen asked her uncle to show her the letters of her name as they appeared in headlines of the newspaper. This experience with Karen's uncle was a source of unending joy to her and undoubtedly an unending frustration to her uncle, who lived with the family, as he was pressed to look through headlines for K's, A's, and on through Karen's name. With a slight twist one evening, it occurred to Karen to ask her uncle to show her the letters of her name *in order*. Wisely, uncle did not cut the letters out of the paper; instead, he printed them on a sheet of paper, and showed Karen how to copy the letters of her name. An important moment for both of them!

We're discussing primarily, but not exclusively, your reading to a child who cannot yet read by himself. However, don't delude yourself into thinking that a child who has learned to read can then read everything. Even though a child is beginning to read, you can continue to read stories with the child which he cannot read for himself. And reading aloud continues to be a fine experience for togethering through the child's tenth and perhaps even the twelfth birthday. Plan a mixed program of entertainment, true-life documentaries and biographies, and even controversial materials about which you hope the child will develop a reasonable point of view.

What's for Real?

Older children and adults know that the words "Once upon a time" are the four steppingstones into a fairy tale and that fairy tales hardly ever happen. But, as you know, some of the best, bloodiest, goriest violence occurs in some of the most popular fairy tales intended for children. Fair princesses are locked in tower rooms, dragons breathe fire, nightmarish fiends carry children away in the dark, witches bake boys and girls into gingerbread—events like these can, without your knowing it, become a source of private worry and fantasy in young children. Without emasculating stories altogether, you can help children to understand the parts that are unrealistic and possible causes of worry.

When necessary help a child to realize how impossibly some situations are exaggerated. However, you will have to look at some things from the child's point of view. For example, to a three-year-old a beanstalk may indeed look as if it grows into the sky. But how could anything as big and blustery as a giant live on the top of a bean vine? On the other hand, if the child has never seen a beanstalk, you're going to have some difficulty in explaining the exaggeration. Comparing a beanstalk with almost any plant in your house or neighborhood may help. In many fairy tales and other stories for children, animals easily borrow from humans the ability to talk, walk, wear clothing, keep house, and have feelings. One advantage of a trip to a pet store, farm, or zoo—as silly as it may seem—is to help a child to understand that real animals don't talk. If the going gets a little too scary in a fairy tale involving animals, you can always smooth things a bit by asking, "Do animals really talk the way they do in this story?"

In many fine stories for children, the events are highly improbable, even though they may sound quite possible. When the child looks puzzled and seems to try sorting out the real from the unreal, possible but unlikely situations provide fine opportunities for you to discuss the differences between reality and fiction. The events in fiction sound entirely plausible, but "any connection with real people and events is purely coincidental," as the saying goes.

On the other hand, you can discuss biography with the child and prove that the person in a biographical story really lived. You can, when the child insists, show that events in history really occurred. The same is true with stories, documentaries, and articles about geography, ecology, and nature; you can prove that the places are really there. I once worked with a high school student named Ron, who didn't read well but certainly had me buffaloed regarding real and unreal events in a biography. "Isn't a quotation meant to be exactly what a person said?" he asked. Yes. "Isn't a biography supposed to be about a person who really lived?" Yes. "Unless the person made record albums, how is it possible to tell what that person really said?" I'd been trapped; Ron didn't quit. "Then direct quotations which can't be proved are really fictional, and a biography contains a lot of made-up stuff about the person, doesn't it?" Yes. And he had me there.

Generally, though, as children grow in their ability to read and understand stories, we can help them to divide events into several different classes—those which can be proved, those which seem real but can't be proved, those which are clearly impossible. Especially with your help in talking about stories and characters, the child can compare story events against what she knows to be real. Concepts of reality are formed and developed after the child learns which things, actions, and qualities can and cannot be perceived.

How about you—do you think Snoopy really has a pool table and an art gallery in his doghouse?

The "Tool" Words

Have you ever tried to learn another language? I've tried both French and German. Unsuccessfully, although I won't starve in a French or German restaurant. The names of things are OK, until I come to rows and rows of irregular forms. The names of the actions are not so good. I wish I could learn the past forms first, since I seem to need them the most, but learning the past before the present seems to be immoral. My real struggle comes with a whole set of words that don't mean much all by themselves. I flounder and sink with words like *weil, beinah,* and *deshalb.*

The "tool" words are not usually used to name things, actions, or qualities. Children cannot associate them with specific, perceivable meanings. Instead, the tool words nail ideas together, create relationships, and establish sequences. Here are some examples. How you explain them to the child depends upon the way these words are used in your conversation or in the context of the materials you are reading with the child.

And, also are togethering words. For good or bad, things, actions, and qualities may be wrapped and tied together with *and.* Things sandwiched with commas and an *and* mean that you get the whole bunch. *Also* adds an afterthought, also.

Or says it's time for a choice. You get one or the other, you get a choice among several, but you don't get the caboodle. Which may be a good thing if you have to pick among disagreeable choices. Which gives you more for a dollar? Six bananas and six pears? Six bananas or six pears?

But is not to be confused with *butt,* but it often is, particularly in the child's own writing. *But* contrasts and separates. It also gives the benefit of the doubt sometimes, as in "William was hurt when he fell, but he'll be all right." One of the classic puns in childhood is built around *but:* "She's got freckles on her, but she's nice."

Too gives children and their reading teachers fits if it's not sorted out from *to* and *two. Too* can be used like *very;* it can be used like *also, too.* Sam and his sister Lindy stood in front of Nathan's, a famous food institution at Coney Island. Their brief conversation boggled me, but not them.

"I'm having a hot dog and french fries."

"I am, too."

"To what?"

"Two hot dogs."

No, not and *-n't* negate the meaning of the phrase or sentence. It's important that children hear these tools and see them unmistakably in reading, because they turn meanings so radically around. Just one of them makes the great difference. For example: "I have more money," "I have no more money."

Very, almost, nearly, quite, just about, and other words like these may be used to intensify or qualify the meanings of other words. One way to rub these words against their meanings is to say a sentence with the word, then without it. For example, "This bucket was just about full, that bucket was full." Which bucket held more?

An irate pedestrian stomped up to the driver's side of a taxi and yelled through the window at the man behind the wheel, "You almost hit me just now. You could've killed me!"

"In New York, buddy," returned the cabby, "almost don't count!"

If is a kind of wish, a way of *spozing.* It's a way of setting the ground rules for another time, place, or circumstance long enough to observe a consequence which may or may not be introduced by the word *then.* "If wishes were horses, then beggars could ride." You'll find plenty of iffing in poem books for children; try "If All the Seas Were One Sea" as a start.

Could and *would* are used like *can* and *will,* but in the past or as wishes and conditions. They don't name actions by themselves, and they sometimes imply a circumstance other than the real situation. *Could* and *would* are a kind of verbal taffy. I talk around these words in conversations and spozings with a child. Did you ever twaddle around with these words in this piece of doubletalk?

> I would if I could, but I can't;
> I could if I would, but I won't.

Should and *ought* may be better known to children, since these words get pushy in sentences. Children frequently hear these words and, later, sometimes spell them as "shudda" and "otta" or even "auto." Aural perception serves the children well enough, but they otta study their spelling.

Because answers why. What follows *because,* as *cause* in the word denotes, is the reason for the result in the sentence. We talk a lot about cause-result relationships, but we more commonly meet those relationships in language as result-cause. Notice that the result often comes first and is followed by the cause: "The forest fire started because a man dropped his cigarette." Younger children often use *because* as if the word itself were sufficient to answer why: "Why did you pour my perfume down the toilet?" "Oh, because . . ."

During, while, until, after, and *next* help to sequence actions, places, and times. Words like these are crucial to a good story, because they tell time without a clock.

Meanwhile is a special word that helps a storyteller to move the action to another place at the same time. The word can even back up the time a bit so that a storyteller is able to keep more than one scene going simultaneously.

Once upon a time, as we've already learned, names a time without a calendar in a fairy tale.

There are other words that may not appear so frequently, but you'll want to watch for them and help the child to understand their meanings—*maybe, perhaps, probably, undoubtedly, espe-*

cially, instead, however, although, unless, indeed (notice how *yes indeed* is yesser than *yes!*).

Feel free to interpolate phrases, which need to be clarified for children, such as *on the other hand, for example, for instance, without a doubt, needless to say.* When the conversation or the reading offers you the opportunity, help the child to notice that a *not only* needs a *but also, neither* likes *nor,* and *either* likes *or. Off and on* means something more than either *off* or *on, now and then* means more than either *now* or *then.*

The purists at dramatic interpretation blanch at this practice of interpolating a story or play script. Knowing, then, that you risk the curse of the great muse Thalia, insert necessary words and phrases as you read tool words. Help the child to understand the words that carry very little meaning by themselves. You needn't interrupt the vocal manner of your character or stop for a vocabulary sermon. Instead, just offer some associative meaning that will help the child to comprehend unknown words and phrases.

Children are likely to encounter many of these words in their own reading by the time they're about seven or eight, but the words will undoubtedly be found earlier and often when you read stories together. Don't assume that the child knows meanings of these words any more than he knows the meaning of *fire engine, blue,* or *ran.*

Writing for Children

When the time comes that you and the child enjoy naming together the things you see in the child's drawings or in other pictures, feel free at all times to write those names not only so the child can see them but also so that she can watch your hand during the forming of the letters and words. Print captions for drawings. Make labels for things in the child's room or anywhere else in the house. Let the child watch you make a grocery list. The child may even want to add "a word or two" to letters that you write to friends and relatives. A child who is surrounded by words and reading is very likely to learn to read. It's that simple.

There are at least a half-dozen major types or schemes for

handwriting which are taught in classrooms throughout the country. Classroom teachers get very feverish about introducing handwriting to their pupils in order to present the scheme they themselves use. I'll confess that when I was a teacher and supervisor in a school system, I used to recommend that parents keep hands off from teaching children how to write— "You want the children to begin correctly, don't you?" In truth, I was actually defending the handwriting system used in the school and protecting the teachers from children who might enter their classrooms with a different writing style.

Well, I've reformed; I still feel that it's not at all important for you to *teach* children to write, but it is important that the children be surrounded by both oral and written language in the home. If you're going to spend all of this time teaching children to perceive and name things orally, then it's high time that they also saw the names in print, whether they read them or not.

Most every writing scheme is divided into two styles. The first manner of writing is called *manuscript,* if you care, a fancy name for printing. This is the kind of writing you will use with young preschoolers in the home as you make labels and captions. The later kind of writing is called *cursive,* in which the letters are joined together. School children about eight or so are introduced to cursive writing; it need not concern you when you are writing for younger children.

Use manuscript or "printing" for one-word labels to name things. Write the common name for things in small letters. The child's own name and all other proper names begin with capital letters and are then continued with small letters. Capital or block letters are rarely used for the full names of anything, since it's more important, eventually, for the child to recognize and read small letters. Letters that become names, like TV, CBS, and NBC, are written with capital letters; so are the new zip code abbreviations for the states, like NY, CA, IL, and MN. The post office or an almanac can give you the two-letter abbreviation for your state.

Make each letter mark as it comes, generally from left to right and from top to bottom. For example, in printing a *d,* notice that it seems to combine a small *c* and a small *l*—write the circle part, then the straight line. The left part first, then the right part next. Try not to back up. Dot the *i* and cross the *t*. For an *i*, make the line and then the dot; for a *t*, make the line and then cross it. Complete each letter before starting the next letter in a word. Again, don't back up. For *I*, write the up-and-down line, then the top, then the bottom. *M* and *N* are exceptions, because you write both sides and then make the middles. *V* is easy, because you draw the left angle, then the right angle. *W* really should be called *double-v* instead of *double-u*, since it's made like two *V*'s touching each other.

When you finish writing the word or sentence, read it all aloud. Help the child to associate what was said with what you wrote—for example, by saying, "This is what you said, and this is the way it looks." You may or may not, as you wish, say each word in a sentence as it's completed. However, teachers generally prefer that you do not name each letter as you form a word. However you say it and however you write it, be sure to sweep over the finished work or caption with your voice; don't hammer out each word as if it were standing there all by itself. To make writing go "clang" with reading, you will want the child to perceive the thing, name it, watch as you make the strokes to form the letters and the words, and then hear the writing read aloud. All of this may only take a moment, but you and the child should not leave the writing until the words are perceived as language and as the child's "thought written down."

The order in which the letters are said or written is the only difference between the twenty-six different letters of our language and the English alphabet. The alphabet is nothing more than an agreed-upon sequence of the different letters. It is not especially helpful to teach your child to rattle off the alphabet in sequence if he can't recognize and name any of the letters at random. Keep in mind that there is practically no relationship between the order of the letters in the alphabet and the order of those same letters in words. When you're reading together or talking about words, the big language experience lies in associating spoken words and sentences with the written words and sentences. However, when you're playing or talking with the letters themselves, perceiving and naming those letters in their capital and small forms and learning to arrange them in an alphabetical sequence is a game by itself. Talking leads to writing, and writing leads to reading.

Defining Words

In addition to the pronunciation of words, children are likely to seek from you one or two kinds of information about words—definitions and synonyms.

"What does it mean?" A child needs words and phrases that build a kind of ballpark in which the meaning of a word can operate. Some words have a number of meanings, depending upon the context in which they are used. Knowing that context will help you to discuss the meaning with the child. Avoid using the word in its own definition. Stick with four-letter words (all of them clean, if you can!) to define the word.

When I was about nine, I wanted to know the meaning of *rape*. I had looked for *rape* in the dictionary, but those were the days when dictionaries defined it in terms like *carnal knowledge without consent*. Although I could read all of the words, the definition was too obscure to get through to me. I asked Willard, my older brother, to explain *rape* to me. He seemed clearly cornered, but he rose admirably to the task. "Do you know what *screw* means?" he asked gingerly. I said I did, and I thought I did; after all, I was only nine. "Then *rape*," he offered, "is to screw a girl without asking her for a date." The definition may not be accurate by your standards, but it sufficed for a nine-year-old.

"What's another word for . . . ?" The child is asking for you to rub some meanings together. If the time is right, the words can open up quite a language experience for the two of you. For instance, what's another word for *heart*? Could be *courage, center, valentine,* or *organ*. If you hear the word, without seeing it, it may also be a *stag deer* more than five years old (*hart*). Again, you need to know something of the word's use and the intention of the user. Hundreds of jokes and puns rely on words in distorted contexts.

Comparing the meanings of words this way is not unlike comparing the letters and the sounds in the word. However, if the child shows very little interest in the letters and sounds but remains interested in the meaning, fret not. After all, if reading is not going to be meaningful, there's not much point in doing it, is there?

If you're a do-gooder, keep at it. Give books and games with words in them, appropriate to the child's age and interests, for birthdays and holidays. I do yet. My gifts generally get tossed aside in favor of the new gadget, toy, or plastic marvel. But a few weeks later, when children have tired of the toys, the books are discovered. And read. And reread. Feel as you wish about acquiring and keeping books for children. Some combination of owning reading materials, trading them with other children, and borrowing them from the library seems to be the most satisfying arrangement.

About a year or so before kindergarten—earlier if you and the child have a special interest in letters and appropriate word games—the preschooler could own at least one ABC book. I prefer the ones that show the letters in both their capital and smaller forms, and, if possible, the letters should be copyable; that is, the child should be able to use them as models for printing, if he's interested in doing so.

If the child has some concept about alphabetical sequence, you may wish to add a picture dictionary to the book shelf. The most suitable picture dictionary for the young child will picture a thing, label it with its name, and have one or more sentences which contain that name.

When the child is about eight or nine years old you may wish to provide a beginning dictionary—the real article with illustrations, entries, definitions, forms, and part-of-speech labels. During this time, if you have an adult dictionary, be seen using it. When you and the child are talking or reading together, invent an opportunity to consult the dictionary regarding information about a word. If you both have dictionaries, the child will look for the word in one, and you will look in the other.

However, before you and the child become abecedarians (howja like that one?), you may want to spend a little time in the ABC corner of the book store or library. Notice that the alphabet books for children are arranged in different ways. First, you'll probably find the label type in which appears the letter, the label, and an illustration, such as, "A is for apple, B is for boy."

Another type arranges topics alphabetically. You'll probably find an animal ABC, an ABC of things in a city, dolls and clothes, things that grow. Deciding which of these alphabet books to borrow or buy depends upon the interests of your child and, of course, the things you see in the book which you will enjoy talking about with the child.

Still another kind of alphabet book uses poems and stories which are overloaded with the letters of the page on which they appear. Each letter may have its own story or poem together with a number of illustrations. The author of such a book may have continued a running story with the same characters throughout.

Generally speaking, the more to see and talk about on the page, the better I like it. I feel that in order to get your money's worth, plenty of *b*-things should appear on the *b*-page. I'm particularly pleased in poem or story alphabet books when the selected letter appears *within* many words as well as *in front of them.*

You'll enjoy making a homemade ABC book from pictures cut out of magazines and junk mail. With them you can tell a story using the things on each lettered page. To add to the suspense, you can climax your story at the end of one page in incomplete sentences. After turning the page, the child finds a thing on the next page which completes your sentence and continues the story.

Don't Get Pushy About Reading

Don't let a teacher tell you to keep your hands off the child's reading. The first-grade teacher in your neighborhood school may love to cavort through her perennially favorite unit called six weeks of reading readiness. Many, many children need and benefit from those early readiness experiences, especially if they have not grown in a language-conscious family unit. It's absolutely amazing how some children enter school from a home life of virtual silence. On the other hand, nothing crabs the teacher's gig like a child who comes to school already knowing how to read. However, teachers are professionally trained to work with individual children, and they should capitalize on the child's reading ability rather than penalize the child for a talent.

If a child indicates to you an interest in the sounds of the words in the language, the letters that stand for those sounds, and even the spellings of the words, by all means you've been invited to do your own cavorting. If and when the child requests, feel absolutely free to explain how the words are put together with letters and how the letters stand for the sounds of a word. Show a great interest when the child becomes curious about words in themselves. That's real side-by-side reading and you'll both enjoy perceiving and naming the words.

Keep clearly in mind, every time you come close to the reading act, that it's far more important for the child to understand what is being read to him than it is for him to read it. When the sounds make sense, that's called comprehension. One day, the child will show an interest in cutting out "the middle man"—you—in favor of making sense from the letters without you. That's reading!

You needn't feel pressed to rush the child into reading. And when the child has begun to read, you mustn't feel pressed to rush the reading act for speed. Keep in mind that sequence—what happened next, that part we've talked so much about in other sections—is the first casualty of speedy reading. It's a fusty comparison, but a good one, that an instructor wouldn't dream of teaching a person how to drive a car fifty miles an hour without first teaching that person how to drive it safely and securely. For a young child, high-speed reading is just like visiting fourteen European countries on a nine-day tour. Both the reader and the tourists have been over all of it very quickly, but actually saw and understood very little.

Helping the child to make connections between parts of a story and comparisons between different stories—going "clang!" after perceiving and reacting—is your overall goal. Reading has a remarkable way of becoming a snap after a rich oral language background has prepared the child for the reading act.

Handling the language orally and seeing it appear on paper at the end of your pencil has a very positive effect on comprehension in reading. Reading readiness or not, those children who breeze through the early years of reading indicate again and again the results of a full language exchange in the home.

13

Sensing Humor

How often do you share a good head-back, deep-from-the-belly laugh with a child? Many say that laughter is innate for every child, but not every child in the world laughs. Others believe that a child's laughter is induced and rewarded in some cultures but not in others. The number of different things and actions which a child perceives as funny may grow with age, experience, and your help.

A child may perceive things and actions, combine them with memories of past experiences, go "clang!" and laugh—a fast, pleasant way to tell or reassure you that "that's funny!"

The Stuff of Humor

Humor seems to be a social thing. Clowns and stand-up comics are quick to say that they prefer full rooms of people for audiences—a "full house" or "SRO"—and that it's very tough to warm up a group who partly fill the room. After adults have met socially and have exhausted preliminary exchanges, notice how they often resort to jokes and anecdotes to become better acquainted, especially if they don't venture into more personal topics. On the other hand, it can be deadly for some to venture a joke too soon. Perhaps you've heard a wife say, "Oh, he's such a card!" as a half-apology for a man who tells jokes too soon or whose stories have been misunderstood or offensive. In a similar way, children warm up to humor after they feel a friend-ship is secure. More than once I've left a joke hanging on my face in front of a child who didn't seem to know me well enough to appreciate my wit (or half-wit, perhaps!). At any rate, humor doesn't seem to be much of a solitary or silent ac-tivity, nor is it something to be ventured too soon with ac-quaintances.

Humor seems to depend on a child's emotions and physical well-being. Tired or sick children may react less physically to something that would be funnier to them at another time. Per-haps you may also have discovered that outrageously funny stories don't make very good reading at the child's bedtime. They tend to rouse rather than to relax the child.

Humor seems to depend on the age of the child. It may de-velop as the child's experiences with realism develop. A knowl-edge of relative sizes, shapes, colors, and "the way things are" sharpens a child's background for realizing the humor in things and actions. A clown on nine-foot stilts will be funny after the child learns that real people are not nine feet high; after all, to a child three feet high, almost anybody six feet high could look nine feet high.

Humor may be defined as nonsense, not in the context of silly language or annoying behavior, which we might call non-sense as in "Cut out that nonsense!", but in those situations which may be rubbed against sense, as in non*sense*. Nonsense limericks can be a classic source of humorous experiences for you and the child, if the child is old enough to rub the ridicu-lous situations against sense. If you read and enjoy limericks together, don't be surprised if the child understands one but not the next, since the child's background and knowledge of real situations either helps her to find the humor in each limer-ick or keeps her from doing so. Don't lump all limericks as suit-able or unsuitable; instead, when you read one that "ain't funny," simply slide it by and go on to the next one.

You and the child, then, flirt with sense every time you talk of funny things. The realistic sense of things, actions, and qual-ities are put askew as you compare what's real and sensible with what's unreal and, therefore, nonsensible. Humor lies in incon-gruity.

*But I don't want to go to the zoo today! If they want me,
they can just come and get me!*

It's fun to feed nonsense into an otherwise ordinary conversation. With a child it's your way of having a joke together about the situation. We'll create a scene in order to illustrate the point. At a pet store Dad and four children admired a brilliantly colored parrot. Dad injected, "Hasn't it got a long, soft, furry coat?"

Harley missed the point completely. We can call his development of humor a "not-yet."

Dominica understood the incongruity, but she did not laugh.

"Dad, those are feathers," she corrected, making her humor an "almost."

Maureen understood, reacted, and giggled. Her giggle was Dad's "understand marker" as well as his applause for making the joke.

Cyril replied. "Yes, if it had roller skates they could sell it as a trained bear." Cyril's use of Dad's comment as the basis for one of his own is the mark of a more advanced comprehension. It meant that he assimilated the joke and offered an additional, humorous comment.

Dad's simple injection of nonsense into an otherwise sensible conversation, together with Cyril's reply, could have continued in quite a stream of impromptu humor. A language exchange like this may be labeled *camping* in some parts of the United States, or it may be called giving the parrot a *send-up,* a term you might hear frequently in Britain. Basically, it's a kind of harmless, very enjoyable tease.

When you're toying with humor as you talk with a child, you'll always know when you've hit the comic jackpot. If you try to "make a funny," and the child either agrees with your incongruity or misses its point, you have an obvious indication of her inability to match your nonsensible comment with what she knows as sense. Mom parked the tiny car in an area between two unusually large trucks, turned to Bea, and said, "Now, if we hear it barking at those two big trucks, you'll have to come out and feed it." Bea seemed to make no connection whatever between the tiny car and a yippy dog barking at trucks, so Mom knew that her humor was met with a "not-yet." If Bea had been a bit annoyed and disagreed, Mom might have concluded that

Bea simply didn't find the connection funny; perhaps the comparison was too new to Bea to be funny. Or, if Mom had received a humorous response from Bea, she would have known that the comparison between the car and the dog was nicely assimilated and they might have enjoyed a good joke together. Bea may, in time, return a nonsensical comment and enjoy a good send-up about the tiny car.

One evening in the winter Jeri had a fine laugh as Yuki, her mother, checked a fur coat in a Chinese restaurant. The checkroom attendant quipped, "Is this coat housebroken or do I have to take it for a walk?" You can consider this kind of humor, then, as a play on language, depending upon the child's developing knowledge of sense and nonsense.

Repetition

Say *milk* slowly and deliberately ten or twelve times. Concentrate on the sound of the word instead of its meaning. After several repetitions, does it seem increasingly ridiculous that a noise like that—one-third hum, one-third burp, and one-third hiccup—could have been invented by anybody other than a clown?

When you're well out of sight sometime, try to listen and peek as two children mimic your words and ape your manner after you've overanimated some bossy caution like ". . . and don't open that fridge again!" Their repetition turns your great act into a caricature which reduces your warning to almost nothing in their laughter. But don't be angry at the children in spite of their threats to your adult power. They are probably well intentioned, and they're indulging in a popular form of childhood humor. Children can reduce almost anything to laughter through repetition.

We adults teach them how to do it. The next time you play and talk with a baby, try and experiment with a goochy goo or two. Your first goochy goo may not go over too well because the child may not consider you to be very funny. The baby may even seem fearful of you. Haven't you seen pictures from a baby's point of view of big-faced adults leaning ominously over a crib? After the second or third goochy goo, the baby may conclude from perceptions that you're not as big a threat as you look and that you don't mean to harm. Several more of your goochiest goos get a smile, but you rarely get a smile on the first one.

Peekaboo is fun for the very young. Peekaboo is a kind of now-you-see-it-now-you-don't game. When the baby puts her hands over her eyes, you aren't there. But you are there all of the time. You are, and you aren't. After several more peeks and several more boos, the dichotomy is reduced to humor, but the baby must remember both conditions simultaneously in order to enjoy the fun. Haven't you seen the look on babies' faces who don't understand peekaboo, leaving you to wave your hands in the air like an idiot? Repetition of pastimes like peekaboo and goochy goo help a child to develop some sense of the there-it-is-there-it-isn't scheme so that they can respond with a smile.

"Ring Around the Rosie" and other statue, freeze, or fall-down games are clearly not fun for the toddler or clumsy child who freezes or falls at the wrong time. It may take several rounds of the game to help a young child understand that control and timed freezing or falling are parts of the game's fun. If you're teaching a game like this to children, be patient and guard against your own pushy bossings when the children fail to follow the game's few directions. Repetition will provide opportunities for the children to get the hang of it.

When you read stories and fairy tales together, the child seems quick to notice the number of repetitious words and phrases, very popular story parts. Children learn to wait for the appropriate moment to say the "magic" words. And you get assistance when it comes time to say, "Mirror, mirror on the wall," "Somebody's been eating my porridge," or "Wolf! Wolf!"

Stories intended for children are often repetitious and episodic. It seems necessary to have three episodes in order to bring a story to a climax. The first and second events are needed to set the pattern and to create the suspense for the third event, which introduces the surprise, the climax, and the end. Mama Bear and Papa Bear notice the traces of a mysterious stranger twice before Baby Bear finds Goldilocks asleep. The wolf blows down the houses of two pigs before he meets his match at the brick house of the third pig. Two billygoats are allowed to cross the bridge before the troll confronts the third goat. Jack shimmied up the beanstalk three times before he aroused the giant sufficiently for a chase.

Children love for these stories to be repeated. In a manner somewhat like the peekaboo scheme, they know that the surprise is coming in the third event, but they act as if they don't know. Not only do children participate in the repetitious words and phrases of a familiar story, but also they would seem to participate wholeheartedly in the surprise as well.

Very seldom, however, do these tales or jokes go beyond the "third time." You may be interested to note this three-part separation in the stories, jokes, and "party pieces" that you enjoy telling. Humor seems to need repetition in order to set up an incongruity.

Incongruous Situations

Incongruities can be funny. The most obvious, perhaps, are the pictures and stories of things that go topsy-turvy—a horse riding a saddled man, the turkey fattening up a plump child for Thanksgiving dinner, a cartoon of a face showing one expression right side up and a different expression upside down. There doesn't seem to be anything wrong with a boy walking a dog, unless the boy is walking in the gutter and the dog is walking calmly along the edge of the sidewalk. The dog is holding a leash fastened to the boy's neck. Who's walking whom? These topsy-turvies may seem silly to you, but you surely went through this form of humor at some age. Sensing humor in the absurd is possible only when the child develops a concept of the real. Something silly must have something real against which to be measured.

Things and actions which cross category lines can be funny. When we talked earlier of metaphors, we mentioned the child's ability to give something the characteristics and actions borrowed from another class of things. A human face on an animal, an animal face on a human, a human face on anything not human—these incongruities can be funny. Is a pumpkin funny? Probably not. But cut eyes, a nose, and a mouth with a big toothless grin on a pumpkin? Funny! Try sketching a simply drawn truck rolling down the highway on oversized wheels. Draw a hot tired face on one wheel; sketch a dizzy nauseous face on another; and show another one, a flat tire perhaps, looking positively exhausted. Borrow the feathers from a bird, and sketch them quickly onto the wings of a jet plane. Another time, sketch a sun on the top of a large sheet; give it pointed ears, long whiskers, and hungry cat's face. You might label the drawing "The Cat Sun Over Mouse Land." With the child, you might discuss and draw mice showing varied reactions to living under a hungry, shining cat.

Human clothing on nonhumans is funny. Millions of children are acquainted with the Cat in the Hat who also wears a necktie and carries a brolly.

If the child shows interest in the letters of his name, you might take one opportunity to draw cartooned faces of people in or on the letters. You might turn the letters into animals in the woods, flowers in a garden, or clothes drying on a line.

Some very funny things happen when one class borrows the actions of another. Recently, Snoopy won an ice-skating championship. Dancing animals and singing flowers contribute to the perennial charm of Disney films. An airsick angel showing the facial symptoms of extreme nausea guards my working area.

A creative mind both perceives and feeds on incongruous situations. I'm told that Cora and Sadie became extremely bored in the women's wing of the retirement home. One day, Cora hit upon a fascinating proposal for Sadie. "Let's take off our clothes and run naked through the men's wing," Cora suggested.

Sadie was aghast at first, but in time the idea appealed to her, too. Finally, she agreed. Cora and Sadie went hobbling and whooping naked through the men's corridor and assembly rooms.

At the same time, Ben and Ralph observed this spectacle

from their seats in the men's assembly room. "Did you see what I saw?" asked the agitated Ben.

"Yup, sure did."

"What on earth did those women have on?"

"Dunno, but whatever it was, it sure needed pressing!" This story is intended to illustrate the point . . . but for you, not the child.

Sudden Change

Any sudden change in position or equilibrium can be fun for oneself or funny while perceiving the change in others. Thousands of people go to amusement parks and pay to submit themselves to brief, sudden changes on rides. What child doesn't enjoy the circling or the bumping of a ride on a small fire engine or a pony? Watching the riders on a merry-go-round can make us laugh; riding on it can also be called fun, although many adults prefer to call it sickening.

Playing London Bridge, hide and seek, drop the handkerchief, and other similar games with children can be great fun for them because of the surprise and the suddenness of the stopping, the catching, the stalling, and the running. Participating in active fun builds that important background of experience that you hear so much about. Later, the child will react with some sense of humor when you talk about pictures, read aloud, or exchange stories about others who are enjoying the jerking, whirling, and whooshing.

Many popular cartoonists employ the suspense of a possible sudden change in their humorous drawings. Knowing what is about to happen to an unsuspecting character in a cartoon makes the situation funny, provided that the child has had some experience in perceiving and discussing actions before or after the "slice of life" depicted in a picture. Notice how the humor of many cartoons depends upon what is about to happen next to a cartoon character who is unaware of his fate.

When a child misses a chair as she sits down, falls over the dog, or drops her milkshake in her lap, the sudden change may cause disorientation and confusion in her mind. The child is quite likely to look where you are and attempt an instant judgment on how you may react. Will you swoop down on her, making all kinds of protective noises about her possible injuries? Will you start a string of abusive and bossy noises about her being so clumsy and stupid? Or will you remain relatively calm, lighthearted, pleasant, and helpful? Such situations for a child can be funny or frightening, depending upon your own reaction to the sudden change. Pratfalls and custard pies in the face probably seem funny only to those of us who've sensed the ridiculous humor of being in the same situation at some time or another.

Exaggerated Proportions

The humor a child senses in exaggerated proportions depends upon her development of a sense for real proportions—sizes, shapes, colors.

The child may measure a humorous proportion physically by a show of widespread arms and the comment "The cat was *this* big," for example. You and the child may exaggerate by comparing the proportion of two dissimilar things, such as "The cat was as tall as a tree." After the child has learned something about weights and measures, you may both share the humor of exaggeration in measured proportions by telling stories, for example, about a "250-pound canary." By the way, how big do you think a 250-pound canary would be?

This type of humor may not be so funny to a child who is not ready for exaggeration. Exaggerated proportions are humorous when the child is aware of the comparison and can make his own exaggerations deliberately. Gross exaggeration may come first, if the child cannot hold well-fixed comparisons in his mind. As his ability to compare things develops, so does his ability to exaggerate for humor.

Keep in mind the size of the child. Perspectives can be misleading. For example, if you are standing in a certain place between the child and a house, you can appear to be "as big as a house." The child may be attempting to determine real size rather than to offer an exaggeration.

The rhymes of Mother Goose offer hundreds of humorous exaggerations for the child to mull and discuss.

Hey diddle diddle, the cat and the fiddle,
The cow jumped over the moon,
The little dog laughed to see such sport
And the dish ran away with the spoon.

Notice the wonderful overstatements in this rhyme that you can enjoy together. The cow jumped over what, for heaven's sake? What did the dog do? And who ran away? Look at the exaggerations you've got to talk about here!

Exaggerations are funny only if the child's perceptions and background of experience offer her sufficient points for comparison. "The Mets need a shortstop with twelve-foot arms!" This comment may be clever to your baseball buddy, but it may be too complicated to be funny to the child. In order to laugh at exaggeration, the child has to know who the Mets are, what a shortstop is, the length of normal arms, and the advantage of twelve-foot arms. If your clever crack didn't go over with the child, save it for a year or two.

Helen and Jamie, friends and first-grade classmates, were sitting on the front steps of a brownstone apartment house. They were consumed in giggles as they repeated a phrase numerous times to each other, "Patinky in panties, panties in patinky." It was time to embellish the remark. Helen stood up, waddled back and forth in front of Jamie, pretending that she had filled her pants. Then Helen sat on the steps once more, and the girls collapsed in gales of laughter. I was reminded of the famous scene in a Charlie Chaplin silent film where a cream pie went down a lady's dress, and she walked wide-legged out of view. Hilarious!

Back to Helen and Jamie. The patinky comment wore out, but the resulting waddle became funny. Each took turns improving the pantomime. Helen waddled like a fat lady, Jamie waddled as if she carried heavy groceries, then Helen waddled like an enormous elephant. They then sat on the steps for a moment to recover from the waddling and the laughing.

At that moment, sheer providence must have placed a

woman at least eight and three-quarters months pregnant on the sidewalk in front of the young girls. Both stopped and stared at the woman in utter disbelief as she continued down the street. Then, at the same time, both Helen and Jamie were reduced to fits of hysterical laughing.

It was not an occasion for praise or blame. Their exaggeration grew from a comment to an outlandish pantomime. And yet, they both realized that they had been outdone in their humor by the innocent walk of an unknowing passerby.

Puns and Riddles

How did the arrows act when they got excited?
   They were in a quiver.
What's the last thing you take off before going to bed?
   Your feet from the floor.
When is it proper to drink milk from a saucer?
   When you're a cat.

Groan if you wish; a groan is one way to compliment a pun.

The humor of a pun is usually based on a word which has two incongruous meanings. It can also grow from a pair of homonyms, two words which have the same pronunciation but quite different meanings, and, often, different spellings. Although it's quite possible for a child to see the humor in incongruous situations and sudden changes when she's all by herself, it's very difficult for her to enjoy telling herself puns. Puns are social; they generally require a punster and an audience, one or more "punnees." Usually, the punster asks a question which sets a frame of meaning around the pivotal word. The answer, instead of being the expected reply, breaks the frame open by presenting an incongruous image or meaning for the main word.

The man in the shining armor got off his steed and felt hungry enough to eat a red, juicy apple. But he didn't know that there was also a juicy worm in the apple, so he ate the juicy apple, juicy worm, and all.

Then the man lay down in his shining armor to have a nap. But the worm didn't nap; he wanted out. He yelled, "Help! Help!"

Another apple worm heard him and cried, "I'll help you! What do you want?"

The worm in the man answered, "Just help me make it through the knight!"

As you can see, a humorous pun may be told in the form of a question and an answer, or it may come across in a joke. Every pun is, in a way, a test of the child's perception and his background of experience. The child must rub together the different meanings of a word or a pair of homonyms to determine if the result is funny. He may not understand the pun because he lacks experience with the meanings of the pivotal words. A pun involves incongruous meanings, and the child must be able to rub two meanings of a word or homonym together. A laugh may indicate that the child has understood; it also rewards the punster.

Sometimes you or the child may insert more than one pivotal word in order to attempt a multiple pun. Here's a triple-header.

A father and three sons raised superb beef cattle on an enormous Texas ranch. Their champion stock was known for miles and miles around. The sad day came, however, when the father died, leaving the large ranch land to be divided equally among the sons.

They divided the land amiably into three pie-shaped parcels, the center point of each section touching the others at one spot. They also decided to build a town in that point where their lands touched. After a great deal of discussion, they agreed upon the town's name and erected a billboard to announce to travelers: "Welcome to *FOCUS*—where the sons raise meat."

Older children and adults compliment a good pun with a groan, a rather sophisticated and acceptable reaction. Be warned, however, that younger children interpret a groan as an expression of discomfort, pain, and disapproval. When you're exchanging puns with a six- to eight-year-old punster, remember to offer a laugh, not a groan, as your reaction and reward for the child's attempt at humor.

Many puns, especially the question-and-answer kind, masquerade as riddles. The differences are hard to spot. Puns play on words. They are, essentially, a form of humor. Although an audience may try, it is not expected to produce an answer to the pun. A pun depends upon a child's ability to hold two different meanings simultaneously in the mind in order to discover its humor.

A straight riddle poses the problem of naming a thing from perceiving information about its parts, its actions, and its qualities. Exchanging riddles may be fun for the riddlers, although riddles aren't necessarily intended to be forms of humor. Twenty questions, for example, is a kind of riddle game; it is fun to play, but it is not a punny game (sorry about that!).

Reading Cartoons Together

As we've noted earlier, the key to the humor of a cartoon often lies in what happened *before* the situation that was illustrated, or what the readers but not the cartoon characters surmise is about to happen a moment *after* the cartoon situation.

As you read cartoons together, don't expect the child to catch on to the humor in every one. If you and the child have shared a laugh and perhaps a comment or two about a cartoon, go on to the next one. The last thing in the world a child needs is a sermon on the humor of something which he has already determined to be funny.

If the child seems puzzled and lingers with the cartoon a moment, trying perhaps to sort out the two sides of the incongruous situation, you may want to ask a question designed to help the child sense the humor. Keep in mind the questions words (the five W's) and ask the child, "What happened next? Why did the man feel that way? Why didn't he see the mudhole?" Something in your question will invite the child to understand and explain the humor. But the child must see it for himself, if it's to be funny. If you tell it all, you'll never know whether the child understood or not.

If the child doesn't understand the humor, your questions get no reactions, and the child does not seem concerned enough to linger over the cartoon for the point, go on to more pictures, something else. Above all, the child can't be raked over the coals as stupid or humorless, if his age, experience, or emotional set at the moment fails to help him make a connection.

A two-panel cartoon may offer a "laugh sandwich." Let's assume, for example, that the first picture shows two men standing on a platform swinging a large bottle of champagne toward a new ship; it's a launching ceremony. The second picture shows the two men looking down from the platform at a large pile of debris with the bottle of champagne lying whole and intact on top. The humor of this situation lies somewhere in the crack between the two incongruous moments which the pictures record. For the child, an understanding of what happened in the middle holds the key to the laugh.

A sense of humor comes from many exposures to funny situations, not just your favorite "great one" of the week.

Telling Funny Stories

When you're trying to size up the child's "funny bone," don't confuse a no-sense-of-humor with a not-yet-sense-of-humor. Assume that the child's humor is there and that it is a-growing. Many exposures and a lighthearted sense of fun on your part will help the child to find it. Certain reactions to humorous situations have been proved to develop as the child grows older.

Ever tried to be funny with the girl at the checkout counter or the teller at the bank? Probably went flat, didn't you, until your "jokee" decided that you weren't trying to be fresh, threatening, belittling, or downright degrading. You are in a comparable situation with the child each time you try to be funny or clever.

The child may not expect you to be funny at some given moment; she may respond with confusion or fear, until she realizes by the look on your face and by your actions that you're attempting to be funny. A child needs a moment's preparation for a joke; although you need not announce the oncoming funny story, the look on your face and the sparkle in your eye can tell a child that fun is coming.

When you're into your "gig," think of throwing yourself physically as well as vocally into your story. Keep in mind that repetition, incongruity, sudden changes, and exaggeration are four of the ingredients that make stories humorous, and then make the most of them. Act as you go! Make sure you're planting all of the clues the child will need to determine that the story is funny. There's nothing worse than a joker who tells an unfunny story, and then announces sheepishly that he left something out.

Make a big production of your story! Give it the pace and the animation it deserves as you progress toward your punch line. A wow of a wind-up . . .

. . . And you're funny! A sincere smile or a laugh is your listener's reaction and your reward. But don't explain your story, or—worse yet—decide that, if one telling is great, two tellings is greater. You're dead if you do.

. . . Or (sigh!) you're a bust! Perhaps the story wasn't really funny, but your telling was absolutely great. Perhaps you told it wrong, got the important parts mixed up, or you lacked sufficient animation. Maybe your young listener isn't old enough or experienced enough to make the important connection for a laugh. Maybe she's heard your "great one" a number of times before, but we won't dwell on that. Anyway, the story is done, and it doesn't really matter.

Don't stomp your story to pieces by trying to run a seminar on it. Don't slink away glum if you didn't make good during your big moment. You can, however, try another one—it better be a good story and it better have a good telling. Or, you can pass and let the child or another in the group tell the next one. And you'd better laugh. It's a strange thing about jokers, but there's an unwritten contract, "You laugh at mine, I'll laugh at yours." The agreement works with children, too.

You or the child may get a mixed reaction in telling a story to a group which differs in their ages. It's quite possible that the five-year-old won't understand, the seven-year-old will laugh, and the nine-year-old will groan or smirk, which you interpret as a compliment to your story.

When the child attempts to be funny, take your cue from the child's intentions. If the child explains a drawing as humorous or tells a story which you know is meant to be funny, enjoy the child's humor, and really let yourself go to share the child's good time. Remember that humor is essentially social. Although we sometimes look oddly at people who laugh a great deal by themselves, we enjoy sharing those same kinds of laughs with others. Privately, you can ask yourself what kind of humor your child is offering, then respond, and return a story that you feel is the same kind that the child will understand.

Also, take time to create humorous moments during a language experience. For example, draw an oval on a piece of blank paper. You can ask, "This will be a face. What kind of a face?" The child decides that the oval shall have a happy face. You can offer a flood of questions as you talk and sketch: "Shall we turn the mouth up or down? Big laugh or little? Who owns the face? A worm? Why is the worm happy? Just found a hiding place from a bird? Where is the worm? In a tin can? Where's the bird that she can't see the worm? Where shall we draw the bird's face? What kind of a face shall the bird have? Sick and hungry? Mouth up or down? Tongue in or out? Why is the bird sick? She just ate another sour, rotten worm?" A worm goes in the bird's stomach, and your story continues piece by piece. At any good stopping point, you offer the child an invitation. "OK, now tell me the whole funny story."

The Measure of Humor

The test is quite simple. There just isn't a better rating scale for a sense of humor than a smile, a laugh, or a hearty ha-ha, when you intended to be funny.

Reply in kind to the child's humor. No smirks, groans, or on-off sneers. Your response may help to knock a sense of humor right out of a child even as you intend to help the child develop it.

A sense of humor is in many ways like the concept of

thoughtfulness, generosity, good nature, and honesty. Children use you as a gauge to measure the effect of their own efforts.

By the way, speaking of laughs, how many adults are convinced that there's "trouble" when they hear laughing from children? When you hear children laugh, are you sure that they're into trouble, up to no good? Can you observe and assess the children's scene before you enter it? What kind of fun are the children enjoying? And what do you want to do when you enter the scene? Share the fun? Or put a stop to it?

Learning what's funny depends largely on learning what's real. If the unusual is funny, the child must have some concept of the usual. Perceiving and naming things, naming the power of things in categories, making comparisons—all of these help a child to build a backboard against which humorous things and actions are bounced.

Have an open, explanatory approach to your child's development in sensing humor. As the child grows and matures, take an interest in the various ways in which he or she may respond to your humor:

- no indication of understanding;
- a serious attitude toward new knowledge;
- laughing at comic incongruities and harmless teasing;
- responding in a language send-up.

And keep your own sense of humor alive and well fed!

14

Where Are We?

All of the areas mentioned in this chapter compete with the child's spot in front of the TV.

All of these experiences compete with the time which the child may otherwise spend watching TV. And don't kid yourself. These activities with the child will compete with the time you yourself feel is important for doing something else. However, if you're going to compete with the child's tube time, you must be eager and ready to give time of your own.

How successfully the experiences in any of these activity areas provide opportunities for language with a child depends largely on you. The activities here don't begin to cover all of the possibilities for togethering, but you'll have to promote the language exchange.

These activities, and any of the others suggested in this book, are intended to bring the adult and the child together in a noncombative feeling of companionship. Stay side by side with the child, guard carefully your bossy sentences, and bite your tongue when you feel an abusive opinion word aimed at the child forming in your mouth.

The child's language, rather than yours, is the big goal and the reward for all of your time and effort.

At Home

These activities depend somewhat upon the child's age. You can feel fairly sure, but not entirely certain, that a child two years old will probably not be interested in the letters of her first name. We've noticed before that a collection of experiences is helpful to develop an interest in another kind of experience. Growth, development, and experience need time.

Children don't outgrow interests as quickly as you might think. A number of activities are labeled "childish" by adults, not children. Don't press upon a child that he's "too old" for some activities he really seems to enjoy. Of course, we're not talking about sucking thumbs and wetting diapers; we're talking about those experiences which may with your encouragement, or at least without your discouragement, turn into hobbies, sports, and vocations.

Take your cue from the child. Let the child's interests in an experience rather than the child's age guide you. If the child is interested in the letters of a name, then you get interested in those letters as well as others. Think of trying an activity with a child a bit like dipping a calf's nose in milk: if the child likes it, continue it—if not, postpone the activity for a later time. You'll want to read and sort through these suggestions to try those which you may think will interest the child and which may promote a language exchange between you. Think of each of these experiences in terms of a "run," and not just a one-shot pastime.

The shapes and the names of the letters and numerals are not the private property of reading teachers. They're there to be perceived and named just like pictures of snowballs, jet planes, and bananas. If a child can perceive a picture of a clock and say "clock," then he can perceive a picture of an S and say "S." He doesn't need to know immediately its importance in the word *Mississippi* any more than he needs to know *9:21 a.m.* when he sees a picture of a clock. But letters and numerals are there for the perceiving and the naming, so feel free to talk about them without pushing the child into reading, the same way you would talk about a picture of a ring without insisting that the child should get married!

Games with Letters

A number of your good times together can come from some-thing as simple as a package of index cards, probably available at a nearby stationery or dime store, perhaps your local drug-store. I prefer the cards that are lined on only one side, so I can print on the lined side when I wish or turn the card over to draw on it or paste pictures on it.

Paste colorful pictures cut from magazines and junk mail of living people, living plants, living animals, and nonliving ob-jects. Name them, tell about some actions they can do, and sort them with discussion into the four different categories. As a game, each player may pick one card from the face-down pile, name it, create a story sentence that tells what it did (with the actions in the past). The player with two or three pictures of the same category, whichever number you agree upon, may put them down rummy-style. You may score the game, if you wish. The player with the most pairs or triplets of matched cards after the main pile is gone, wins.

Look together for more colorful pictures to paste on another set of index cards. Find two or three things that begin with each letter of the child's name or with each letter of the entire alphabet. Print the initial letter of the name on the back of the card. Each of you can name the picture, identify the initial let-ter, and confirm the answer with the letter on the back. Match pairs or threes that begin with the same letter. The back of the cards will confirm the match. As the child tells the letters in order of his name, he may find a picture named with the same letter. The cards, either the pictures on one side or letters on the other side, may be sorted and arranged in alphabetical order.

With your help, the child prints each small letter of the al-phabet on one index card, mixes the cards, and tries to name each letter. Help the child to print each capital letter on an index card. Mix and then name them. You and the child can match the small letters to their capital letters. Each set of letters may be laid in rows in the order of the alphabet. If you wish, you can work together to print a second set of small letters and capital letters, each on its own card, but in a different color.

You can match these pairs of small letters with the capital letter of the same color, you can match the small letters with the small letters of a different color, or you can pair off the matching capital letters. As a grand finale to the activity, you can sort all letters both capital and small as well as those printed in different colors into piles of four and arrange them in alphabetical order. And, of course, you can use letters from all of the cards to spell any words in which the child seems to be interested.

Work together to identify and cut out letters or words from magazines and large newspaper headlines to make the child's name, address, and telephone number. Create letters and stories by cutting out the needed words and placing them on sheets of scrap paper. This is also a special way to make invitations and greeting cards.

At the Typewriter

If you have a typewriter and are willing to let the child use it, you can share some fine experiences in watching words appear before your eyes. Sometimes you'll find an old typewriter at an auction or rummage sale. Perhaps, because I depend so much upon a typewriter myself, I am enthusiastic about introducing school-age children to this easy alternative way to produce language. At an early age, children become entangled in the wonders of cameras, stereo, and tape recorders—why not typewriters as well? I don't know about you, but typing is my greatest single convenience.

Type a line of five to ten letters at random, leaving three or four spaces between the letters. The child may copy each letter immediately under the one you typed. Peck out the alphabet in order, then ask the child to identify the letter and type it below the letter you wrote.

Type the child's name, address, and telephone number. Teach the child how to copy this vital information, both on the typewriter and by hand.

The child may dictate a sentence caption for a drawing she just made. You can type the caption as a model. Then assist, if you're needed, as the child copies your model on a gummed label (mailing labels are fine) and sticks the caption to her drawing. You needn't fuss about the carriage shift until the child shows an interest in how to create capital letters.

Diagrams and Maps

When a child indicates an interest in the various parts and functions of the body, ask a local storekeeper for enough wrapping paper to match the child's height. Or, better yet, cut open brown grocery bags from the supermarket and tape them together. The area of the paper should be large enough for the child to lie on it. Trace the child's body with a heavy pencil, crayon, or magic marker.

Afterward, the child may add the details of fingers, fingernails, toes, facial features, and hair. Print labels in small letters on index cards—a pair of labels when two are needed—that name *arm, leg, hand, stomach, head, ear,* and other parts that the child seems curious to identify. These labels can be as general or as detailed as the child wishes. Include, if desired, *wrist, knee, elbow, navel,* and other details. Draw and label the *vagina* or the *penis* and *testicles,* if the child's interests awaken. The child can identify various body parts and you can introduce the labels, a few at a time, when the child shows an interest in the word.

Draw a map of any room, the whole house itself, the block you live in, or even the neighborhood. A map is, after all, a kind of picture from the point of view of a fly on the ceiling, an airline passenger, an astronaut, or maybe an angel!

Fold a large piece of paper lengthwise in half. On the top half you and the child may discuss and draw what you see on the opposite side of the street. Then walk across the street, turn the sheet upside down, and proceed to draw the opposite view on the other side of the street.

Calendar Before Clock

It seems easier for a child to grasp the idea that whole days, rather than hours and minutes, can be given "number names."

The idea that time constantly changes on the clock and that each passing hour and minute has its own number name can wait until the child has a firmer grasp of numerals and a concept of *day*.

An old calendar for any month can help you to introduce the numerals to a child. Together, cut the numerals 1 to 10 from an old sheet of a large calendar, and paste them to index cards. Don't be in a hurry to introduce the written words just yet— The numerals and their names will do nicely for now. The child may learn to identify the numerals by their names and also to lay them in a sequence from 1 to 10. Mix them, and show them to the child one at a time, asking the child to name each one. In the same manner, the child may show them one at a time to you for naming, except that the child must watch to see if and when you offer the wrong name for a numeral. Try it every third time or so.

Cut and paste numerals 1 to 10 from another month so that the child may match and identify the numerals in pairs. When the numerals through 10 seem secure in the child's mind, continue these same steps of naming, sequencing, and matching with the numerals 1 through 30. Add the numeral 31 a time or two to act as a kind of "joker" in the deck.

Along the way, as the child grows in familiarity with the numerals, you both may use them to make and answer problems in adding and subtracting. You have also paved the way to introduce time concepts.

Use a calendar with extra-large squares for each day in order to draw some indication of the weather—suns, clouds, raindrops, snowflakes—which you both observe each day at a given time. The child identifies today's date, and either draws the weather symbol or sketches a tiny picture of an appropriate action for today's weather. When you both desire a break in the weather forecasting, you may use the space to mark birthdays, special events, and countdowns for approaching holidays. If you prefer, you and an older child may use the calendar diary-style by writing a story sentence of a memorable happening for each day.

The day will come when you feel that the child is ready to

learn about time on the clock. An approaching birthday or holiday may provide you with an opportunity to give the child a clock as a gift for her room. Whether it ticks, flashes, or hums, be sure that the child's first clock contains all of the numerals for all of the hours. At first, a sweep second hand is unnecessary and may be even confusing to the young child inexperienced in telling the time.

On a large piece of wrapping paper or opened-up grocery bag, trace a large circle, leaving room both inside and outside for numerals. Using a real clock as a model, ask the child where each numeral should go, and place them inside the clock as accurately as you can. Fasten two movable hands—the big hand obviously longer and thicker than the little hand so that the difference is unmistakably apparent to the child. Outside the circle over the twelve write *o'clock;* below six write *thirty* and *half-past.* Write outside one, *five after;* outside two, *ten after,* outside three, *fifteen after* and *quarter after;* outside four, *twenty after;* outside five, *twenty-five after.* Similarly, outside seven, write *twenty-five till;* outside eight, *twenty till;* outside nine, *fifteen till* and *quarter till;* outside ten, *ten till;* outside eleven, *five till.* At any chosen time, look at the real clock, help the child to place the hands of the paper clock in the same positions, then read the time. When you play with the clock together, practice the hours first, then the half-hours, and then the sides of the clock. Naming the time formally—such as *nine twenty-two* or *four thirty-seven*—may come later, although the recently developed digital watches and clocks make this kind of time quite easy to read. At any rate, give the child the advantage of age and experience in learning to tell time precisely. Don't push.

o and O

Your child's teachers will undoubtedly appreciate your calling o "zero" when you talk about numerals and calling O "oh" when you talk about letters. Using the terms "zero" and "oh" helps the child to realize that it's not the same symbol all of the time. Learning to dial the telephone depends on the child's perception of the difference between O in MNO and o after 9.

When you talk with the child about dialing numbers on the telephone, be sure to teach the child how to dial the two or three essential emergency numbers. Post them in big, easily readable numerals by the phone, discuss them, explain how important it is for the child to be able to dial them. And yet, caution them against dialing playfully.

Manipulating Groups of Things

You can play and talk in three ways about clothespins, hair rollers, buttons, large pieces of pasta, stones, and other objects commonly found in or near your home. These different ways won't matter much to the child, but you may be interested in the range and the growth with which the child may use objects in groups.

First, these things may be used as unnamed objects. They may be counted, combined, grouped, divided, measured. The identity of the objects is not essential in these activities, since these are operations which the child will eventually learn as she groups almost any kind of objects.

Second, the objects are named as a group and their specialized functions are identified. The utility of the object and the function for which it is designed become important in this kind of activity. Clothespins may be somewhat similar to paper clips, although their clipping functions differ. Pennies may be used in some ways like buttons, but each group of objects may be used in quite different ways.

Third, things within a group may function beyond their normal utility, according to a child's creativity and imagination. Paper clips may become wire fences on the child's model farm. Clothespins may be painted and dressed to become toy people. Pennies may become stepping stones or a terrace for a miniature house. Buttons may become stars when pasted to a painted night scene. Hairpins and facial tissues may be turned into butterflies to decorate a coffee table. In each of these examples, the thing performs in a creative function beyond its normal use.

In the Kitchen

Plant a white potato in a leftover jar and half a sweet potato in another. Day by day, watch and measure their growth. Compare the differences in the two kinds of potato plants.

Plant the fruit or vegetable seeds that come from any fresh food. Fill an empty clean jar full of paper towels and shove the seeds down between the towels and the inside of the jar where they are in full view. Keep wet. Planting lima beans or other hard but uncooked seeds will surely reward you with something to watch daily. How about planting an onion which may already have a sprout?

Use the brown shopping bags from the grocery store to make costumes, maps, and murals. Cut the two side panels from any brown bag, fold them together, and tie or staple the folded sides. Presto! You have a four-page book for pasting pictures, coloring, collecting autographs, or keeping a diary. The more shopping bags you staple, the bigger the brown book.

Whether the child can read or not, follow a recipe together to make almost anything. Help the child to notice that recipes generally contain three different kinds of language—names of utensils, names of ingredients, and directions (bossy sentences in a row, remember?). When you have an opportunity, point out to the child how an ingredient becomes a mixture, a mixture becomes a dish, a dish contributes to dinner, dinner becomes leftovers, leftovers become garbage and garbage becomes pollution. Another example of how a thing can have many different names. If the child is interested, compare things to note the differences in their form and their ingredients; for example, waffle-pancake, biscuit-muffin-cupcake, broil-bake. Read recipes aloud as you prepare the dishes. If the child is able, request his help with measuring ingredients. Make a little extra dough, batter, meatloaf, or other gooey mixture, and let the child get the feeling of his own artful cookery. The child will eat what the child makes (but that's no guarantee!).

The child may even take an interest in turning one of your brown bags into a recipe book.

Play store with empty containers. You can even save the

prices by opening the other ends of containers. Suppose that you can't decide which of two competing foods to purchase. Ask the child to give you a "commercial" on which food is better and why.

"Fixing" Things

Come out of the kitchen and into the fix-it shop. Children seem to enter an age when old clocks, bathroom scales, radios, TV sets, motors, appliances, and almost anything else which is mechanical become the "stuff" for the repair shop. After you've removed the electric cord and plug from any old appliance, let the child take it apart to see what's inside and how it works. The child may wish to save, sort, count, and name the various parts. You might work together to build collages using mechanical parts and wiring. Then sketch in details and outlines. Some parts may also be used to create actual working models of gears and other thingamajigs. You might have a good time and outrageous fun creating a Rube Goldberg machine.

Work Times, Play Times

We haven't said too much here about a child's family jobs, which consume some of the child's time and compete with the spot in front of the telly. Your discussion and sharing of household duties is a part of the child's contribution to the family unit. Children can learn that living as a family involves a blend of work times and play times, both of which may be made to be pleasant—at least, they don't have to be unpleasant. It's not the mere exchange or reward for work that counts; it is, rather, the mixture of activities which may offer the child the security of a routine.

Jeudi Hunter tells of her relationship with her son at home: "I have found it most important with Alistair to tell him what is happening." For example, one morning Jeudi told Alistair that they would work in the kitchen, and then they would play a game. By sticking to routines as promised, Jeudi and Alistair established a strong bond of trust. Alistair was satisfied each day to wait for Jeudi's attention and to help her when he could, because he was sure that she would keep her promise and not let him down. Knowing that Jeudi was there and could be depended upon to keep her promises, Alistair also seemed quite willing to meet unexpected circumstances and to venture toward new experiences, with her when they were together but without her when he was alone.

Sentences about the future, like the forecasts about tomorrow's weather, are opinions about what is to come. To children, these sentences may also constitute promises. Daily, dependable routines—both household duties and game times—are comfortable when the child can rely upon the promises of the adult who predicts them.

On an Outing

You may decide on a short "go" of an hour or so for just the two of you. Perhaps you've planned a half-day pleasure jaunt with your child and a young friend or two. Maybe your outing has turned into a full day's excursion for the whole family of adults and children together. But however your time and destination vary, certain ground rules for the outing remain the same.

Most outings cost money. Before you leave home, discuss how much money may be spent by each child in addition to the regular cost of carfare, any admissions, and meals. You can guess a reasonable amount. If the child is old enough to count money, remind her after each expenditure during the day of the remaining available funds. When the child wants to make another expenditure, mention briefly how much money will be left after the cost of the current whim. Older children may wish and be able to manage their own special allowances.

There are people at parks, zoos, beaches, and amusement areas whose livings depend upon their aggressive ability to persuade children to spend money. Managing and discussing the day's expenses and learning how to make choices that involve money may provide for both of you opportunities to exchange language or to argue, and you can easily have it either way. Briefly planning a budget and keeping the child aware of costs are intended to cut the child's pleading when the money runs out. Planning also minimizes the child's attempt, often very successful, at bargaining or downright extortion. I don't think that children on a day's outing really expect overindulgence because they probably don't know where it starts, but they will surely attempt to find the limit of your generosity. Plan ahead in your own mind where the good time of seeing and doing things together stops, and the nonrewarding acts of pleading and overindulging begin.

"Air and water" everybody—that means you and everybody—the very last thing before you walk out the door. On any bright pleasant day, I see hundreds of children swigging down large cans of soda in parks and other public places, the middle of nowhere, you might say. When your child guzzles twelve ounces of bubbly, you *know* that you'll be confronted with a trip to the restroom very soon. Mrs. Leppert carries collapsible plastic cups when she and the children go somewhere together. They all share one soda—less for each to drink, fewer trips to the toilet, and a very companionable thing to do.

Wherever you are, keep a quiet, private eye open for signs indicating which way to the restrooms. One of the best ways to promote a pleasant day anywhere is to cut down on the odds of an unpleasant situation when you hear the words, "I have to go!" And when one goes, everybody goes.

If four or more children are going along with you, you might try the buddy system. Pair them, making each responsible for knowing always where the other buddy is and what he's doing. Having the children in pairs may save you from making a lot of adult noises and bossy sentences at the children one at a time.

Beforehand, talk a bit about where you intend to go and what the child may expect to see and do, especially if it's a new experience. If your city has public transportation, get on a bus some morning and ride it to the last stop. It may not sound like much to you, but the child will probably love it. A bus map may show you some of the more interesting routes and indicate places where you may want to get off and visit. If you big-city people are accustomed to underground transportation, try rid-

'N ya wanna hear what my dad yelled to another driver
who cut in front of us?

ing the surface bus for a change. The ride may take a little longer. But what do you care? There's more for you and the child to see, and you may discover some things that you didn't know you'd missed on all of those subway rides.

Even though you've lived in a city for years, visit, telephone, or write to the tourist office or convention bureau to find out what the city offers as sights to its out-of-town visitors, especially to children. Look in your local telephone book to see what you'll find listed under "Tourist." Ask at local hotels and motels for the recommendations they give their guests who wish to take children sightseeing. Or write to the mayor of your city and sign your child's name. The mayor will surely find somebody to reply to the child's letter. All in all, you may be quite surprised to find out "what's here" that you didn't know about. Travel folders and the local newspapers also give you news on what to point out to the child and to discuss during your visit.

If your destination is too far for a half-day's trip, then plan ahead in your own mind how you'll vary the pace of your time together. As you move along, look for a place to sit and rest awhile every now and then, when you can talk quietly about what you see, what you've seen and done earlier, and look over together any folders or brochures that you've collected along the way—or just sit silently together for a while. If the child is accustomed to a rest after lunch, provide a rest in a car, on a bench, on the grass, or in some quiet spot. Whenever you feel the heat going up the back of your own neck, grab control of yourself and simply say to the child that you need a rest and that you want the child's company. And sit down!

When you visit museums together, don't expect to see everything within the walls at one time. Pace your strolling and viewing. Don't stay too long; perhaps you can ask to go outside awhile and then reenter the building. Children generally aren't nearly so interested in two-dimensional paintings, charts, and posters as they are in the three-dimensional stuff—dinosaur's skeletons, carcasses of historic airplanes and boats, mummies, armor, models of pyramids and Indian villages, things they can look into and walk around.

Concepts of history won't mean as much to a youngster as the size, shape, and color of things, what they did, what a strange object was used for, and some comparisons with the child's here and now. Almost any child I know will go ape at old trains, cars, and science-action exhibits. And surprise actions, too! Just find the lightning machine in almost any science museum and watch the children of all ages from infancy to senility gape and jump at the event.

When the children can explain and describe things for you, by all means let them do it. You don't have to be the perpetual expert; on the other hand, welcome the child's interest in showing you what things are for and how they work. I eavesdropped on an overeager grandmother and her grandson as they observed the actions of a complicated toy on the second floor of New York's great mecca for toy freaks. Grandmother began the dialogue.

"You wind it up and it runs."

"No."

"Then it runs on a battery."

"No, it doesn't."

"Let's get a clerk over here to show us how it works."

"No."

"Don't you want to know how it works?"

"I already *know* how it works."

The deflated grandmother, without additional questions or comments, walked away from the toy and the grandson.

Who wanted to know how the toy worked? Count the words as a simple measure of who got the most from the language experience, and yet the experience broke the pair apart instead of bringing them together. What simple question could Grandmother have asked in the first place?

In these days of ice-cream wagons, hotdog carts, soft-drink machines, and an unbelievable assortment of quick-food counters, fewer and fewer children have ever been inside a genuine restaurant. Children may not even believe that some restaurants don't sell hamburgers.

Your child may become restless when the food doesn't arrive at the table in thirty-two seconds flat. She may squirm, ask to leave the table, or want to go to the restroom, just for something to do while the adults eat leisurely and dawdle over their coffees. More than one food handler has fallen over children darting through the main service aisles of restaurants. I was once a food handler, and I can tell you this for sure.

Try to strike a happy medium at the restaurant table—the child remains patient a bit longer, and you dawdle over coffee a bit less. Include the children in your adult conversations; they're there, and they want the time to go as pleasantly as you do. Play "I-see-something" riddles in which you give a word clue about a thing's size, shape, color, one at a time; after each clue, the child attempts a guess at the thing you have in mind. Try "hot-warm-cold": you keep a thing and its place in mind, and as the child names things, you say *hot, warm,* or *cold,* according to its proximity to the goal, the thing you've chosen. Also, you can discuss outrageous hiding places—for example, by asking, "If I were a plate (napkin, coffee cup, stove, a glass of milk without the glass), where would I hide?"

If you wish, bring along a book, paper and pencil, or something diverting for the child to read, sketch, or color while you eat. After all, you deserve a rest if you've given the past several hours to the child.

Ask the manager or cashier for a menu to take home. Not only can it go in the child's brown-bag scrapbook, but also you can use it to play restaurant at home, providing a good follow-up as well as a preparation for the next visit to a restaurant.

Wherever you are and whatever you do, watch your threats. "If you do, we'll . . ." or "If you don't, we'll . . ." becomes a very foolish game during which children undoubtedly feel forced to comply, challenge, or cry.

Timing and pacing are important. Plan enough time for a good, relaxed outing, and don't strain the child's endurance— or yours. Unkind words, confrontations, and tears of fatigue can replace togethering when you're away from home too long. Take a lesson from the best entertainers in the business, who leave the stage while the audience still wants a little bit more. Go home before it's too late!

In the Car

Before you leave on a longer trip, write to the State Tourists Office, State Capitol Building, the capital city and ZIP code (available in an almanac or at the post office) of the state where you expect to spend some time. In the letter tell where you plan to go, and ask for information on sights and events of that area. Mention specifically that you are interested in places and events for children. You'll receive a reply from somebody. Use the child's name for the return, if you wish, but you may want to add a note indicating that your request is valid. After the child opens the replies, sort through the pictures and brochures for the places that you may be able to include in your travel.

Along with your other paraphernalia, pack a shirt box or shoe box with paper, crayons, pencils, paste or transparent tape, blunt scissors, and perhaps a supply of those grocery-bag scrapbooks which we mentioned earlier. The child may also be old enough to enjoy an inexpensive aim-and-click camera and some film, a great way for the child to record memorable perceptions.

When you're the driver, your prime concern is the car and the road. Insist upon cooperation from the children (and the adults, too) so that you aren't distracted as you maneuver the car through difficult traffic and unfamiliar roads.

The child hears and notes the language you use at the other drivers in your way, at the police officer, and at teenagers on their bikes zigzagging through traffic. Why do children seem so quick to pick up all of your profanities and abusive words? When you blow out those half-dozen vocal blasts on the road, you may be repaid in kind by the child with the same language. Later, a stressing situation for the child may evoke the same language that you yourself used when you were frustrated. Adults are the prime sources of all kinds of language for children. Children perceive the situation and your vocal reaction; it's quite natural for them to react with the same language in similar situations that upset them.

On the highway, if there are two adults on the trip, you can agree that one will be the pilot and the other will be the program director. If you're the passenger, steer the conversations, as much as you can, to what you perceive as you travel; after all, that's one of the reasons for the trip.

Play "I Spy." Each passenger in turn determines something that everyone is to look for—a woman wearing white shoes, a hitchhiker, a spotted horse, a sign advertising milk, for starters. The first finder says, "I Spy!" You may with experience wish to compound the list to two or three items before the game's winner is decided.

Or try "One-Something, Two-Something." First, look for a single thing, such as one white horse. Then, two red barns; three chimneys on a house. Continue your "somethings" until you perceive a group of ten. No winners this time; it's a group effort.

As you travel down the highway, one player may say, "I see something red." The others have an opportunity to ask about the perceivable size, shape, or actions of the thing; but one guess only, and if you're wrong, you're out. A variation of this game is called "I see something *k*." The players must look for something in the immediate scene whose name begins with *k*. Another variation is "I see something that begins like *c*at," or, "I see something that rhymes with *mouse*."

Play "Zoo" with the pictures of animals you see on the advertising signs along the road. During a given time or a number of miles, perceive, name, and record all of the animals in the signs that would start a good zoo.

You can help older children to develop a sense of distance when you ask, "What's the distance to that farmhouse on the hill straight ahead?" The driver can give you a speedometer reading at the starting point and again at the farmhouse. You can then compute the distance and determine the best guess.

Learn together to identify the international traffic and recreation signs. One well-known publisher displays these signs inside the front cover of road atlases with an explanation for what each one means. The child may even check off each sign as it's seen along your route.

Play letter, word, and number games with the license plates

you see on the cars ahead of you. Help younger children to read the numerals and the letters in the order they appear on plates. If you're driving through a state where many letters are included on the plates, look for an *a,* then *b,* then *c,* on your way through the alphabet. As a child gains some experience with letters, ask him to read and alphabetize the letters in any one license. Also, perhaps you can take turns to name a word that begins with the first letter, reading from left to right of each license.

As an older child, I learned a license-plate game which I still enjoy playing. I try to make a sentence of words, each word beginning with the license's letters in order. For example, assuming that the license is *QED 589,* my sentence might be *Q*ueens *E*at *D*ogfood; 457 ILS, *I L*ove *S*aturday! Allow *ex-* for X. Get the idea?

In a similar way, you and the child can play with the numerals on licenses. Look for one, then two, then three, and so on to ten. Name all of the numerals in a license, and then rearrange them in their numerical order. You can take turns and add the numerals on a license plate, keeping score to decide who may win after five or so rounds.

Older children may enjoy playing "Lucky Seven." Together or in turns, you can see how many different ways you can add the numbers to seven. For example, if the plate reads *AT 34316,* notice that there are four different ways you can select these numerals to add to seven. You can play this with "Lucky Ten" or you can prepare a child to play cribbage by using the plates to add combinations to fifteen.

Nothing can make many adults feel more lost and desolate than not knowing where they are during the course of a trip. The same is undoubtedly even truer for children. How many times during your travels do you hear children ask, "How long will it be till we get there? Where are we now? What time will we get there?" Let the child watch as you mark the map, even if the child can't read it. Explain what a map is, why it's needed, the route you'll take, how far you're going, and how you'll know when you're getting close to your destination. Look for and read the mileage signs that indicate when you're getting

223

closer to a checkpoint. Explain to the child where you expect to turn, when you may see a lake, your next rest stop, where you intend to stop for lunch, how much longer before you cross a bridge, or when and where you expect to cross a state line. Try along the way to give the child something to look forward to. Anticipation can shorten a long trip and motivate perceptions.

Utilize the scenery for language as much as you can, but sometimes it runs out. Then, you can rely on the good ol' standbys—word games, hide-and-seek ("If I were a doughnut in this car, where would I hide?"), and counting games like *buzz*.

But the passengers may wear out, too. It's not necessary to see-hear-do every single inch of the way. Encourage the child to have a nap toward the end of the trip in order to feel awake and fresh at the end, especially if you're to meet people at your destination. Who enjoys a cranky, tired kid when you're saying hello to relatives or friends?

I believe in scrapbooks wholeheartedly. For children and myself, I prefer a scrapbook of a trip to slides or film. A scrapbook can offer more to remember than a photograph album, although photos easily become a part of the scrapbook. The shirt box or shoe box with the child's supplies can also hold the scraps. Or else, a plastic shopping bag, a large manila envelope, or one side of an inexpensive flight-type bag can be the "scrap heap." Depending upon where you go, the child's collectibles include airline magazines, the remains of a used flight ticket, baggage checks, maps showing the traveled route and dates of stops, menus and restaurant receipts, admission stubs, hotel receipts, promotional brochures of hotels and amusement areas, post cards (both the free kind and the ones you purchase in special places), dematched matchbook covers, sections of any local maps showing visited areas, programs of entertainment and sports events, transportation schedules, interesting clippings from local newspapers, visitors' guides—anything with a date, place, time, or amount that helps a child to remember some moment on the trip.

Slide and film showings may be your own way of showing your trip to your friends. The scrapbook is the child's own individual way of showing his trip to his friends without your having to set up all of the picture equipment. Consider, too, that films move relentlessly onward when they're shown, leaving only a moment or two for you to comment with the young traveler about the scene and events. On the other hand, the scrapbook provides a dependable sequence and outline which the child can use to tell at his own pace and stop for comments, questions, and answers. Experience has proved to me that real language opportunities with a child lie with a scrapbook and photographs rather than slides or films. Just look at all the things to talk about that a scrapbook can hold that slides and films will never show.

Using the materials from the supply box, the child may at almost any time draw quick sketches and add captions with a date, place, and a story sentence or two. The series of drawings may be sequenced and scrapbooked at home later, another scheme to promote language among young friends.

If your travel budget allows, help the child to select a record album or two which seems appropriate to a place or event during your trip. Mark the date and the place of purchase on the jacket. Also, look for inexpensive pamphlets and books about memorable areas and attractions which may interest the child. At home later, you have a fine visual or aural memento of your travel which provides a long-lasting language experience.

Before they leave home, Martha helps her son Charlie to print or type gummed labels with the names and addresses of several friends and relatives to whom Charlie may expect to write post cards during the trip. While waiting for their breakfast, Martha and Charlie discuss briefly what they did the day before, where they were, and the date. Charlie sticks a label on a post card and prints a story sentence or two. During one trip, Charlie insisted on sending post cards to himself instead of his friends. He stuck labels, licked stamps, and wrote brief stories to himself each day. At home, he sorted his own post cards by date and shared them with his friends. In this way, he said, his friends got their post cards, all right, but he got some, too.

Meeting People

One quite predictable human trait, not just in our culture but in cultures through the ages, is that people hang on to whatever it is that they call home. When people move or travel, they tend to take their culture with them and preserve it or defend it in unfamiliar areas.

It may disturb children to learn that hamburgers and milkshakes are not available everywhere in the world, although the instant-food syndicates are trying hard to remedy that. The currencies of other countries are not "funny money." And many progressive people in other countries consider "quaint" to be a put-down for their daily customs, holidays, scenes, and architecture.

You and the child can display an attitude of arrogance and superiority, or you can express a sincere, genuine interest in perceiving and understanding the countries of others. You can call up the excellences of home while you're away (and home has a way of becoming better than it really is when you're away from it!), or you can ask to learn more of the customs and daily routines of the areas you visit. Hotel employees, salespersons in shops, and cafe cashiers are polite but unappreciative when you hold out a handful of the local currency and say, "Take what you need, it all looks the same to me." It is not Monopoly money to those people. It's hard cash. Don't belittle their valuable currency any more than you would your own.

According to Genesis, God scattered the people of the Tower of Babel and gave them different languages in order to separate them more completely. But He didn't state which language He preferred over all of the others. You and the child do not speak the "preferred" language. You speak only one of more than five thousand of the world's different tongues.

Therefore, before you leave home, take some interest in discussing the food of the country you'll visit with the child. Make some effort to discuss the value of the foreign currencies, if your child has a concept of the mechanics of money. You might also do a little research on the courtesy words of the languages in the countries where you'll be traveling. Words and phrases like *bonjour, bitte, grazie,* and *de nada* are sure to be warmly wel-

comed when sincerely offered. And the child will have an opportunity to say them often.

If the child can read, the words in an unfamiliar language
are sure to interest her. Discuss the different names for commonly perceived things—the names of different stores, foods
on a menu, signs and directions on doors and in public areas,
especially the appropriate words for the restrooms. If you're
traveling in Britain, you and the child will be interested in the
different names for many things, even though you have the
same language. Develop an ear-without-ridicule for the different dialects and vocal tones when you hear English spoken
in another region or country. As always, the dialect that differs
from yours is certainly not inferior to yours.

God must have enjoyed listening to many languages, because
he created so many of them. Point out languages in which you
may not understand the words, although the same alphabetic
letters are used. You may also perceive and discuss the use of
unfamiliar letters in the alphabet of another language. Also,
you'll be sure to notice languages in which the alphabet is entirely different, such as Japanese and Arabic.

More and more in my own travels, I've seen people carrying
tape recorders. They not only narrate what they see as a kind
of diary for their trips, but they also record various sounds, for
example, the traffic in Piccadilly Circus, a train pulling out of a
station, and an announcement spoken in several languages by
the flight attendant during a jet take-off. Understandably,
some people in another region or country remain quite skittish
about having their language recorded. They may not like to be
considered a tourist curiosity.

After you and the child make some friendly contact, however, you may want to ask if they'll exchange some language
with you for the benefit of your recording; perhaps they'll tell
their names, their addresses, something about the areas in
which they live, and what it's like to live there. Perhaps the
hostess or the manager of a restaurant will explain some of the
names of the foods on the menu, if the restaurant is not too
busy. A new friend or host may offer you a lesson in the local
language.

Whether you're traveling or at home, as one way to mix and

talk with people, your child may become interested in collecting autographs. An inexpensive autograph book, a blank telephone or address book, or a homemade small scrapbook decorated with the child's drawings can provide the start. The child may collect signatures of the family, relatives, friends, neighbors, acquaintances met on a trip, neighborhood shopkeepers, business people, and visitors to your house. The signers may also be invited to add a note or quick sketch. The activity is a guaranteed language maker.

Watch different adults as their children pursue a friendship. One adult stays out of the child's scene, relaxed and interested, as the child makes friendly actions. Another intervenes, probably wisely and thoughtfully, when the child seems to intrude unwanted upon another person. There is a third adult, however, whose motivations I question, the one who becomes the interrupter and the intruder, sometimes quite unnecessarily, as the child and the other person seem to be getting along. Could that third adult feel the threat of competition and begin making adult noises designed to end the acquaintance because of mild jealousy?

With some exceptions, children have an uncanny way of making friends. From Lihue to Lugano, I've watched friendly, nonabrasive children collect acquaintances, adults as well as other children, almost as if by a prearranged appointment, in hotel lobbies, buses, swimming pools, airline terminals, and beaches, almost anywhere they have a moment or two to exchange a smile and to get their things going. I've seen children become acquainted in only a few moments with both young and old persons who didn't even share the same language. It's a *something,* a childhood charisma, that either many adults outgrow or they finally manage to tamp out of older youth.

Today's teenagers get acquainted with each other much more easily and quickly than I did at the same age. But they seem less ready to cross the age gap in amiable, courteous conversations. A shame, really, isn't it? I wish it were otherwise, because I thoroughly enjoy talking to people who are younger than I. And, with my each passing birthday, there seem to be more and more of them!

15

About Death

Children learn to cope with many different kinds of loss—
the loss of a toy, an article of clothing, coins, an ice-cream cone
dropped on the sidewalk, a seat on the school bus, a minor
privilege, a defeat in a game or contest, among others. Some of
these losses may be recovered or replaced. Others cause the
child to strive for greater ability and strategy. To a favored
child, the loss of material things implies replacement, and
unless the child is given some time to experience the feelings of
"doing without," the concept of loss is forgotten in the anticipation of the new.

Children are more deeply affected by other losses which happen less frequently—a pet that died or ran away, a favorite
teacher who left the classroom in midyear, a family member
who lost a job, a friend who moved away, or a parent who left
the family unit because of separation or divorce.

There are also more subtle, unseen losses for which the child
will undoubtedly need your understanding and guidance, such
as the loss of attention because of the arrival of a new baby or a
new step-parent.

Loss can be renamed *misplacement, change, deprivation,* or *sharing.* You'll help the child deal with any of these losses in side-
by-side language experiences.

Much more serious is the loss to death of a loved neighbor or friend. But the ultimate loss is the death of a parent or other close family member.

If you are the next of kin, the chief mourner, the family's adviser, a trusted friend, or other influential person, you can arrange a funeral and the related events as simply and economically, or as elaborately and expensively as the family's wealth and traditions provide. This chapter won't try to explain the traditions of funerals. So if we talk, for example, about an open casket, and you don't believe in open caskets, keep in mind that some family groups believe in viewing the body. You'll only compound the problem by explaining your personal feelings about funerals, especially to children, during these grief-filled days.

On the other hand, we very much want to ease the feelings of loss and correct the misconceptions that children harbor as the result of death, regardless of the family's customs. Comfort and condolence will guide your actions and words at this time.

Language exchange with children at a very upsetting, difficult time is the purpose here—just as language exchange with children is the purpose for all of these pages.

"Zap, You're Dead!"

To an adult, death is final and irreversible. To a child, however, death may be viewed as dramatic but temporary.

When choosing sides, some children may insist on playing the cops, while others clamor to be the robbers, since the robbers have more fun and they get to "die." There used to be a time when nobody wanted to be the Indians unless they could wear the feathers, tie up the cowboys, threaten them with torture, and be promised an audience for their highly dramatic death scenes. Nowadays, the Indians win more and more of the battles, and both sides mock their battles until the last child spins to the ground with an arrow "straight through the heart."

Children play space war. They hunt and gun down monsters from other planets. They zap each other with intricate death-ray guns. But in none of these games does the concept of death need to be associated with permanence, since the children get up at the end of each game and start to play again.

He says he wants to be a cop this time, 'cause all the robber gets to do is play dead.

TV-soaked children watch movies, situation shows, and violent cop stories. Even if they cannot read, they can tell you when the cast of fictional characters is presented in the roll-up, indicating those people who were paid to play dead. They see a famous actor or actress die in one film, only to be starred in another "Million Dollar Movie" on the next night. Children know that Frankenstein cannot stay dead; he is burned, frozen, buried, and drowned in quicksand, only to revive for the next sequel.

Children may watch the television news with you and find it difficult or impossible to believe in the gore of reality. They may see a body removed from a smashed car or a dead person carried out of a burned building on a stretcher, and then they see the roll-up at the end of the news. Can they assume that those names also include the cast of the characters who were paid to play dead? You know it's news, but it may be simply another TV show to the children. Again, there is no need to associate death with a permanent, final condition.

One day, though, as the child tests his perceptions of reality against his growing memory of events and his language experiences with you, he will begin to discern that there is a difference between fictional TV shows and factual news. One day, a death will occur within the family unit or nearby in the neighborhood—a sudden fatal illness, an unfortunate accident, perhaps a disaster nearby. Statistics support the likelihood of a sudden, shocking death in a car accident of a family member, neighbor, friend, or classmate. Then, the concept of death becomes real, permanent. The time for the sharing of feelings and the answering of questions has come.

Face this first: You can't possibly protect your child from the actuality of a death. You may harbor the attitude that children will have enough problems when they're grown, and they don't need this. But you can't treat death as a "problem," since it's more real in your daily lives than milkshakes and birthday parties. Closeting the child from death, grief, and related events may only compound the child's fears, which are engendered by curiosities, child-to-child tales, and perceptions without explanations. The eventual reckoning with reality may become more awesome. Time somehow permits fantasies to become more and more structured unless discussions and some open experiences with death help to enlighten the child.

Psychologists, anthropologists, and clergy can offer a number of explanations for death. The three that follow may give you some ground work on which to help a child reckon with the loss of a person through death, but your own experiences and your religious feelings will add more to your language exchanges.

1. Death is eventual for every living person, animal, and plant. Families of living things reproduce themselves. Living things must have room and nourishment to grow. Living things age during their periods of growth and life. Imagine how crowded the earth would be if all living things from the beginnings of time continued to grow and age, but nothing died. Life for everything has its time, and then it dies so that living things which follow can also grow and age naturally. It is the growth of living things which perpetuates our earth. But where there is life, death must also exist.

2. Death provides an opportunity for others to prove their benevolence and compassion. Life isn't made up entirely of cheeseburgers and french fries. The language of emotion between family, neighbors, and friends is learned and used during periods of stress, sadness, and grief: "What can I do?" "If I can help in any way, just call me." "I just wish that there was something I could do."

The desire to say kind words like these and to do thoughtful actions during a period of grief can help to prove to the child and to reassure each of us that we are able to think generously and compassionately about something besides ourselves.

3. Death provides an opportunity to reaffirm the feelings of love and friendship among the living. Families reunite during the first days of the mourning and the funeral. They touch each other. They say and hear consoling words. They exchange stories and anecdotes about their relationships with the dead person. They reaffirm their vows of familial love. They bring each other up to date on their lives, and they promise continued contact.

233

Vows and actions of friendship are also exchanged among the living friends and the neighbors of the dead person. A neighborhood or a community may come more closely together through a common loss. In this way, death provides an opportunity to strengthen and reaffirm the ties among the living.

Consoling Another's Child

When you offer your sympathy to the family of a dead neighbor or acquaintance, there is no need to ignore the child, to pretend that the child doesn't exist among the family members. The child has feelings, too, and is suffering the puzzlement as well as the pain of loss. When you speak consoling words to a bereaved adult, speak some consoling words to the bereaved child as well. Sit, bend, or lower your face to the child's eye level, but don't condescend yourself mentally to a childlike manner. Assume a side-by-side attitude. Resist the temptation to sound like the Voice of Doomsday when you talk of death or the child's loss. Remain straight-voiced, honest, and sincere in your language exchange with the child.

It's possible that the child may never have seen you before and doesn't know your name or anything about you. Introduce yourself, saying your name very clearly, as you would to any adult stranger. State your relationship with the dead person to the child. Perhaps you were a fellow employee, a Rotary Club fellow member, a golf or fishing buddy, on the same bowling team, a church friend—whatever. In a quiet, calm way, take time to tell the child who you are and why you are offering her your condolences.

If you wish, share one of your feelings or memories about the dead person with the child. Be cautious, however, not to build insurmountable goals in your language exchange, such as, "Will you be a good golfer one day the way your Mom was?" "Are you going to grow up to be a lawyer to please your daddy?" "Now, you'll want to try very hard to make your grandmother proud of you."

Be mature in your conversation with the child. Don't allow yourself to wallow in phrases like "Oh you poor baby" or other infantile gibberish. If the child is struggling to achieve some composure in his grief, don't blow it. Maintain your own mature but sincere manner with the child.

Watch to see that you do not overenergize your own feeling of grief and sympathy with the child and his family. Oversolicitous adults, with a "you poor little child" attitude, can create additional, unnecessary difficulties. If the child's loss was sudden and perhaps violent, such as an accidental drowning or a suicide, adults can too easily scoop up children in their own overreactions of frenzied grief. With excessive carryings-on, the child will sense quickly enough that something to wail about has happened, become frightened without really knowing why, take the cue from the adult, and react with a mixture of fright and frenzy that will resemble a bizarre grief. Let yourself go in private, if you wish, but when you are with the child, hold tight to whatever manner you wish the child to emulate.

A child learns the conditions of grief by perceiving and responding to the actions of grief-stricken people. These are the days when a child learns the meaning of sympathy from sympathetic people. The word parts in *sympathy* means *feeling with,* a togetherness in emotions. Your manner and your words are being perceived by the child, who will eventually be able to name them as sympathetic.

In a similar way, the word parts in *compassion* mean *suffering with.* Compassionate actions include not only sympathy but also your desire to assist or support a person in a difficult time. You can believe that the child is perceiving and responding to your words and manner even though he's mainly concerned now with his own feelings of loss and grief. One day, when the child wishes to be sympathetic and compassionate with another sad friend, you can believe that the child's actions may reflect your own behavior.

Feelings of compassion make neighbors and friends want to help. You may want to invite the child to come have lunch or supper with your own children. The bereaved adults may welcome a bit of peace and quiet because of your gesture. But don't keep the child to the point where she feels isolated from her family.

235

A child's trauma about death and loss is created by others and not by the child. Shock is a reaction from a combination of perceptions of the actions, words, and responses of others. Something that seems not so much to the child at the time can become unnecessarily heightened, distorted, and spiced with frenzy, a fearful memory that the growing child must choke down and hide for a lifetime. How many people do you know who harbor such fearful memories of loss that they can't speak reasonably of death?

Sharing Loss with Your Child

You and your own child will have to deal with at least these four ingredients, among others, of mourning. First, mourning surrounds the child with an atmosphere of disbelief. Before these days, the child could perceive and therefore believe in the presence of the live person. In dozens of unpredictable ways, those perceptions which once were taken for granted are now being replaced by voids or substitutions. The child must test the reality of each feeling concerned with the loss. Betty found her daughter sitting on Grandmother's bed at an odd hour in the early morning. When asked why she was up, Betty's daughter merely replied, "I had to see if Gram's bed had been slept in."

Mark came through the door into the kitchen and said, "Mom, the lawn still isn't mowed. Dad always mowed the lawn."

Second, mourning disorganizes the routine of the family unit. The disruption results in inaction for some of the family members and action to the point of exhaustion for others. Children are puzzled and even disgruntled because they can't do what they used to do, and during the days of mourning they can't do anything else. Doctors will agree that mourning brings on periods of disorientation as well as inconvenient, unpredictable periods of fatigue. Together with the arrival of relatives and the visits from friends, the unusual household activities are sure to upset the child.

Third, mourning turns once-pleasant memories and associations into sources of confusion and anguish. The toothbrush by the bathroom sink, the scent of a familiar perfume, the miscellaneous contents of a wallet or purse, a once-favorite television program, a Bible verse or table grace—dozens of minor connections can bring a temporary breakdown for you or the child.

Fourth, mourning raises fears and mistaken ideas about the future. When the child tends to believe the loss, the question will undoubtedly arise, "What are we going to do?"

One trouble with grief is that it doesn't provide much for a child to do. Bereaved families often take the child out of school for a few days, but mourning leaves almost no activity to substitute for the school experiences. Manage things for your child to do, or ask a family member or friend to take over the child's activities, but not to the point of long separations or isolations. If relatives or friends must go to meet a plane, send the child to the airport with them for the ride as one of the family's meeting party. Send the children together with another family member for lunch somewhere, an informal run in the community park, a home movie or slide show at a neighbor's house. You simply can't deactivate a normally busy child without having some problems. Funeral periods may become very busy for adults, but make sure you do not leave your child alone and unoccupied.

Silence and separation is no way to share your loss with your child. "Go to your room" is a bossy sentence associated with punishment, not grief. It's very easy for a child to infer that he is being punished for some action (perhaps even the person's death) when he is cut off and kept away from the other bereaved family members.

Share your feelings of loss with the child, honestly and matter-of-factly. It may not occur to your child that you are also feeling disbelief, disorganized, and that your memories and associations hurt, too. Talk simply about your perceptions and feelings that combine to make the condition in you which you call *grief*. Exchange the language of your emotions with the child during this period of stress. Your feelings can be shared, and so can your words.

At times, you'll need to supply the words and sentences

which help your child to name his feelings, since the child's experience with such loss has not been enough to provide for him an appropriate vocabulary of words and expressions.

Remembering a song or a special gesture may bring tears when you and the child are together. These associations occur on very sensitive nerve ends. Be assured that time and your talks together will alter these moments. Meanwhile, talk frankly with your child about crying as one reaction that may accompany loss. Some men and women cry while mourning, and some do not. Tears may come unexpectedly, and they should be allowed to flow. "Unsissify" the act of crying for a boy. Psychologists reassure us that crying is one of the reactions which may accompany feelings of sorrow in both men and women.

Remorse must be the most painful and self-destructive emotion regarding the death of a close relative or a dear friend. There seems to be no easy way that a child may completely throw off the guilty feelings which may result from a word said, a word not said, an unkind action, or an inaction when action would have been appreciated. In short, a child may feel that nothing was done when there should have been something, or a something was done when there should have been a something else.

Children may remember times when they were mean to the dead person, said they hated him or her, and wanted that person dead. Children may not always act in loving ways, but it's time now for you to dwell together on the consistencies of loving actions that make people love each other, and not on the occasional unkindnesses. Loving kindness for the dead person may not necessarily have been characterized by wholly and exclusively affectionate actions. Remember, though, to explain to the child that *love* names the consistency of the relationship, and not every fragment of it. Children must not be made to absorb guilt for unkind actions for which they can no longer apologize or make explanations.

For heaven's sake, don't begin using the child as your own confessor so that you may transmit your own feelings of remorse. Think of language and actions that cleanse, that put the sad experience behind you.

"Daddy said last Saturday that he wanted to take me on the merry-go-round, but he died."

"OK, you and I will enjoy one ride together on the merry-go-round as Daddy would want us to do."

You need not (and perhaps cannot) venerate the saintly aspects of the dead person. However, you can in easy ways be the "keeper of the flame," especially of those memories that may otherwise decay in the anguished child's mind.

Children can get fed up with the protracted illness of a relative. Let's face it, long illnesses usurp the time of the attending adult, which the child may also long for. The terminally ill become the topic of prolonged conversations and planning sessions; children may yearn to change the subject. The loss of a long-sick relative can actually be a relief—without associated guilt—for children who believe that they'll soon have their parents to themselves and the family routine back to normal. In these cases, don't instill guilt where it doesn't exist. Shaming won't do the child any good, the dead person any good, or you any good. The child has been starved for your time, attention, and conversation, and you are now in a position to provide it.

Easing Misconceptions

Eavesdropping, which as you know by now is one of my sources of information, isn't a good source of firsthand language exchanges between bereaved adults and children. People struggling to overcome the first days of fresh grief don't seem to appear in stores, parks, and public vehicles. If they do appear in public, they certainly don't talk freely of their loss. Most cultural traditions encourage private expressions of grief among family and the most intimate of friends.

I was quite shocked at the mysterious silences, childlike expressions of fear, and apologies for headaches, chills, and sick stomachs I observed in people—all of them adults, mind you—when I asked them about their experiences with death, dead bodies, funerals, and grief. Stories poured out—a woman almost fell into a casket when she was a little girl; a dead eyelid opened as one man approached the coffin to pay his respects;

239

another man dreamed that the corpse was sleeping with him in bed; the bottom dropped out of an improperly built casket and "Aunt Tootie" dropped into the street behind the hearse; a teenaged boy swore that the casket was exchanged for another as the hearse made its way to the cemetery. Good, gothic stories which, I'm sure, improve with the tellings. However, almost nobody offered me a reasonable story of how the concept of death became clear and understandable to them in a pleasant, reassuring experience.

If adults can believe such fearful and unreasonable tales, what must the children involved in death and funeral rituals conclude from their experiences? It's no wonder that many children think of death with the same histrionics that accompany a Vincent Price horror movie.

You may consider the child's fears and false ideas to be immature. That's because you're mature, and the child's understandings don't agree with yours. But the child's misconceptions may be quite reasonable when we consider how our language may have engendered those ideas in the beginning.

Euphemisms about death are vague, polite words which we prefer to use instead of those which are more precise. Some words, fine for another time, become more blunt than we can bear during periods of mourning. The euphemisms we use when speaking of the dead, the funeral customs, the burial equipment, and the church services may ease our own adult minds, but they mislead children.

Death is not a perceivable person or thing. In a Midwestern weekly newspaper, I was astonished to see at the top of the obituary column the shadow of a Father Time carrying an antique scythe next to these words: "Many answer the summons of the Grim Reaper." We've mentioned earlier that, for children, most things exist as perceivable before they're internalized. It's easy to find death pictured as a skeleton enveloped in a white or black cloak. Halloween costumes and decorations always include skeletons, ghosts, coffins, vampires, and other personifications of death and the dead. Children tend to picture death as a "somebody" lurking in the shadows and appearing suddenly from mists. The dark is often associated with death; it's not at all unusual to find the house of a bereaved family brightly lighted throughout the days and nights during a period of mourning. Many children have been known to run and hide from the thought of death and the awareness of a dying person.

The dead don't "play dead." They do not rise at night in funeral homes and cemeteries to wander and dance. Whistling as a child walks by a cemetery is sure to keep the bodies in their graves, since nothing in the tune is likely to disturb them.

The dead are not "asleep." When a child hears that a dead person looks asleep, he can reasonably and logically assume that the dead will awake. Why not? The child does it every morning and after every nap. On the other hand, the comment may be inverted and cause some children to fear sleeping and others to fear sleeping in the dark. From the child's point of view, it's quite logical for her to feel apprehensive when you are taking a nap, since the sleeping body can look to the child like a dead body. Many adults still teach children to say the bedtime prayer which includes the line "If I should die before I wake."

The dead do not "go away" or "pass away" or "pass on" or "leave us," and they are not "the dear departed." Any child hearing these words can logically assume that *going away* means *coming back, leaving* or *departing* means *returning* and *reuniting*. If these euphemisms for dying are to be believed, then *death* may be imagined as a place where people go temporarily, like Philadelphia and Dallas, and that the dead have some kind of round-trip ticket. The conclusion, quite logical in a child's mind, raises a host of questions. When will the dead come back? Why did they go? How can they get there in a box? How can they come back if they're in the ground? These questions and doubts in the child are based on our own desires to protect ourselves from the final and unmistakable words *die, death,* and *dead.*

The dead do not die as a punishment to the living.

Why did he do it, Mom?

What did you do that made him want to get even with us?

Maybe he didn't love me any more—why didn't he just say so?

If she loved me, why did she want to go away?

I must have done something wrong! What did I do? What did I say?

These questions arise, and the child's fears behind them deserve to be put down by your calm thoughtful answers. Even if the death was a suicide, certainly you don't want to hang the motives around the child's neck.

Similarly, some children protest, "It's not fair!" Then, you must explain to the child that the dead person loved life as much as you and the child do, and the dead person had no actual intention of committing a "foul play."

Death is not an omnipotent, omnipresent spirit. Your child may say, "Once I wished she was dead, and now she's dead." Death has no ears to hear the words and the wishes of children. Contrary to the words of some romantic tunes, wishing does not make it so. Chance remarks don't shoot people or give them heart attacks or run their cars into trees or consume them in fires.

Your time and your language exchanges will help the child to understand that death is final and irreversible. The physical functions stop. Dead bodies don't move, breath, feel pain, or think. And, above all, people don't return from the "land of the dead."

Death is a natural and permanent end of life. Yes, accidents may occur unexpectedly and unnaturally. Normally, however, the older people have come to know and understand that they will eventually make room for younger people. And from this point, you may want to talk with your child about the spirit of the dead person in whatever manner is appropriate with your personal beliefs and religious opinions.

The Funeral

One massive word count indicates that the word *funeral* appears only thirty-eight times in a computerized analysis of grade-school materials which included a running text of over five million words. More than half of these rare thirty-eight appearances were in materials intended for students in grades seven, eight, and nine. To give you some idea of the rarity of the word *funeral* in children's reading, *birthday* appeared *241* times, *love 735* times, *born 637* times, *dead 590* times, and *death 518* times.

In a more detailed word count, *funeral* appeared in a few children's readers, English and social studies textbooks in the fifth grade, and a few more in the sixth grade. According to the same wordlist, the word *dead* commonly appears in materials for grade three, and *death* was found frequently in the textbooks for grade four. We can conclude, then, that eight-year-olds read about *dead*, nine-year-olds about *death*, but they must wait a couple more years until they are introduced to *funeral*. Why can't a pupil logically ask, "People die, but what happens to them?" It seems to cast a reflection on the adult authors of textbooks, who can write about death but cannot seem to bring themselves to write about disposal.

There's very little in the experiences of children to prepare them for the intense period of time between death and funeral, and, especially, for the funeral ritual. Since Jessica Mitford's book *The American Way of Death* appeared, there has been much debate about the manner and customs of disposal. Dissatisfaction with funerals, costs, and the questionable practices of funeral directors rage among adults. But they don't touch children in direct, memorable ways. Instead, what children perceive are misty, candlelit tales of formidable castles, graverobbers, the living dead, mad scientists, vampires, and unsavory undertakers.

In a big city the funeral home or mortuary may be largely ignored, since it may look very much like a store or the bank next door. In smaller or less-crowded areas, however, the funeral home becomes a place of deep mystery for the child, who stares at it curiously from the window of the car or as he passes it on his bike. He peeks into the windows and watches every movement around its front and back doors. He sees people standing in small groups on the front walk, and occasionally he passes at a time when a casket is being moved from the home to the hearse.

Beyond the melodramatic tales on television and perceptions in passing a funeral home or cemetery, a child's real experience probably occurs from watching a funeral procession. Don't you share a silent but intense curiosity to peek into the passing hearse and stare at the following flower cars? Do you tend to glance into the first cars carrying the bereaved family to see what you can see? I do. Children do. Far from attempting to be anonymous, the cars in the funeral "parade" often carry small flags on the fenders or burn the headlights in some communities to invite your respect for the dead person and the mourners. In many less-hurried towns, the drivers of other cars often turn to the side of the road and stop in respect to the passing procession. During this momentary break in the travel, the young passengers often get a good look at the entire entourage.

When you see a funeral procession, there is no need to shield the child or stand in silence. Instead, you may want to explain simply and calmly what is happening, what is in the hearse, where the flowers came from, who is riding in the cars, what happened before the procession started, and where they are going. Feel free to provide brief, satisfactory answers to the child's questions, if any, before you proceed.

It's not unusual to find city children who've never been inside a cemetery. They may pass them on a school bus, public transportation, or in your car. However, the families of small-town children often include a drive through the cemetery when they "go for a ride." It's very common in smaller communities to stop at the cemetery plot on a pleasant afternoon to pick up, clean up, and prettify the area around the graves. I still remember my childhood experiences of visiting the family plot, where it was my job to scrub the pigeon droppings off the gravestones. Memorial Day, the first Sunday in spring, and Veteran's Day were traditional occasions to decorate the graves, to greet and talk with others who were doing the same, and to stroll through the cemetery paying our respects to recently buried friends. For me, cemeteries do not hold unpleasant associations, and they should not be fearful areas for your children. It's an appropriate place to stand quietly with your child beside a grave of a relative or friend and to talk together about the relationship of death to life as well as to answer the child's questions.

244

If the child requests a funeral for a dead animal or pet, don't hesitate. The child's perceptions and reactions eventually go "clang," and he associates death with some kind of ritual—a service, a procession, and a burial or some other method of disposal—but he may have no concept of the language or form for each part of the procedure. You'll need a few flowers, a container which may be padded and decorated if the child wishes, and a place where you expect to dispose of the dead thing after you pay your respects. The procedure and the elaborateness of the details depend upon your own personal beliefs, but in some way you'll help the child to understand the events which surround a death.

In short, help the child to "get it together" from your talks associated with funeral processions and from visits to a cemetery, and with a mild introduction to the events surrounding a death. The child needs inclusion and explanation. The child needs answers to his questions. And, above all, the child needs some background of experience to assist him when death occurs in his family.

We've mentioned before that the realities of life begin to awaken in a child at about the age of six or seven, give or take some months and depending upon the child's experiences. Santa Claus, who used to be a jolly old man with a long beard and red suit, metamorphoses into the spirit of giving. The stork no longer brings babies in little blue and pink blankets. And little boys and girls get tired of hearing about the puppydogs' tails and the sugar and spice inside them.

You may decide that it's time for the children to join the family and participate in a funeral service, or part of it. If you feel that the actual funeral may be too much of an introduction for the child, arrange with a relative or friend to have the child meet you after the service in order to participate in the procession, that part of the service with which the child may already be familiar. The interment service, if you have one, is usually brief. The child may then be with the family during the final moments of the service. For an introduction, you may consider that much of the child's participation to be enough.

If you decide that the child will attend the funeral service, you may wish to take her to the funeral home beforehand to

245

see what's there, to satisfy her curiosity, to meet a few of the people who may call while you're there, and to answer any of the child's questions. If the service is to take place there, you may wish to show the child where you'll sit together, how you'll get to that place, who else and what else will be there. Explain who will be with her throughout the service, and discuss simply what will happen. If the service is to be in a church or other place, you will undoubtedly need to explain, side-by-side and simply, how the dead person will get to that place and what will happen there.

There may be no need to mention (but I'll mention it, anyway) the importance of taking the child to the toilet the last thing before going into the funeral service. Funeral homes, chapels, and churches have restrooms. And funerals don't wait while you meet a child's emergency.

Some psychologists suggest a trip to the funeral home on the death of a neighbor, acquaintance, or a distant relative. Without the mourning accompanying the death of a closer family member, you and the child can explore the funeral home and talk about the experience. Be calm and prepared to discuss the child's questions, since you are primarily arranging this visit for him. There is no need to overexplain, overemote, get sepulchral, or tell the child more than he wants to know. Let the child perceive fully and ask what he wishes. Your manner with the child will be easy, honest, and side-by-side.

Caution! Be sure to hang onto yourself and to keep your own fears from permeating this unique language experience.

Grief and Curiosity

While you may be coping with your own feelings of fresh grief, including an uncontrollable outburst now and then, the child is juggling two rather distinct reactions. First, the child is struggling in a much more inexperienced manner with his own feelings that accompany loss. Second, the child is undergoing an intense curiosity about dying, death, bodies, bones, and spirits.

You can share emotions with the child when you discuss the

memories of the dead person, the kindnesses of friends, the comforts of reunions, and the visits with relatives. But you can expect to be brought up quite short now and then when your sharing is interspersed with questions which may seem to you abrupt and brutal.

If I pinched Dad right now, what would he feel?

How soon does a body become a skeleton?

Does a body smell after a while, like the trash?

Do mice and bugs crawl around in there?

These, among others, are the questions of the child who is displaying the natural inquisitiveness of a learner. If the child is to cope, he must ask and learn. If he is to fight fears and misconceptions, then he must have the truth.

At some time, you must decide whether to grant a child's wish to see a dead body. When that time has come, the child may be too small to see over the edge of the casket. Instead of lifting the child unsteadily for a glimpse, move a solid chair or stool to an appropriate viewing place and help the child to stand squarely on it. The two of you will then be side-by-side and quite steady so that you can discuss comfortably your perceptions and answer any of the child's questions.

The time may also come when the child will ask to touch a dead body. The desire may result from a combination of curiosity, in which the child wants to experience the perception, and grief, in which a touch may prove the reality of death.

I'll confess to you that I was well into adulthood before I touched the hand of a dead person—my older brother—in a deliberate attempt to dispel some fears and tales that I had collected since childhood. I can now testify that nothing stained my hand, I didn't leave purple marks on the body's skin, no eyelids fluttered, no skin fell off that dead hand, and nothing moved. The fearful childhood fantasy was put to rest in that gentle touch of a brother's hand. It felt cool and still, but not unpleasant.

Decide as you wish regarding your child's request, but keep in mind that the child is expressing a curiosity. How you reply may or may not provide the structure for a longstanding fear. Although some families do touch or kiss the dead person's face as part of a farewell ritual, the hand may be quite enough for the child's first experience.

There is no need for you to volunteer the unpleasant details of the person's dying moments, especially if they were prolonged, painful, and difficult. If the child asks, provide honest answers without overdramatizing to achieve a gothic effect. The time may come when the child exhibits an intellectual curiosity about what happens when a person dies and how death is determined. Arrange in advance for a doctor, your firsthand authority, to answer the child's questions during your next office visit.

It's all right for you to leave the door open on the spiritual aspects that you honestly don't know and can't answer for the child. After all, who has all of the answers about the mysteries of death and dying?

Reading About Death

If the child is able to read independently, she can help to satisfy her own curiosity. Nonfiction books giving the straight story about death and dying don't seem to be too numerous, but there are fictional stories and poetry on the shelf that may help the child to discover feelings that she recognizes when they are expressed by the characters in the narratives. Children who haven't coped with loss will also be curious to read how the characters in the story felt and what they did to understand about death.

Stories about wilting tulips, funerals for birds, and dead dogs may satisfy young readers for a while as they make some generalizations about the life cycle. The more curious reader will wish for more substantial circumstances about the death of real people. For some children, reading about dead pigeons and pets after a period of mourning can be as unsatisfying as hearing about the birds and the bees after they have seen their parents in bed together.

If the child can't read and you would like to share some books about death, read them for yourself first. Seek satisfying answers to these and other questions:

248

Does the book tell specifically what you want to share when you read it together?

Do its religious and emotional overtones support those you want to discuss with the child?

Is the book too vague and nebulous, or does it seem to have a definite point which it sets out to make clear for the child?

Does the book stress the process of dying, the life cycle, suicide, animal deaths, memory, establishing substitute relationships, dispelling fears and fantasies, funerals, fatal diseases, drug overdoses, or histories and customs?

And, very important, who died in the story? And how?

Reading together about death aids the child as well as yourself in sharing the non-uniqueness of loss. It may also help you both to relieve tension, especially those induced by aloneness and silence, just by the act and the time you spend together.

Helping Your Child to Recover

Earlier, we talked of the actions which may accompany mourning—disbelief, disorganization, distressing memories, and apprehension. During an indeterminate period following the funeral, after the relatives have gone home and the family quiets down to life without the dead person, the loss will continue to be tested and found to be real. The security of a daily routine will again reorganize the family unit and restore the child to his daily activities. Tears may no longer accompany memories. The family will speak less and less sensitively and frequently of the dead person, and life will readapt itself with time.

Moments of grief will continue to be evident in some action, and times for togethering will undoubtedly occur. As in the first chapter of this book, you must decide when and whether to enter the child's scene of sadness, and how. You may decide to exchange language. On the other hand, you may share a moment of touching and embracing, and perhaps no more. Crying will happen sometimes. Avoid being bossy about "brave little men" and "only babies cry." Your subtle directives may only build a trap for yourself during your own sad moments.

Share your religious convictions freely, as and when you wish, because that's what religious beliefs are for at a time like this. Keep the goal of comfort for your child in your mind. Share your feelings but not your own unfounded fears—worms that crawl in veins, hair that continues to grow, live burials, and all of that baloney.

You may be thinking about wills, estates, and financial provisions. But, for the moment, contain your fears about income and eventual care for the child. Discussions and family plans will come, but at a calmer time.

When the child seems to seek your comfort and company, be accessible. Emotions in the child don't hold well until after you return from the office or the hair stylist. It's a time for a side-by-side experience, time for you to listen, to answer, and to reassure. If you cry together, share your tears without guilt, but get on with it. A child's sufferings may be alleviated by sharing, by acting in impulsive, pleasant ways (go unexpectedly to have an ice-cream cone together!), and by time. A child's feelings of aloneness may be relieved as simply as by togethering with you in the kitchen, coloring at the kitchen table where you are ironing or cooking, reading a comic book in a comfortable chair near the desk where you are paying the monthly bills.

Get things going again for the child with his friends and your neighbors. Don't isolate him from playmates; discuss with other parents ways of getting your child back into "the gang," especially if the child's young friends seem afraid or hesitant to play because of their own fears of death—a real possibility.

The child can help you with the activities following the funeral—licking stamps, signing thank-you notes and acknowledgments, pasting mementoes into the memorial book. When you clean out the dead person's drawers and closets, discuss those things which the child would like to keep as his own.

Marsha's mother died when she was eleven. Marsha said she had no apprehension of breaking up her own home with her father until an aunt invited her to move to another city to live with the family of relatives. The point here is that you must be prepared to deal with the child's apprehension, but don't instill in children an unnecessary fear of what will happen to them afterward. By a remark, an invitation, or a suggestion, undoubtedly well meant, you may start an issue that wasn't there and that may be hard to settle.

Certain perceptions will cue tears in children as they may bring sad moments to any of us. Nine-year-old Jim, who had attended the funeral of a great-uncle sometime before, began to hear in his mind's ear the tune of "The Old Rugged Cross," which had been played as background music at the funeral. He broke into tears unexpectedly while doing math problems in his fourth-grade classroom. He was not immediately willing to explain the behavior to his teacher, who was at a loss to help.

If you paint an overly rosy picture of an existence after death, you run some risk of convincing the child that life beyond death may be better than the child's present reality. Fantasizing about flying around on wings, sleeping on clouds, wearing starry crowns, and reuniting with pets, friends, and family members can lead the child to wish, perhaps, for death as an entrance to some kind of an eternal amusement park. Explain, according to your beliefs, the eternal conditions for the dead person, but do your best at the same time to stress the continuance of a satisfying life for the child. The here-and-now must have its goal and its satisfactions for the living child.

After all this, don't be surprised if the child's grief span is quite short. The child may be eager, even fidgety, to get back into school, to play ball, to see favorite TV programs, or to go to the pancake house. Do something for the child that resembles the normal round. Take your cue from the child's desire for normalcy, reestablish your own routine, and get going again!

When the Child Consoles Others

When the child becomes a sympathetic consoler for another person, you may be needed to help her choose the appropriate words to say. Rehearse the words with a bit of role-playing, if she seems unsure of her manner and language. Reassure the child on the appropriateness and the sincerity of her efforts; and, again, be ready for questions. The spoken language of the emotions helps her to develop language for expressing feelings and for acknowledging the feelings of others. Through the child's own experiences in consolation, she learns the answers to these questions.

How does grief feel?

What do sad people do?

What do sympathetic and compassionate people do?

Dealing with the loss through death of another person can strengthen the mental and the emotional fiber of the living. The circumstances surrounding the loss—dates, times, places, the weather, flowers, music, friends, long-unmet relatives— become memorable, but they need not become unpleasant. The child's perceptions and reactions go "clang" after a loss, and insights result.

Given time, an awareness grows of the connection between death and life. A quiet peace replaces grief and depression. Relationships among the people within the family unit become more closely knit. Vows and actions reaffirm the ties among friends and neighbors. Insights develop about the purposes of a robust, happy, and useful life.

Illness and death are indeed given to some among us in order to prove the benevolence and the compassion of others.

16

When I Grow Up

A really good textbook teaches a child how to get along without it. As a matter of fact, there are two things in school that a child must learn to live without—the textbook, and the teacher.

It's true at home, as well, that children must be taught to live beyond their parents. Add it up. A child under ten today will spend half her life in the twenty-first century!

I'm sure our parents and grandparents fretted (as we do) about what this old world is coming to. Your child faces adulthood in a liberated world that already intimidates many of us. But fret or not, wish it were so or wish it weren't, you must anticipate the future that your child faces—and the child must be prepared to cope with it.

Beyond you.

Working for Pay

A teacher in Texas asked the first-grade students how they would spend $100. After the children had time to think about, describe, and draw pictures of their expenditures, their teacher had an opportunity to discover just how far the children thought $100 will go in this world. One young economist got a lot for his money by "buying" a new house and a new boat. Another sport "ordered" a new car and a new television with a remote control. One girl was quite sensible when she decided to have a new bike, but she blew the budget when she also decided to have a trip around the world. Another family-minded chap budgeted for Mom's ring, Dad's car, and a pup for himself.

Try the $100 spending spree with a child who may be from five to seven years old. You'll discover that children are not automatically equipped with calculators and ledger sheets. With patience on your part, you can help children to realize the value of money, not only because they learn how to spend it, but also because they learn that it is generally earned. When you have an opportunity to talk about currency—coins and bills—include straightforward, non-bitchy comments on where money comes from, how it gets into the household budget, the meaning of wages, salaries, fees, commissions, and bonuses. Even if you don't expect the child to remember the terms at a certain age, she'll realize quickly enough with your help the need of working for pay. There is no real reason for children to comprehend careful spending if they do not understand the time and effort involved in earning an income.

When your child can count to ten and group things by fives, you can informally and pleasantly introduce ten pennies, two nickels, and two dimes in your language experiences with money. Help the child to count the pennies to ten and group them into fives in order to talk about the nickel. Your counting experiences and groupings of the pennies and the nickels will eventually help the child to discover that ten of the pennies or two of the nickels make one of the dimes. Ten of the pennies and two of the nickels make both of the dimes.

You can expect that the child will confuse the dime and the nickel a number of times. The nickel is larger, and the child may logically conclude from perception that the nickel should be worth more. After all, the child's experiences with candy bars, pieces of cake, slices of bread, and chunks of fresh fruit have led him to believe that bigger means more. You might try Hazel's explanation to her nephew. She turned one dime face up and the two nickels and ten pennies face down. Then she told the story about the "Little King" who owned the ten copper houses and decided to sell them for the two silver castles.

Introduce the quarter after the child has the pennies, the nickels, and the dimes up to twenty cents sorted out clearly in his mind. Take plenty of time in discussing change up to twenty cents, since these understandings will also be valuable when you talk about paper currency.

You can easily play store now. After opening the *bottoms* of small cans and jars, you can mark prices on the top. Mark at least ten items serially from 1¢ to 10¢, including more than one item for each price, if you wish, but nothing more expensive than 10¢. Take turns buying, selling, and making the correct change up to 20¢, adding the quarter when you are quite sure the child can handle it.

You can follow a similar pattern when you introduce the half dollar, although some areas of the country rarely see them. Of course, the dollar culminates the play of making change with coins.

When the child has a good grasp of the coins and change-making for amounts up to a dollar, you can play store with other items—cans, bottles, boxes, and other tagged merchandise, especially non-grocery items. You can mark the prices in round figures. If you think the child can make change, use the actual prices already marked on the items. Give the child an opportunity to draw copies of the bills—five ones, two twos, two fives, two tens, and one twenty. Discuss with the child the important ways of telling the bills apart. Then, play at buying and selling items and making change for the bills. When the child expresses an interest in combining the paper bills with the change, there you go!

Without arranging seminars on the economy for the young child, take numerous opportunities to talk briefly about the costs of running a store, of buying wholesale and selling retail, and something about the number of times an item may be bought and sold during its journey from the original producer to the consumer.

Many child psychologists advise that an allowance need not be earned. Instead, they say, it is a device to learn financial responsibilities and to make reasonable choices as a young consumer. If you agree, you'll hesitate to supervise too strictly the child's use of an allowance. Gradually, however, you'll talk together about where the money which provided that allowance was earned and by whom. You will be able to communicate that independence as an adult is related to the ability to earn a sufficient amount of income and to live within it.

Talking About Work

Horsepower, pneumatics, and electronics have largely replaced physical manpower—and I mean the grunt-and-strain kind—in almost every modern American working place. People don't generally carry or drag heavy stones up inclines to make buildings any more. They don't dig with trowels or wooden scoops, except in gardens and window boxes on weekends and holidays. The old covered well at the back of the lot and the wood-burning kitchen stove have been largely replaced by modern (and very expensive) electric systems. And yet, our attitudes about "a woman's place" and "a man's work" remain unbelievably behind today's times.

Modern pushbutton-and-lever technology has moved much faster than people's attitudes about the strength and intelligence needed to operate machines. Moving dirt by pushing wheelbarrows, once reasoned to be work for a man's strong back, is now accomplished by operating enormous sod gulpers. It is reasonably considered as work for a person, man or woman, who knows how rather than for a muscular, half-naked male.

"It isn't ladylike," and yet women are making good livings by driving trucks, hacking in taxis, repairing telephone lines, painting houses. Well, today's fine jobs for women that "girls just don't do" are endless and exciting!

It never was a compliment to say to a boy, "You climbed that tree (or mowed that lawn) like a girl." But the reverse is equally true. Your compliment can smack of sexism when you say to a girl, "You climbed that tree (or mowed that lawn) like a man."

Many little girls may actually still believe in the Sleeping Beauty syndrome. But, instead of waiting to be rescued by their Prince Charmings, they may be waiting to be rescued from

CLICK

If enough mothers do that, think of all the people you'll put out of work!

GRRROWR

bossy, overbearing adults. A number of little girls—like Frieda, Charlie Brown's friend—may wait for others to admire her naturally curly hair. So do many big girls. But today's children are learning that *beautiful* is the name we also give to beautiful actions, and that *beauty* is a condition which should not be used as an excuse to avoid what could be an interesting involvement with life, another condition called *work*.

You are one of the workers that a child perceives. How do you feel about your own job? Are you ashamed that you aren't doing what you think is a "man's job" or a manly job? How do you feel about being a homemaker, if that's what you are? How do you feel about the child's becoming a homemaker? Do you still think that girls should wear short skirts and tight sweaters, stay cool, and do nothing? Where do you think a woman's place should be? And how do you feel about the kind of people who earn livings as doctors, writers, people in the fashion businesses, nurses, teachers, bus drivers, politicians?

If you are a homemaker, and you enjoy being a homemaker, don't dump trash on your head every time you mention something about being *just* a housewife or that "you don't work because you keep house." Instead, talk with both boys and girls about the tools which help you in your work, and emphasize that single men and women must do all of this for themselves. When a mother works, the father and the kids should offer to help out. More and more of today's couples are drawing definite agreements which state who does what in the house.

Girls can be free to choose if they wish to become homemakers, but they should not be forced or forecast into the role. Homemaking is one of many jobs for girls, or it may be combined with going to business. Bite your tongue when you hear yourself about to say, "It's too hard for girls." The comment implies that girls aren't smart enough or strong enough for the discussed work. When you hear the comments, find out what the speaker means by *too hard*. Does it mean difficult physically or intellectually? You may want to follow the discussion from there.

Some boys and girls state readily that they want to get married, and that's fine, but it need not be commended with gusts of approval. There's no hurry in getting married. Single people can lead lives that are as rich and full as those of married people. Or as empty, meaningless, and unhappy. Welton's grandfather often said, "If you do or if you don't, you'll often regret it!"

These are the days which test the truths and uncover the fallacies about work, both inside and outside the home. Single girls have babies. Single adults adopt children. Men, too. Thousands and thousands of mothers have full-time jobs. Separated, divorced, or widowed men manage businesses and maintain children in their homes. More and more adults are becoming self-employed. They're learning the convenience and the financial benefits of working at home. To them, "going to business" may mean walking six feet to a desk or studio.

To work at home, to go to business, or to mix the two may be a matter of choice for the child and not a mold into which the child must fit. There's nothing, for example, on a fork lift or a school bus that says only men may drive it.

A man's self-worth depends upon his enterprise and not necessarily upon his title or his actions in a business. I have worked with men unable to make decisions, afraid of crossing the boss, weak and emotional in their reasoning, and inactive in their jobs. However, they are not less than men; they are less than able, assertive, and confident. These words actually name how we feel about business actions and not how we feel about the men or women who occupy the positions.

Watch those special words you use to describe jobs. A girl who writes stories is a writer or an author, not an author*ess*. A doctor is a doctor; you need not call her a woman doctor. The same is true for women who work as scientists or car dealers. Similarly, you need not call him a *male* nurse or a *male* kindergarten teacher. That *male, female,* or *woman* adds a kind of "golly, ain't that unusual!" context to your titles, overly emphasizing the sex of the worker instead of the nature of the work.

As a rule of thumb, use a title that refers to the work rather than the worker. Jobs that are titled with -*man* may easily be renamed—for example, *mail carrier, chairperson, fisher* (not *fisherman*), *firefighter, police officer.* A *flight attendant* is not a euphemism for *steward* or *stewardess;* it is a more apt description of the work rather than the sex of the worker. Again, the emphasis is on the action instead of the person.

Girls and boys may play together with the same business-oriented toys—a boat, a printing set, a model plane, cooking equipment, and art or craft materials. Real-estate, stock-market, and business-management games may easily be bisexual.

Surprisingly, the books in the library won't help as much as you think to minimize sexism in occupations. The stacks are still full of books that dwell on careers for boys, careers for girls, 100 jobs for men, 100 jobs for women. If you wish, try one of the books on the child and ask, "Why can't women do this job?"

Better yet, clear your own mind of stereotypes and open the widest possible range of vocational choices for both the boys and the girls. A life's work should be chosen, satisfying, and successful for meeting one's ambitions. It should not be an unhappy drudge, chosen only because it fits an adult's outmoded concept of "what's fit and proper."

The point is that there is no point in comparing men-jobs with women-jobs. The success of any child's future in the year 2001 will depend on a carefully balanced mixture of flexibility and specialization. If the era becomes more and more technical, men-jobs and women-jobs may be nonexistent, because much of the work as we now know it may be done in highly computerized, "solid-state" ways.

Uniforms and Markers

There is a feeling of fellowship when people wear some article or accessory to announce the individuals as a group to all outsiders and to bind them together as "we"—outlandish caps at a ballgame, red blazers at a convention, black leather jackets, bank uniforms, provincial costumes at a festival, football helmets. There's a practical reason for costuming a group, too. Have you ever noticed how much easier it is to watch baseball or to tell the star from the chorus line when you're watching color TV? You can tell the officers from the troops when they're subdivided by uniforms and marks within the general clothing scheme.

These differences are conversation makers when you and the child are watching uniformed or costumed groups of people. Also, discuss how you might identify a police officer when you need one. Talk with the child about why some police officers wear plain clothes. If you're at an airline terminal, show the child how to identify an employee of a particular airline. Compare the differences of uniforms that indicate who works for which air carrier.

One of the reasons why the staff of a hospital often wear white coats is so that they won't confuse each other as patients, visitors, or unauthorized persons. In television comedies and farces, point out, even if briefly, when the comedians wear a costume, uniform, or the accepted dress of an institution in order to hide or otherwise muddle the plot.

Notice the different kinds of uniforms worn by working people in your neighborhood. Mention, for example, that one benefit from wearing a mail carrier's uniform is to announce to the neighborhood that the carrier is not a meddling or dangerous stranger.

Uniforms serve a protective purpose as well. Firefighters don't wear uniforms to impress onlookers. Ask, the next time you and the child are near a fire station, how each piece of outerwear is designed to protect the firefighter from the dangers of the job. Talk also to a construction worker about why the hard hat must always be worn on the building sites. Ask a welder to let the child look through the mask and to explain why it must be worn. The baseball catcher and the umpire both wear pads and masks that the other players don't wear; talk together about why. When you're together in any of these areas, talk with children about why butchers, bank tellers, barbers, druggists, cooks, florists, gas-station attendants, printers, plumbers, dentists, carpenters, and others wear special coats, aprons, or other clothing when they work.

Tina says that she used to explain the markers worn by employees every time she took Karla into a large, strange store, so that Karla would know whom to seek if she and Tina ever became separated. You can probably arrange for the child to interview briefly almost any person wearing an emblem, a security clearance badge, or other identification in order to learn how the wearer earns a living and what the wearer had to learn or do in order to wear the marker.

Never underestimate the child's possible interest in your conventions or sales meeting badges. After you've attended a meeting, bring home your own badge for the child; it will give you a fine opportunity to tell the child why you wore it, where you were, and what you did there.

Tools, Instruments, Devices

I worked in the offices of a New York publishing company for a little more than eleven years. Sometimes, when I was in town and when other things weren't going very fast (or very well), I would meet small groups of students and their teachers who had previously requested a visit to see the operations of publishing. I explained briefly the work of the people who sat in small cubicles reading copy or typing. We discussed the artists who assembled the pictures and print on the pages and designed covers. We talked briefly about the unseen salesmen who sold the material we published. On one occasion, after saying goodby to a very attentive, friendly group, I saw them unexpectedly once more in the main-floor foyer, but they didn't see me. I heard one child explain, "But Mrs. Forbes, where are the presses and all the other stuff? Golly, we didn't see nuthin'." Thinking, typing, sketching were not what that group wanted to see; they wanted *action!*

When your child is too young to talk about the background and training needed for a job or the daily routine of a profession or office position, you can instead discuss the tools, instruments, and devices which those people use in their work. Whenever you can, take advantage of an opportunity to visit offices or sites where you will see people working with tools— the shoe repairer, the optician, the pizza chef, the baker, the dry cleaner, among others.

Point out, when appropriate, the tools and instruments which people use in their work as you look at pictures in magazine stories and advertisements. One way to ease your concern about the child's TV viewing is to look in your local guide for job-oriented documentaries. Young children are very likely to be fascinated by stories of steel mills, railroad yards, and fish hatcheries. As you listen to the TV news commentators, make a word game of listening for the titles of occupations during the course of the news—mayor, construction worker, miner, union official, White House aide. Also, talk as you wish about the tools and the equipment these people use as you watch the news, or try to name the instruments and devices shown in TV ads.

You may talk about the equipment people use in earning a living in two ways. First, talk about the thing a person might need in order to build a wooden flower box, put a light fixture in the closet, bake a loaf of bread, or paint the bathroom. Second, you can talk about the tools themselves, whether you see real ones or pictured ones. Discuss with the child what it's for, how a person might use it when working, and the names of the occupations of people who might need one of these tools.

Feel free to talk about the tools and devices you use in your own work, such as the dictating machine, the typewriter, computer discs or tapes, a T-square, a change machine at the checkout counter, whatever thingamajig that makes your work easier. If you take the child to visit your place of work, don't fail to point out and explain the instruments and equipment that you normally use in your work, those things at the office which you call "mine."

Also, discuss the tools, the appliances, and the devices which both men and women use in the business of homemaking. Vacuum cleaners and automatic washers don't come with instructions that say only women can operate them. When the appliances break, isn't it wise for both the woman and the man to know how to repair them? Go through the tool box or the closet, that place where you keep all of the stuff to help you run the house. Name the things. Tell the child why, how, and when you need them. Instead of talking about the man-tools and the woman-tools, keep the possibilities of sharing the equipment in the house as flexible as you can. After all, when you work to keep the house going and when you have a particular talent or an inclination for chosen chores, the child should realize that sharing the home duties becomes a matter of choices rather than stereotypes.

The Job Cluster

I can sit here at my desk while I work on this book, and I can feel very alone as I write. I can delude myself into believing that the work in the life of a writer is very lonely and self-contained. And yet, I can only begin to list the hundreds, perhaps thousands of people needed to get these words from me to you.

Business executives (who signed the contract and paid the bills?).

Editors (who made the pencils and the office trappings for them?).

Typists (what about paper, erasers, carbons, typewriters? Who taught them how to type before they came to these words?).

Typesetters (who made the type, the ink, and the complicated machines for all that?).

Artists, designers, proofreaders, salespersons, freight handlers, packers, truck drivers, bookstore managers, and store clerks . . . Well, you take it from there! It's enough to make your head swim.

With your child, try to name just a few of the occupations in the job cluster that put a box of chocolate-chip cookies or a can of tomato soup on your kitchen shelf. Be sure to include yourselves in the producer-wholesaler-retailer-consumer list.

When the TV program gets dull, join your child in identifying some of the people who must earn a living to help present the show you're watching. The people in front of the camera, unless the show boasts a "cast of thousands," are easily outnumbered by the workers that you don't see. A TV program generally offers you the advantage of the roll-up at the end of the show—the list of the people who worked on the production together with the titles of their jobs. Many of these job titles are worth additional conversation—key grip, chief gaffer, set designer, and montage director, among many others.

Visit a nearby construction site often—a new house or apartment building, a road construction, or an electrical, drainage, or communications installation. Give your child plenty of time to watch the work. Try to perceive the project from more than one side, if you can. Talk with the child about the job of each worker you see, the special clothing or uniform, any identification markers, tools, and power equipment. Perhaps one of the workers may be willing to tell you more about what they're building and how they're going about it.

What you're observing at the site is the process, and process is discussed using actions in the present. What happened before may be narrated in story sentences using actions in the past. For example, you may ask the child, "What did they do yesterday? What are they doing now? What do you think they will do next?" Trips to the same construction area will provide a number of opportunities for you and the child to perceive any changes in the construction.

All of these workers become real when you talk about them. The jobs they do become a part of the broad range of choices available to children as they think about their own lives as adults.

Your rule of thumb, then, is to broaden the range of possibilities rather than to restrict it, to make pleasure and pride in work as important as wealth, and to present homemaking and business as compatible rather than separate in the minds of both girls and boys.

17

A Matter of Attitude

We haven't been deeply involved in the psychology of why adults *don't* want to talk with children. All the way through this language workout, however, one question hovers near us. Sometimes it's implied, sometimes it's asked outright. *Why do you want words with a child?*

- to indicate your general disinterest in any language exchange?
- to make unmistakably clear that you don't intend to be interrupted?
- to attempt proof that you know more than the child knows?
- to put down or put off the child for you-forget-why?
- to punish through rebuke, isolation, a dramatic show of non-love?
- to remind the child of your power, threatened or actual, real or imagined?
- to wound with a couple of verbal shots right between the ears?
- to reveal your lack of knowledge, your willingness to listen and learn?
- to express your pleasure for the child's warm, welcome company?
- to share a particularly pleasant moment, or a sad one?
- to answer a question, to ask one?

Dad, if the lion got loose and ate you up,
what bus would I take home?

- to offer a point of view, to elicit one?
- to share something funny?
- to play around together in the wide world of verbal non-sense?

Having words with a child boils down to assessing your own attitude. Are you entering the language experience to get something off your own chest, to have something straight once and for all, hurray for your side? Or are you more interested in the words, opinions, feelings, and language development of the child?

Oh yes, there'll be a verbal exchange either way. One way, you're likely to win on the word count, and the experience may even be memorable. But uneasiness may also gnaw within you, and you may feel less close to the child than you did before.

The other way, you may conclude that you've listened considerably, a task worth time-and-a-half for many adults and parents. You seem to know something about the child that you did not realize a while ago, something that you're glad you bit your own tongue to learn. You feel closer to the child. There may have been a moment that lingered between you before you parted. And the child still seems close to you, out of sight and yet still "there."

A matter of attitude, that's what it is.

I was toy-tinkering in the hectic fun-and-games department of a large store during the holiday season. I came upon two boys, Alain and Delmar, watching the progress of a magic trick being performed by a clerk in a magician's costume. The clerk-magician showed both sides of a small, unpressed handkerchief. He spread it on the counter and held its corners down with his hands.

Slowly, the center of the handkerchief rose, giving the effect of a tiny tent with a center pole. A dramatic trick, I admitted.

But I'm generally less interested in the "sponse" than in the response, so I watched the boys more carefully than the tiny tent.

Both boys maintained suckling-pig faces, trying to get the magic effect together and explainable. Alain said, "What made it do that? What's in there?"

"What do you think's in there?" asked the magician.

"Boy, I don't know!"

"Well, *that's* what's in there."

"Wow!" Alain said, turning to Delmar. "I'm gonna find my mother and ask her to buy me one of these."

"Man, what are you gonna tell her you want?"

"I don't know."

"You crazy, Alain? Your momma ain't gonna give you good money for an I-don't-know!"

I don't really care whether Momma gave Alain the money or not. The overwhelming point is, Alain had something to *talk* about. He'd perceived something to relate in a story. He was full of reactions that begged both for words and a listener. And he was primed to do a "commercial" to rival an advertising agency's most persuasive pitch.

What do you think Momma did? What do you think she said? Did she fire off a few sharp verbal shots? Or did she exploit the experience for the language possibilities within it?

After all, Alain cannot develop his own abilities to understand and use the language by talking to himself.

But you've read that somewhere before, haven't you?

Index

actions, 45-48
action vs. reaction, 12, 17
active vs. passive concepts, 39-40
adolescents, 83
adults:
  as models for children, 143, 157
  participation in learning, 71
  See also Family; Learning experiences and games; Parents; Reading and reading readiness
adverbs, 30, 176-79
advertising:
  development of, 96-97
  premiums, 97
  print media, 104-106
  See also TV
after, 178
allowances, 111-12, 255-56
  See also Money
almost, 78, 177
also, 176, 177
although, 179
ambition, 157
and, 176
animate vs. inanimate classes, 38-39
antonyms, 117-20
arguments, 138-40
  arbitration of, 140

entering into, 138-39
  loaded questions in, 139-40
  teaching children to settle, 139
assumptions about children, 93-94

bad breath as deterrent, 14
because, 178
behaviors, 120-22
body language, 18-19, 51, 146-48, 150-51
  in children, 147-48
  cultural rules about, 147
  descriptive words for, 151
  between parents and children, 148, 151
  side-by-side position vs. confrontation position, 16, 56, 147
  and social space, 147-48
  in sports, 148
  between teachers and children, 148
boredom, 122
but/butt, 177

camping, 190
can/will, 178
cartoons, 193-94, 195, 200-201
  "laugh sandwich" in, 201
  See also Humor